CHOOSE
COSTA
RICA

CHOOSE COSTA RICA

A Guide to
Retirement
and
Investment

John Howells

GATEWAY
BOOKS

Copyright © 1996 by John Howells
Cover Design by Amy Neiman
Cover Drawing by Ed McElligott
Photographs by Alan Cohen, John Howells, Don Merwin, Charles Pastor
Edited and Designed by Donna S. Lee

Printed in the United States of America

Gateway Books

Oakland, CA

Distributed by Publishers Group West

Library of Congress Cataloging-in-Publication Data

Howells, John
    Choose Costa Rica : a guide to retirement and investment / John
    Howells. -- 3rd ed.
        p. cm.
    Includes bibliographical references and index.
    ISBN 0-933469-26-8 (pbk.)
    1. Retirement, Places of--Costa Rica. 2. Investments, American-
-Costa Rica. 3. Costa Rica--Guidebooks. I. Title.
HQ1063.2.C8C67   1996
917.28604'5--dc20   96-28955
                                                              CIP

10 9 8 7 6 5 4 3 2 1

Contents

Introduction

This book is the third edition of *Choose Costa Rica* and the result of 23 years of travel in and writing about Central America. The two years since the last edition of this book have seen much change in Costa Rica, and this new, thoroughly revised third edition reflects this.

Before I began doing nonfiction books, I was a freelance writer; my specialty was writing travel articles on Latin America. Why Latin America? Partly because of the warm climates (I hate cold weather) but mostly because of the gorgeous scenery, exotic foods and the friendly people who live there. Places like Mexico, Guatemala and Costa Rica naturally beckoned with tropical warmth and picturesque surroundings. I always hated it when my research was completed and I had to return home! Thankfully, my wife and I have solved that problem. We purchased a condominium in Rohrmoser, a suburb of San José, Costa Rica, and recently constructed a home near the beach on the Pacific side of the country.

Choose Costa Rica is intended not only for retirees like me, searching for an affordable, interesting lifestyle after leaving the workplace, but for those nearing retirement age who are casting about for ideas for the future. This book is also designed as a guide for those individuals who manage to have part or all of the year free for doing exactly what they feel like doing. It's for the professor on sabbatical; the school teacher on a summer vacation; the construction worker with chronic winter unemployment; the executive who can take a leave of absence. This book is also for the self-employed individual who can trust his business to others while he enjoys life *now* instead of waiting for that "someday" which may never come. *Choose Costa Rica* is specially oriented toward those who seek a "new start," who might wish to invest time and resources into launching a new business career as well as enjoying a fascinating lifestyle in an exotic foreign country.

Although this is partly a travel book, the emphasis is on "how to do it" rather than "where to go." A hotel, bed-and-breakfast or a restaurant may be mentioned from time to time, but only as an adjunct to the narrative and should not be taken as my personal recommendation. Directing you to places to stay and dine is the job of the many excellent travel publications such as Frommer's *Costa Rica, Guatemala & Belize on $35 a Day,* Blake and Becher's *The New Key to Costa Rica,* Ellen Searby's *Costa Rica Traveler,* the *Tico Times* book *Exploring Costa Rica,* or Fodor's *South America on $25 a Day,* just to name a few.

About prices quoted throughout this book: they are accurate as of the time of writing, based on the current dollar exchange rates in Costa Rica. In the spring of 1996 the Costa Rican currency, the colón, was valued at about 200 to the dollar.

After you read through this book, maybe you'll understand why Costa Rica has such a good reputation among North Americans and Europeans. You might even find a niche there for you and your family.

Chapter One

Switzerland of the Americas

One of the more common descriptions of Costa Rica is "the Switzerland of the Americas." At first glance, Costa Rica differs so much from Switzerland that one might wonder how it earned this title. True, both countries are of similar size (although Switzerland is actually a bit smaller—one of the world's few countries with that distinction). But Costa Rica is lushly tropical, continuously swathed in luxurious green vegetation, a place where coffee, sugar cane and mangoes thrive, and where snow never falls. Costa Rica would seem to be the opposite of Switzerland, with its snowcapped peaks and rocky terrain.

Yet, the more one travels in Costa Rica, the more apparent are the parallels with Switzerland. Both are peaceful, progressive countries where democracy and stability are hallmarks. Although Costa Rica's tropical beaches are incongruent with the Swiss terrain, the higher mountains rival the rugged beauty of the Alps. The lake area around the Arenal volcano could easily pass for parts of Switzerland—during the Swiss summertime, at any rate.

Even closer similarities between the two countries appear in their philosophy of life and economic structures. Both are places of small farms and small businesses, with an air of prosperity and a feeling of equality among citizens. Both countries have renounced aggressive militarism, diverting resources—that otherwise would be consumed by wars—toward education, medical care and services for the good of all. In short, both places are

NICARAGUA

Caribbean Sea

Lake Arenal

Flamingo

Nicoya

San José   Limon

Jacó

San Isidro

PANAMA

Pacific Ocean

Golfito

Costa Rica

affluent, happy and tranquil. Both are locations where North Americans can feel at home, safe and welcome.

There are differences, of course. Costa Rica is closer to the United States and Canada, making it more accessible than Europe. Costa Rica enjoys a dramatically lower cost of living. And, best of all, Costa Rica has a climate that can be enjoyed year round by those of us who hate wearing snow boots and earmuffs. The higher elevations enjoy spring-like temperatures all year; flowers bloom everywhere and seem to glow in the crystal-clear atmosphere. The countryside is so fertile that fence posts sprout and become trees despite all the farmers' best efforts. Crossing over the mountains, you drop down to tropical lowlands where North Americans own plantations of coffee, macadamia nuts, black pepper and other exotic crops for export.

People who have traveled all over the world affirm that Costa Rica's beaches are unsurpassed anywhere. Its various climates offer choices of weather as perfect as you could hope to find any place on earth (unless you are a skier, of course). Steep-sloped mountains, topped with cloud forests, ferns and exotic wildlife, tower over fertile farmland dotted with hundreds of neatly maintained homesteads. Flowers bloom everywhere; often entire trees bear so many colorful, scented blossoms that green leaves are hidden. As if this weren't enough, the small towns are every bit as neat and clean as the countryside and are blessed with friendly Costa Rican hospitality. This is truly a country of superlatives.

A Unique History

Costa Rica stands out in this hemisphere in many ways, but its biggest contrast is with its Central American neighbors. When you drive across the border into Costa Rica, or when you step off an airplane arriving from another Central American country, you know immediately that you are in a special place. Relative affluence stands out in contrast to the grinding poverty of most other Central American locations. People of neighboring republics all point to Costa Rica as an example of the kind of world they would hope to imitate. "If Costa Rica can be prosperous, democratic and free," the envious neighbors ask, "why can't we?"

Clearly, there are light-years of difference between Costa Rica and the other Central American countries. How did it get that way? Why is there so little poverty and so large a middle class in comparison with neighboring countries? The answers to these questions can be found in a series of historical events, some accidental, some planned.

In 1502, when Columbus happened upon Costa Rica during his last voyage to this hemisphere, he anchored at present-day Limón and dispatched an expedition ashore. Chances are, Columbus himself waited on the ship for a report from his landing party. His explorers returned with news of an inhospitable jungle, impossible swamps, plus ferocious natives who owned but a few paltry ornaments of thinly-pounded gold. In short, the Limón Coast offered little to excite the imagination of these early explorers. They quickly moved on without attempting colonization.

According to legend, Columbus gave his new discovery the name "Costa Rica" or "rich coast." Actually, the name probably came from another explorer, Fernández de Córdoba, as he charted the Pacific side of the isthmus some 30 years later. Impressed by the magnificent forests, fertile lands and abundant wildlife of the Nicoya peninsula, he coined the term "Costa Rica" as he established a settlement in 1539. The Caribbean coast that Columbus discovered was left virtually untouched and ignored by Europeans for several centuries. In part due to the isolation of this Pacific Coast settlement, and in contrast with the fast colonization of other parts of the Americas, Costa Rica grew very slowly.

As a rule, the Spanish Crown granted huge tracts of land to the conquistadors as a reward for their services. Indians were considered a part of the land, and although not exactly slaves, they essentially belonged to the enormous haciendas, forced to work as peons for the aristocratic conquerors. In places like Peru, Mexico or Guatemala, the Indians meekly accepted their new rulers and continued working the same lands as before, paying tribute to new overlords. However, the Indians of Costa Rica (like their cousins in North America) proved to be determined, fierce fighters who resisted the idea of accepting the intruders as their superiors. Experts in defending their heavily forested lands, the natives simply withdrew farther into the jungle when defeated. They clearly weren't interested in farming land for the pink-faced intruders. Archaeological evidence suggests that at least some tribes were headhunters, possibly culturally related to the Jívaros of Colombia, whose warriors dangle their enemies' shrunken heads around their necks as ornaments. In short, these people were definitely not likely candidates for docile field laborers.

This left the newcomers in a position they hadn't counted on. Instead of being lords over huge estates and overseeing gangs of laboring peons, the Spanish conquistadors were forced to work the land for themselves! This required hard work and a marginal existence on small, family-run farms. From the beginning, all were equal in their struggle for existence. Even the royal governors had to raise chickens and tend their own gardens to avoid starvation. Small wonder many early settlers moved on to easier pickings; others ignored the country completely.

Costa Rica's development got off to an inauspicious start, and it remained a backwater of Spanish colonization, all but forgotten over the ensuing centuries. It grew in its own way, ignoring the ineffective Spanish governors sent by the royal court of Madrid. Costa Ricans lived a calm life, isolated and unaffected by events in other colonies. In fact, in 1821, when Spain granted independence to the Spanish colonies, Costa Rica was the last to know (and probably cared the least). For all practical purposes, it had always been on its own. Independence was no novelty.

Fortunately, Costa Rica's first president turned out to be a progressive leader, a visionary who wanted to see the country develop socially and economically. He was convinced that growing coffee for export could be a major economic breakthrough, a key to modernization. Coffee profits could build roads, schools and cities.

But the country was scantily populated. More people were needed to grow coffee in order to fulfill the president's dream. Consequently, free land was offered to anyone willing to plant coffee trees. Since coffee production in Costa Rica is ideally suited to small farms, European families began immigrating to take advantage of Costa Rica's opportunities. They came from Italy and France as well as from Spain. Instead of huge plantations owned by a few wealthy families, as in other Central American republics, thousands of small farms sprang up, selling coffee beans to merchants who processed and exported the product. This resulted in a tradition of independence and equality, with a preponderance of middle-class farmers and a few moderately wealthy, coffee-exporting families. The spread between rich, middle class and poor was much narrower than anywhere in the hemisphere, and remains so to this day.

Troubled times in Europe during the last half of the 19th century sent new waves of economic and political refugees to the Americas, seeking a chance to "start over." The standing offer of free land to grow coffee was irresistible. The ranks of small farmers grew even larger. These refugees, often imbued with contemporary Europe's liberal intellectual and political philosophy, contributed heavily to the notions of freedom, democracy and individual rights that were already in place.

This is not to say that Costa Rica didn't develop a wealthy oligarchy of elite families whose position rested upon their control of coffee exports. But because of their tradition of being "self-made" families and their respect for hard work, their mentality was different from that of the arrogant Spanish conquistadors who worshiped royalty and privilege.

Free and compulsory education was an early development, starting in 1869 and setting a tradition of literacy that ranks Costa Rica higher than most countries of the world—including the United States. A university was founded in 1844, staffed in part by intellectuals who fled Europe's political and economic maelstrom. These and other modern European traditions developed in Costa Rica in stark contrast with the medieval, feudal heritage of Mexico and other Central American countries.

A Peaceful Democracy

Costa Rica is a country where North Americans feel very much at home. It is a country of law-abiding citizens, a place where you don't feel shivers of apprehension at the approach of a policeman or a heavily-armed soldier. (You have to have traveled in a brutal police state to appreciate this last statement.) Costa Rica is a country where juvenile gangs and graffiti are the exception, not the rule. It's a place where your conscience isn't continually assaulted by obvious poverty, beggars in the streets or social injustice. It's a place where North Americans feel comfortable living in just about any neighborhood, not forced to huddle together in enclaves of other expatriates for mutual support. That's not to say Costa Rica is crime-free (is there such a place?), but compared with most places in this world, the country has a safe feeling.

One reason we North Americans like Costa Rica is because Costa Ricans are so much like us. They look like us, act like us and think as we do. They are open, friendly and egalitarian. Most of us feel at home in Costa Rica. (The only other Latin country where I feel this way is Argentina.) Costa Rica has avoided the problems that have mired her sister Central American republics in a quicksand of turmoil and tragedy. Costa Rica's devotion to democracy and peaceful cooperation with its neighbors enabled the country to retain its enviable position as a showcase of prosperity, respect for law and personal freedoms.

A century-and-a-half tradition of free and honest elections forms the basis for today's political life. Instead of frequent coups d'etat, so common in neighboring countries, Costa Rican governments change by balloting. Although members of the same affluent families win office frequently, they are civilians and intellectuals and, for the most part, are working for the good of the country as a whole, not just for one particular class. In 1889, a revolution threatened when the defeated incumbents almost refused to recognize the election results. But at the last minute they decided to accept the will of the people, thus reinforcing a tradition of democratic process.

A truly significant event that totally separated Costa Rica from the ranks of other Central American nations occurred in 1948. The ruling party decided not to recognize the results of a disputed election and refused to give up power, ordering new elections because of the closeness of the vote and accusations of fraud. A crisis of democracy threatened. Pepe Figueres, a charismatic member of one of the wealthy families, stepped forward to lead an uprising against the illegal government and its attempt to use the army to hold on to power. The result of this successful revolution (the first and only in Costa Rican history) was a movement to abolish the army and replace it with the Guardia Civil, a civilian-controlled police force comparable to local police forces in the United States.

This was a brilliant and bold step. Barracks were turned into schools. Ex-soldiers were given jobs building roads. Money which would normally be absorbed by military corruption and graft was devoted to highways, education and medical care. Today, 27 percent of the national budget goes to education and culture. Public money pays for four universities, three symphony orchestras, and five autonomous state publishing houses. Of the gross national product, about 10 percent is spent on medical care, and there is a physician for every 700 inhabitants.

Some North Americans shake their heads in dismay at the lack of a standing army. They ask, "Without a military, how can you defend your country from aggression?" The answer is simple. The function of a Central American military has never been to deter aggression; its duty is to protect the *rulers* of the country from its *citizens,* to keep the people in line and maintain privileges for the military and the country's financial elite. Democracy doesn't stand a chance when armed soldiers bully candidates, threaten voters, conduct the election and then count the ballots! Are we surprised when generals win the elections?

Election day is Costa Rica's most important holiday, a riotous celebration with a joyous spirit that goes far beyond mere politics. Voting is mandatory (non-voters pay a token fine), but few citizens would think of passing up the fun and excitement of an election. Weeks prior to election day all parties campaign vigorously, with folks everywhere waving their party's flags, cheering enthusiastically when a car displaying a favored flag drives past, or booing good-naturedly when an opposition flag passes by. On the day of an election, all stores and businesses are closed, and all transportation is free. Buses, taxis, even private cars are expected to stop when someone indicates they want a ride to a polling booth. In practice, most autos will stop for anyone who waves and asks for a ride in whatever direction the auto is headed. After all, this is a fiesta!

It's interesting to note that many Costa Ricans, when they move from their home towns to another part of the country, do not change their voting registration to their new address. Because transportation is free, this is an opportunity to return to their home towns to vote and to visit friends and family at the same time. Parties, reunions and celebrations are a most important part of election day.

Voters must dunk their thumbs into indelible ink to prove they've voted (and cannot vote again), and this purple digit is worn as a proud badge of civic duty. Automobile drivers honk their horns and wave their discolored thumbs in the air as they drive along the streets, to show everyone they have voted, while shouting, "Have *you* voted yet?" There are so many horns blowing on election day that it sounds like New Year's Eve at midnight, all day long.

The result is a country intensely dedicated to notions of democracy. All segments of the political spectrum, from extreme right to far out left are represented; all are totally legal. Yet middle-of-the road parties always garner most of the votes. Despite vigorous campaigning, the Communists used to receive two percent of the vote, but have fallen to around one percent as party members became disenchanted with failed Marxist experiments in neighboring Nicaragua and elsewhere.

This is not to imply that there is no poverty in the country, or that Costa Rican workers are among the world's best paid. But compared to most Latin American countries, workers here enjoy excellent working conditions and government guarantees of fair treatment from employers. Even those living below the poverty level live far better than in most other countries, including the United States. You'll see few, if any, "street people" or panhandlers on Costa Rican streets. Children never beg. As a friend observed, "Among the world's poor, Costa Rican poor are the most affluent." Food is plentiful, medical care and education are free, and there is always a network of government, family and friends to help in case of disaster. Open-air markets have a tradition of giving food to the poor, with vendors handing out their surplus to those asking. If a family wants land to grow food, the government does its best to set them up with a farm. With all of this, welfare isn't necessary.

Yet, wages appear to be extraordinarily low to us *Norteamericanos*. How can a worker be expected to survive on, say, $200 a month, much less be considered well off? The answer is that even though the cash salary is small, fringe benefits connected with the job make a big difference. In addition to his cash salary, a worker is guaranteed items such as sick leave, at the rate of 50 percent of his salary, from the first day of illness up to a lifetime of disability. Workers receive a month's *aguinaldo* or Christmas bonus every year and a minimum of two weeks' paid vacation every year. Medical care is free and top quality. Women receive six weeks' maternity leave (at full salary), and all receive a pension upon retirement. It isn't necessary to put aside money for the kids' college tuition. Education is free, a basic right provided by the government. Therefore, a worker can spend his entire salary on living expenses without having to put a portion aside for illness or medical emergencies. These benefits are guaranteed by law, and everybody knows exactly what their rights are. At the present time, there is a shortage of help in many areas of work, and anyone who wants to work can find a job. The result is that employers have to pay more than minimum wages in order to ensure competent workers. This is in contrast to other Latin American countries where the minimum and maximum wage is usually the same.

When you measure these benefits and put a cash value on them, you'll find Costa Rican workers are ahead of many North American. In the United States, a pitifully inadequate medical insurance policy costs a worker more than many Costa Rican workers' total earnings! Since few low-paid U.S. workers can afford insurance, one short visit to a hospital pushes them into hopeless poverty. Sick leave? In the United States, a large part of the workforce has to do without that "luxury."

Easy Access

For the past several years, North American tourism overseas has been on the decline, particularly travel to Europe. Out-of-sight prices overseas discouraged Americans from traveling or living overseas. At one time, Europe was considered a bargain place for travel and retirement—but prices in many European countries have risen steadily and now exceed those in North America. In the midst of this softening of foreign travel and retirement, Costa Rican vacations became more and more popular. Tourism increased by 336 percent from 1988 to 1994. (In 1995 the growth slowed, which may be a healthful sign.) The larger U.S. airlines and European charter services are gearing up to handle the hordes of travelers who are discovering the joys of pocketbook-friendly vacations in Costa Rica.

Another thing North Americans appreciate about Costa Rica is the ease with which they can enter the country. A Canadian or U.S. tourist traveling with a valid passport has only to present it at the airport for a 90-day visit, which can easily be extended a couple of months without much of a hassle.

Without a passport, a tourist card is needed, which can be obtained by presentation of a birth certificate and identification with a current photo, such as a driver's license. Some tell me they've been granted a tourist card with a voter's registration card. Tourist cards are available at any Costa Rican consulate, from your travel agency, from the airline, or even at the airport when you disembark from the airplane. But I highly recommend carrying a passport. It's inexpensive and serves as the ultimate in identification, especially for driving a car, cashing travelers checks and performing other financial transactions. You'll be surprised how many times you'll be asked for your passport or to write your passport number on an official form.

Usually it's an easy matter to obtain one visa extension; a travel agent can take care of it for you. If you don't care to bother, you can simply exit the country—with a short sojourn in Nicaragua, Panama or one of the nearby islands belonging to Honduras or Colombia—and re-enter after a three-day stay. Be aware that in 1995, the Ministry of Immigration threatened to tighten the rules on folks who do too many of these in-and-out trips to avoid applying for residency. At the time of writing, the rules are still being applied leniently. This will be discussed in more detail in Chapter Twelve, along with the rules and procedures for getting permanent residence.

Speaking of permanent residence, according to a U.S. State Department source, about 40,000 American citizens live in Central America. This doesn't tell us much about North American retirees or investors since many of these 40,000 are naturalized citizens or aliens who returned to their country of birth to retire. However, a good number are native-born Canadians or U.S. citizens who choose to work, operate a business or retire in Central America. As best as I can tell, about 20,000 North American citizens live in Costa Rica—some full time, others making their homes here seasonally. My best estimate is that 6,000 of them are retired. Exact figures are impossible to come by. The percentage of Canadian versus United States citizens is difficult to say with precision, but you can be confident that plenty of Canadians are represented. A few North Americans live in other Central American countries— Guatemala, Honduras, Belize, and even El Salvador and Nicaragua—but their ranks are scanty compared with Costa Rica.

Because of its small size and economically homogeneous native population, Costa Rica lures a much larger percentage of North Americans (and foreigners in general) who are "starting over" or living part time in this exotic, semi-paradise. Furthermore, you'll find these newcomers scattered all around the country—almost every nook and cranny has a few of us living there—instead of concentrated in enclaves or colonies, as is the case in many foreign countries.

Like Mexico, Costa Rica eagerly welcomes tourists, seasonal residents and retirees, but Costa Rica places fewer restrictions on newcomers. The government makes it easy to own property or start a business. You can do either even while holding just a tourist visa. To become a *pensionado* in Costa Rica, you only need prove $600 a month retirement income. For those who aren't retired, yet who would like to live in the country or to manage a business, the requirement is $1,000 a month income. Happily, these amounts can easily cover a couple's basic living expenses, something unthinkable in most parts of the world. Just consider the living standard you'd maintain in the United States on $600 or $1,000 a month! In Costa Rica, on $1,000 a month you can afford a maid or a gardener, at least part time.

Two other conditions make Costa Rica special as a destination for part-time or full-time living. Most important is the almost-perfect weather. The central plateau is wonderfully temperate, with thermometer readings virtually the same the year round, and the beaches are wonderfully tropical yet not overly hot or humid, similar to Hawaii, except for the prices. The second favorable condition is Costa Rica's exciting investment climate. Instead of placing barriers to prevent foreigners from going into business, as do most countries in the world, Costa Rica encourages foreign investments. To lure investors, the government offers tax incentives and duty-free imports. Again, you don't have to be a citizen or even a legal resident to own property or conduct a business. You can do it on a tourist visa! Not many desirable countries permit you to do this.

Pre-Planning for Costa Rica

One publication I strongly recommend for anyone considering Costa Rica for anything more than a short vacation is San José's English-language newspaper, the *Tico Times*. If you read every issue, from front to back, including the advertisements, by the time you actually get to Costa Rica, you will know so much about the place you will feel as if you are returning home. The classified ads keep you up to date on rental costs, housing prices and what second-hand furniture and appliances sell for. Display ads tell you what you should pay for a hotel room or a bed-and-breakfast, the best places to dine or where to go for a beach excursion. The news columns are well-written, with complete and unbiased news of what's happening in Costa Rica as well as in neighboring countries—news not available in other English-language newspapers. Featured are articles relating to foreign residents, governmental actions or changes in law that may affect them, as well as news of social activities and club events. An extensive letters-to-the-editor section prints opinions of tourists and residents alike, telling of exceptionally nice places to go and which places are rip-offs, giving opinions about the country, kudos and complaints, political views, and just about anything you can imagine. By all means, start your subscription several months before you leave.

A second essential publication for your initial trip is a good travel book. U.S. and Canadian bookstores are loaded with excellent travel guidebooks packed with information you need on bus and plane schedules, hotels and places you'll want to visit—in accurate, non-flowery language. It's best to purchase your guidebooks before leaving home; they are sometimes overpriced in Costa Rican bookstores, partly because of customs duty. You'll need this additional information because *Choose Costa Rica* is not intended to be a comprehensive travel book; it's a guide to retirement, long-term living and investment in the country.

Choose Costa Rica also tries to avoid making recommendations on business services such as real estate agencies, simply because of the impossibility of being able to vouch for reliability or character. Personnel can change; brokerages are sold; and Costa Rican real estate agents aren't bound by the strict rules of ethics common in the U.S. and Canada. Your job is to investigate, make inquiries and make your own, on-the-spot selections. When business services or travel agencies are mentioned, it isn't as an endorsement of their reliability, but simply as a starting place for checking out the field. At the time I interviewed these business representatives, I was impressed by their knowledge—but that says nothing of their competence or honesty. These are judgments you must make for yourself.

Finally, I emphatically urge that you make no decisions about permanent moves or business investments without spending several months "on location," getting to know the country, meeting the people and learning what it's all about. Find a good lawyer before making any financial moves, one recommended by someone in the North American community. Above all, don't hand your money to someone simply because he or she also comes from Omaha or Ottawa and has an honest face. Honest faces and firm handshakes are the mark of good swindlers! Costa Rica has suffered its fair share of sweet-talking Gringos with designs on your pocketbooks. There's something about a foreign country that tends to bring out latent larceny in some people. Later on in this book, we'll discuss ways to protect yourself from these low-lifes.

Why "Ticos"?

Throughout this book you'll see the term "Tico" used when speaking of Costa Ricans. This is the appropriate nickname for a Costa Rica citizen, just as "Gringo" is used for North Americans in general, and "Yankee" for a citizen of the United States. The term "Gringo" is an accepted nickname, both for Canadian and U.S. citizens—no one takes umbrage by it, because Ticos mean it in an almost affectionate way. And, Costa Ricans call themselves "Ticos" when distinguishing themselves from foreigners, instead of the more cumbersome "Costariquense."

The name "Tico" comes from an archaic practice of using the sound -*tico* on the end of a word as a diminutive instead of the normal -*tito*. For example: whereas a Mexican would say *momentito* for "just a tiny moment," some Costa Ricans (not all) might say *momentico*. Thus a kitten would be a *gatico* in Costa Rica, but a *gatito* in Mexico. Not all Costa Ricans use this ending, but enough do to keep the tradition alive.

One uniquely Costa Rican term, solidly ingrained into the language, is *pura vida.* I suppose this would translate as "it's a great life," but in effect it means "okay," "cool," "all right," sometimes as an emphatic "aw-right!" A clerk in a store, instead of asking, "Would you like anything else?" might ask instead, "*Pura vida?*" A gas station attendant may ask, "Is your oil *pura vida,* or should I check it for you?"

Chapter Two

What's Costa Rica Like?

Costa Rica is a small country, even though it doesn't appear so from the standpoint of the traveler who is driving a rental car from one end of the country to the other, over winding roads, uphill and down. Every turn in the road brings a new vista, something else to contemplate. Actually, the country contains a little less than 20,000 square miles, much of it almost unpopulated.

Travel articles and guidebooks traditionally describe Costa Rica as being "the size of West Virginia," but that's not really accurate. Some travel writer must have said that years ago, and others automatically repeat this misinformation. The truth is, Costa Rica is smaller than West Virginia by 20 percent. To be more accurate, let's say that Costa Rica is about the size of New Hampshire and Maryland with poor little Rhode Island tossed in for good measure. Would it help to say that Costa Rica is about half the size of Kentucky? If that makes the place sound small and insignificant, we can balance out the equation by pointing out that Costa Rica is larger than Albania, Denmark, Belgium, Holland or Switzerland (plus a handful of countries you and I have never heard of).

Yet, few countries of any size offer such a diversity of scenery and climate or such a wide variety of flora and fauna. Probably no country in the world devotes as large a percentage of its territory to national parks and wildlife refuges. About 27 percent of Costa Rica's land is thus protected. These preserves range from cloud forests to tropical beaches, from volcanic craters to jungle swamps and inland waterways. The park system is a major drawing card for tourism.

Costa Rica's bewildering assortment of wildlife includes 850 species of birds—more than three times as many as in the United States and Canada combined. Representative mammals are monkeys, coatis, jaguars and ocelots, as well as sloths, tapirs and agoutis. One evening, down on the Pacific coast, a large anteater ambled in front of my car, its long snout almost touching the ground in front with an equally heavy tail drooping behind, looking very prehistoric. Turtles, colorful frogs and toads of all descriptions are found, as well as crocodiles and iguanas. Snakes? Of course. They range from huge boa constrictors to tiny coral snakes. Experts say there are more varieties of butterflies in Costa Rica than in all of the African continent; over 2,000 species have been collected so far and more are being discovered. The number of orchids and bromeliads confuses the mind. This is truly a naturalist's paradise, drawing visitors from all over the world.

Many tropical countries offer beaches and vacation accommodations, but nowhere else in the world can a tourist find such a combination of beaches, tropics, friendliness and tropical wonder that's accessible year round.

The Costa Rican government recognizes this unique asset and actively involves its citizens in both the preservation *and* exploitation of nature at the same time. How can you protect and exploit the environment? Just one example: by hiring local people to guard and preserve endangered turtle nesting beaches, jobs are created. Beach villages then become tourist attractions, complete with motels, restaurants and shops, thus creating even more jobs. Visitors from all over the world can now visit cloud forests, turtle nesting beaches and nature preserves—in comfort. In the process, they leave much-needed foreign currency with Costa Rican businesses and banks.

Many North Americans and Europeans are scrambling to join this bandwagon and, with government encouragement, are investing heavily in tourist businesses, particularly in motels, restaurants and endeavors of a like nature. Some enterprises become instant successes, with full bookings and plenty of business. One Canadian, who started a motel on the Caribbean side of the country a few years ago, showed me the registration book for his 12-unit facility, saying proudly, "This place has an occupancy rate of 98 percent during the tourist season and over 60 percent during the off season." I asked for a room, but was told, "Not until next week. I'm booked solid." This process of expansion did, however, slow significantly in 1995. The tourist industry didn't collapse or anything like that, but instead of an expected 10 to 20 percent increase in tourism, there was only a 2 percent boost. (Details about starting and operating businesses in Costa Rica are presented in Chapter Ten.)

A Country of Contradictions

Before readers are left with the impression that things are perfect in paradise, that Costa Rica is the best of all worlds, let's examine some contradictions.

The first contradiction: even though the Costa Rican government is totally committed to preserving the environment and tries to control illegal deforestation, it also permits foreign companies to bulldoze forests to make more banana plantations. The government puts large tracts of land into biological and wildlife reserves, forest reserves, national parks and Indian reservations—yet at the same time farmers and agribusiness cut down forests on private tracts at a faster rate than anywhere else in the world. The economy destroys in the name of progress while the government tries to preserve in the name of conservation. But at least the government does try, and its efforts are improving.

Another contradiction: the growth of ecotourism in Costa Rica brings hundreds of thousands of visitors to enjoy the ecological wonderlands, but large numbers of visitors tramping through delicately balanced wilderness systems threaten to destroy the very ecological treasures that lure them to Costa Rica in the first place. For this reason the government raised admission fees to National Parks in an effort to cut traffic to some extent. Some say the increase was merely to bring in more revenue—that may well be true—but it did indeed lower the number of visitors and traffic in National Parks.

The fee increase had a beneficial side effect in directing more business toward private ecological parks and developments. However, the tourist industry raised strenuous objections to the higher fees, claiming it hurt business. So the government offered a deal: "You cut the hotel rates 15 percent, and we'll reduce National Park entrance fees by 60 percent." The result is that entrance fees to National Parks, which had ranged from $5 to $15, are being reduced to a fixed price of $6 for all visitors, and over 100 hotels have agreed to lower their rack rates by 15 percent. If this weren't attractive enough (pending Congressional approval, as of Spring 1996), the government has proposed eliminating its 3 percent lodging tax and its 15 percent sales tax for foreign visitors.

Yet another contradiction in Costa Rica is the increase in petty crime among such a peaceful population. In fact, the major criticism this book has received in the past was that it didn't place proper emphasis on the increasing crime rate in the larger cities. I have to admit that I've had a propensity to overlook this problem, probably because I feel the problem is lightweight compared with other Latin countries, and is almost insignificant when matched with most United States communities of similar sizes. Any increase in crime rates can be considered a natural phenomenon which parallels the rise of crime back home, although on a more minor scale. We'll discuss crime in more detail in Chapter Seven.

Some will disagree, but to me a bigger annoyance than petty crime is Costa Rica's substandard roads and heavy automobile traffic in the larger cities. From time to time, public anger initiates a concerted campaign to eliminate the monster chasms and bottomless pits that are euphemistically referred to as "potholes." Once stirred into action, government workers do a remarkably fast job of smoothing things over. Unfortunately, when they turn their attention elsewhere the potholes begin making a determined comeback. Some day they'll make a movie: "The Pothole That Ate San José."

Combine treacherous pavement with too many automobiles on the Meseta Central's street system and you have a situation that encourages taxi rides into congested parts of San José. Fortunately, cab rides are cheap, and over 7,000 taxis roam the streets, so you don't have a long wait between rides. The problems of potholes and heavy traffic in the city will always be another of those fly-in-the-ointment nuisances you'll have to accept if you want to live in paradise. Nothing's perfect. The farther you get from downtown San José, the less the annoyance. When really deep into rural areas, the biggest obstacle to driving might be a herd of cattle being driven down the gravel road, or a sow and litter of piglets ambling across the way.

Another situation, which could become a problem as foreign population increases, is foreign ownership of most of the coastal lands. Although the Costa Rican people are friendly, gentle and welcoming, they cannot help but feel some level of resentment as they see foreigners bid up the price of property until it is out of their price range. (The big-money players are heavily represented by German, Swiss and Italian buyers.) At present, this level of resentment is low, and it's balanced by an appreciation for how foreign investment is creating jobs and helping the economy. Where my wife and I own property, the local people tell us they'd rather see foreigners own the land, because Ticos tend to clear-cut the forest to make room for cattle. Cattle ranches create few full-time jobs compared with businesses and residences on similar lands.

Visitors and foreign residents can do little to resolve these contradictions, but they need be aware that problems do exist and may crop up in the future. The best they can do is try to minimize their impact upon the natural resources of the country. None of these problems have gotten completely out of hand, and solutions are constantly being sought by the Costa Rican government. But as is the way in any democracy, the going is slow and cumbersome. Just be aware that not everything is perfect in paradise—but for my money it's still paradise!

Menu of Climates

For such a small country, Costa Rica has an astonishing variety of climates. From the misty mountain tops of Talamanca or Monteverde to the almost desert-like northern Guanacaste province, from the permanent spring weather of the Arenal area to the jungle lushness of the Caribbean coast, Costa Rica has every kind of climate one might desire. The exception is frozen snow and bitter cold, but you don't want that anyway. Yes, there are seasons, but the differences between them are minimal; mostly measured in differences in rainfall rather than in temperature variation. Unlike many other world vacation spots, Costa Rica isn't a one-season destination; almost any time of the year can be a perfect time to visit. For those who live here full time, the seasonal changes add spice to retirement. September and October are probably the least popular months, though, for these are the rainiest ones.

In Costa Rica, people transpose the meanings of winter and summer. They call the months of December, January and February "summer," or the "dry season." These are the months that children take their "summer vacation" from school. To a Costa Rican, "winter" means June, July and August! Conversations can become very confusing when Costa Ricans and North Americans discuss the seasons, with summer and winter having opposite meanings for each. To avoid misunderstandings, I generally say, "June, July and August" instead of "winter," or I'll say "dry season" and "rainy season"—then everybody knows what I mean.

The dry season, which actually begins around the last of November and lasts until the end of April, isn't parched and arid as the name might imply. Occasional showers keep plants and lawns pleasantly green and flowers blooming in the higher parts of the mountains, where most folks live. On the Caribbean coast and the area around Lake Arenal, the "dry season" is just a figure of speech; rain knows no seasons here. Some Pacific coastal areas are truly dry during December, January and February, looking much like California during its summer, when rain rarely falls.

The "winter" months of June, July and August—also referred to as the "green season"—are actually cooler than the "summer" months. This is because of almost daily rains and the evaporation effect. A common misconception is that "rainy season" means continuous downpours. Typically, even in the most rainy parts of the country, the day begins with glorious sunshine, with blossoms glowing in the sparkling clean air and birds singing happily. Then, rain starts falling between two and four o'clock in the afternoon. Some places Jou can almost set your clock by it. A heavy downpour sends people indoors for a couple of hours. Then sunshine returns, and the world is once again refreshed. Other sections of the country enjoy sunshine all day, with the rain falling mostly at night. This is the "best" rain, for falling asleep to the drumming sound of raindrops on the roof is a delight. And, it's not often that it rains every day; several days in a row can be perfectly dry.

Because most North Americans customarily think of the tropics as a place to visit in their winter season—to escape the snow and ice of their homelands—they are often surprised to find that the rainy months of June, July and August are the favorite time of year for many who live in Costa Rica. "You can't really appreciate this country until you've experienced our winter months," says Graham Henshaw, an expatriate from England. "Everything is green now in January, but when the rains start in May, the grass changes to an even brighter emerald color. Flowers that only bloom in July and August are absolutely stunning. Winter is my favorite time of year."

To further complicate matters, what is true of the mountain valley environment around San José isn't necessarily true on the Caribbean side, which can be flooded with sunshine while the capital is awash in *aguaceros* (rainstorms) and vice versa. The truth is, no matter what time of year you choose to visit, you're guaranteed a serving of nice sunny weather—and probably some rain as well.

Weather in the tropics is largely determined by altitude. At ocean level, the climate is a year-round summer; at moderate elevations, year-round spring is a better description. The higher you go, the cooler it gets. A sweater or jacket can be worn almost every evening of the year in higher elevations. Your travel wardrobe should include shirts, sweaters and jackets you can peel off or pile on, depending on whether you're dining at a beach restaurant, visiting a volcano, or traveling somewhere in between. Be sure to bring rain gear and sturdy shoes if you plan any jungle exploring, plus sunscreen for visits to mountains or beaches; the tropical sun is persistent at all altitudes.

On the northwest Pacific side, the dry season is exactly that, with very little rain falling from November until the beginning of May. The grass turns brown, and many trees lose their leaves just as they do in North America in the winter. But the reason for leaf loss is to conserve water, not because of frost and freezing weather. There are some evergreen trees, but even some of these lose a large portion of their leaves. It isn't as bleak as it sounds, for many of these trees replace leaves with brilliantly colored blossoms, for this is the time of year to attract bees, butterflies and other pollinating insects.

Even on the dry Guanacaste coast you'll find microcosms of green environments tucked away in the interior valleys, where sporadic rains are coaxed from the westerly Pacific winds. Farther south along the Pacific coast, the dry-season rainfall is even more frequent, keeping things pleasantly green during the driest months. (You'll find a weather chart at the end of this chapter that provides statistics on the microclimates of Costa Rica.)

Insects and the Tropics

An odd thing about the weather checkerboard of Costa Rica is that, contrary to what one might think, the more humid areas are not necessarily the most insect-plagued. Of course, bring your insect repellent, but I'm convinced that you need it less in most places in Costa Rica than you do in the American Midwest. Along the forested Pacific Coast and the Nicoya Peninsula, where the insect varieties are amazingly abundant, mosquitoes and flies pester you far less than in the dry, almost desert-like parts of Guanacaste. On the humid Caribbean coast, where rain can fall almost any time of the year, and where bugs can get so large you'd think they've been taking hormones, household cockroaches and flies are not nearly as plentiful as I've seen in Houston or New Orleans. (I've seen many different kinds of beetles, but surprisingly few cockroaches in my Costa Rican travels.)

In parts of Costa Rica, even in the most tropical locations, many people don't bother with screens on their windows. Of course, the rainy season in some areas will make a liar of me, so keep repellent with you. This is particularly advisable when staying in one of the areas where dengue fever has been reported (mostly around the outskirts of Puntarenas and Liberia). There's a vigorous campaign underway at present to eliminate the mosquito that spreads the flu-like ailment.

Why flies and mosquitoes are relatively scarce might seem puzzling. But I believe the answer is that the physical environment in Costa Rica is largely intact. The natural enemies of pests like flies and mosquitoes haven't been eliminated by pesticides, chemicals and other methods as they have back home. By day, birds of all descriptions flit back and forth, snacking on insects, keeping them in balance with nature. Many birds consider houseflies to be special treats. By night, squadrons of bats keep up the good work, finishing off mosquitoes before they get a chance to do much damage. According to one naturalist, a small bat can catch about 600 mosquito-sized insects per hour, and a large colony of bats will consume thousands of pounds of insects every night! (There are over 30 species of bats in Costa Rica.)

Meanwhile, lizards, geckos and chameleons patrol the walls and corners of houses, cleaning up cockroaches and water bugs before they have any chance to infest the kitchen or make a condominium out of your bathroom. The fearsome-looking praying mantis sometimes prowls about the edges of rooms, snapping up bugs that the lizards miss.

My wife and I have additional help in keeping our Costa Rica home bug-free. From time to time, our house is invaded by army ants. They march in formation up a concrete column to the veranda and spill over the floors in a busy wave of housecleaning. They remove moths and other night-flying insects that committed suicide against the porch lights the previous night, and they scour the baseboards, corners and low cabinets in search of bugs, beetles and insect eggs. Scorpions flee in terror; they have no defense against army ants—if they tarry, they are dismantled and served for breakfast. Even snakes fear the ants. We simply stay out of their way or prop our feet out of range while we read a novel, until their 20-minute cleaning expedition is finished. We say goodbye and thank them as they continue on their way to their next house cleaning duties.

Not that insects can't make one suffer. Some very small creatures made my last trip to the Pacific beaches memorable for several weeks. These were the dreaded "no-see-ums," a generic name given to any tiny bug that bites without your knowing you are being attacked but makes you suffer afterwards. In this case they were probably some kind of mini-sand flea because they got me on the ankles and lower legs. However, it was my own fault;

I should know better than to stroll along the beach at dusk without repellent on my bare legs.

Now I'm going to reveal a personal discovery concerning these bites: it's a salve called Panalog. This is an all-purpose antibiotic and fungicide that veterinarians routinely prescribe when treating cats and dogs for infections, rashes and general skin problems. If you have a dog or cat, you'll probably have some at home. I've found that a dab of Panalog on a mosquito or no-see-um bite not only stops my itching, but heals the puncture almost immediately. The only known side effects are an occasional urge to chase Buicks and a tendency to scratch behind your ear with your hind foot.

It's claimed that Costa Rica has more species of insects than anywhere else in the world, and I believe it. Once, in Cahuita—on the Caribbean coast—I was about to enter my cabin when I encountered an enormous beetle. It was about the size of a large teacup, shaped like a giant ladybug and the color of an olive drab army helmet. Feeling brave, I gingerly picked it up by its back, correctly figuring that its wicked-looking legs couldn't reach around the shell. I carried it to a nearby restaurant and proudly displayed my beetle to the people sitting at the bar, figuring that I'd raise a few eyebrows. The bartender looked at my discovery with a bored expression as he remarked, "Yes, those little ones are females." It turned out that I was holding a rhinoceros beetle, possibly the largest bug of the entire insect world. They tell me the male, which fortunately I never happened to confront, grows to a length of 10 inches, sports enormous horns and is colored in brilliant metallic hues.

Earthquakes

All along the mountain chains that stretch from the tip of South America to Alaska, you will feel earthquakes. As a Californian, I've become accustomed to them and seldom experience more than a slight feeling of excitement when windows start rattling and my desk sways a bit. We Californians expect to have several minor quakes a year, and every 25 years or so, a big one.

So it should come as no surprise that Costa Rica has its share of shakes and tremors—actually more than its share. The really big ones here are spaced by decades instead of generations. Yet, Costa Ricans are just as calm about earthquakes as are Californians. After all, compared with the 700 or so tornadoes that slam the midwestern and eastern parts of North America, claiming 80 to 100 victims each season, an occasional shaker seems relatively mild.

The last big tremor—a whopping 7.4 on the Richter Scale—hit the Caribbean coast near the city of Limón in April of 1991. Older structures suffered the most damage, particularly those not constructed to modern-day standards. However, by the beginning of the next tourist season, much of the damage had been repaired, hotels were operating, roads were open to traffic and tourism was going full blast.

A few months after the quake, I visited Cahuita, not too far from the epicenter. Expecting to see a lot of damage and hear horror stories, I was delighted to learn that there were no fatalities in the village and that, except for one major building (which had been made of non-reinforced cement) and a few other smaller structures, the town came through relatively unscathed. Cahuita construction is of wood, which may shake, rattle and twist, but doesn't usually tumble down.

Costa Rica's 7.4 shaker claimed about 40 lives, one of the worst ever. But compare this earthquake with the one in Iran the year before; it was 7.5 on the Richter Scale and claimed over 50,000 victims. A horrible 6.9 quake in Armenia in 1989 killed 25,000 people; one in Costa Rica the following year was just as strong yet nobody was killed. Why the difference?

One answer to this question, besides lower population density, is sensible construction methods. Costa Rican homes and businesses are designed with earthquakes in mind. Costa Rica has prohibited the use of adobe in constructing homes for more than 80 years. This is the only nation in the hemisphere with a ban on adobe, a material with a tendency to collapse and bury earthquake victims. Wood, reinforced concrete block or stressed cement is infinitely safer. Instead of picturesque tile roofs, which can crush inhabitants under tons of heavy beams and broken tile, most Costa Rican roofs are of ordinary-looking corrugated aluminum, plastic or iron. These lightweight roofs may slide about during a quake, but they won't collapse and kill people by burying them.

An interesting feature of the 1991 quake was an uplifting of the coastline. The force raised the land as much as five feet near the town of Puerto Limón and a foot and a half at Puerto Viejo. Coral reefs are now dry land, at the edge of surf where fishermen once hauled in crab, shrimp and red snapper. This lifting of the land from the sea is a wonderful example of how the Central American land bridge was formed some two or three million years ago when quake activity began pushing the land ever higher. Geologists find coral fossils on mountain tops now 9,000 feet above sea level.

WEATHER.
MOISTURE & MORE RAIN
ON THE CARRIBEAN SIDE.
& DRIER ON THE PACIFIC SIDE.

Temperatures and rainfall for selected Costa Rican locations.

Location	Avg.	Jan.	Feb.	Mar.	Apr.	May	June	July	Aug.	Sept.	Oct.	Nov.	Dec.	Year
Alajuela	Highs	81	83	85	85	82	81	81	81	80	80	80	81	81
	Lows	62	62	63	63	64	64	64	63	63	63	63	63	63
	Rain	0.3"	0.5"	0.6"	3.3"	10.8"	10.8"	7.2"	10.3"	13.9"	13.6"	19.9"	1.2"	92"
Golfito	Highs	91	92	92	91	90	89	89	90	89	89	89	90	90
	Lows	71	72	73	73	73	72	71	71	71	71	71	71	72
	Rain	6.3"	5.8"	8.2"	11.2"	19.2"	17.8"	18.4"	22.3"	28.1"	28.1"	22.6"	11.8"	200"
Cahuita	Highs	86	86	87	87	87	87	86	86	87	87	86	86	86
	Lows	68	68	69	71	71	71	71	71	71	71	69	69	69
	Rain	12.7"	8.4"	8.2"	11.0"	11.3"	11.8"	17.1"	12.5"	5.8"	8.2"	15.6"	17.8"	140"
Nicoya	Highs	91	93	95	96	91	89	89	89	87	87	87	87	87
	Lows	69	71	71	73	73	71	71	71	71	71	69	69	71
	Rain	0.2"	0.4"	1.0"	2.8"	11.0"	13.0"	9.8"	12.2"	16.0"	16.3"	4.6"	1.0"	88"
Manuel Antonio	Highs	87	87	89	89	89	87	87	87	86	86	86	86	87
	Lows	69	69	71	71	71	71	69	69	71	71	71	69	71
	Rain	2.9"	1.4"	2.4"	7.0"	15.7"	17.3"	18.4"	19.1"	21.1"	25.8"	15.5"	6.8"	153"
San José	Highs	73	75	77	78	78	78	77	77	78	77	75	77	77
	Lows	59	59	60	60	62	62	67	62	60	60	60	59	62
	Rain	0.4"	0.2"	0.5"	1.8"	9.0"	11.5"	8.6"	10.0"	13.3"	13.3"	5.7"	1.6"	75"

Meseta Central

to Lake Arenal

San Ramón   Sarchí   Grecia
                        Poás
                                Alajuela
Atenas   Heredia
            Rohrmoser-   San José
La Garita   Pavas
            Colón   Cartago
Orotina   Santa   Escazú
                Ana

to San Isidro
del General

Chapter Three

The Meseta Central & Beyond

Those North Americans who make Costa Rica their home—part time or full time—fall into two categories. They either insist on living in the temperate zone or shun that for the more romantic tropical zone. Each group can't understand why the other group wants to live where they do.

Costa Ricans are also divided about which is best, tropical or temperate. But half of the entire population chooses to live in the higher reaches of the country, more or less in the middle, in an area known as the Meseta Central. This is an undulating basin surrounded by a mountain range that starts near Costa Rica's border with Nicaragua and marches south until it crosses the border of Panama. This range is known as the "Cordillera," a picturesque complex of high ridges, valleys, peaks and tablelands, perpetually covered with green vegetation and teeming with wildlife. The mountains vary from rounded promontories to the rugged peaks of the Talamanca Range, dominated by 12,600-foot Cerro Chirripó. Valleys and rolling tablelands are interspersed between steep mountains and volcanic formations, providing fertile agricultural space.

San José, the largest city in Costa Rica, nestles in a wide depression about halfway down the Cordillera, at an altitude of 3,750 feet above sea level. The city of 275,000 inhabitants is surrounded by dozens of satellite towns and villages, and with small cities such as Heredia, Alajuela, Escazú and Cartago perched at various elevations on the uneven plateau. About 15 miles wide by 40 miles long, this break in the mountains is called the "Valle Central" (Central.Valley) or the "Meseta Central" (Central Plateau), depending on who is speaking. From just about any point in this area you are treated to views of the high mountains that form a half-bowl around the Meseta Central. This is not only where most Ticos live, but it is the most heavily populated area in Central America.

Towns and villages surrounding the capital have grown to the point that it is sometimes difficult to tell exactly where one ends and another begins. Although greenery and small farms are abundant, much of the Meseta Central blurs into a loose suburban complex.

Why so many choose to live in the Meseta Central is a question answered in two words: superb climate. This is the land of perpetual spring. Daily high temperatures are almost always in the 70s—creating newspaper headlines on occasions when the thermometer climbs into the high 80s. Low temperatures are always in the 60s. Understand, these aren't average temperatures, which can give a distorted picture, but average high and low readings. Because Costa Rica is so close to the equator, temperatures vary little between summer and winter.

Even this weather doesn't please everyone; some prefer temperatures in the 80s and even 90s, others feel more comfortable in the 60s and low 70s. Fortunately, in Costa Rica, it's possible to "fine-tune" your weather simply by moving a few kilometers in one direction or another. Temperatures and weather patterns are determined by altitude in the tropics. Just a hundred feet higher or lower elevation makes a difference. A 15-minute drive from anywhere on the Meseta Central brings you to a slightly different climate, with more or less rainfall and warmer or cooler temperatures.

Each town or community brags of having the "best climate in the world." Each is perfect for at least some folks. Alajuela is proud of being a few degrees warmer than San José, while Escazú is happy about being a few degrees cooler. Poas boasts about being even cooler than Escazú, and La Garita brags about its rating by

Escazu is slightly cooler than San Jose.

National Geographic of having one of the three best climates in the world. The wonderful thing is that all these choices, however slight, are freely available to you. (The weather chart at the end of Chapter Two illustrates this diversity of weather.)

San José

San José, the capital and business center of Costa Rica, is a comfortable place to live despite its large population of about 275,000. Although downtown streets throng with shoppers and automobiles, neighborhoods a few blocks away can be tranquil residential areas. San José doesn't suffer from the widespread slum zones that plague many U.S. cities. You'll find modest neighborhoods, to be sure, and a few run-down areas, but not the starkly depressing ghettos so apparent in some large United States cities. Truthfully, I've found few residential neighborhoods in San José where I would feel uncomfortable or ashamed to live. There is a slight smog problem in the downtown streets—mostly caused by belching diesel trucks, buses and taxis—but it's nothing when compared with cities like Athens, Los Angeles or Rome. Continuous cross-breezes keep the atmosphere super-clean except in the immediate vicinity of a bus or truck.

As you might expect, the farther from the business center, the better the housing. However, this isn't because of a decaying city core, as is the case with some U.S. cities; it's because the center is taken up with businesses, hotels, restaurants and uncountable shops and stores. For some reason, people from all over the valley feel a compulsion do their shopping in downtown San José. This is mostly from habit and the fact that shopping is something of a social event. By the thousands, crowds of shoppers amble along the streets and avenues, checking out window displays, making purchases and gossiping with friends. Most could shop in their own neighborhoods, but it's more fun this way. So many pedestrians pack the main downtown avenue (Avenida Central) that the city has been forced to turn part of it into a mall. During peak periods, pedestrians turn the rest of the downtown section into a virtual mall by filling the streets, forcing drivers to detour around Avenida Central.

Although just about any neighborhood in San José is comfortable, North Americans are predisposed to congregate in some of the more costly areas. This is understandable, since they tend to be more affluent than Costa Ricans and can better afford upscale neighborhoods. The western edge of San José attracts a large number of foreign residents, particularly around the Sabana Park area (Sabana Sur and Sabana Norte), the upscale neighborhood of Rohrmoser and some areas of Pavas. Better supermarkets, nicer restaurants and amenities such as tennis clubs and attractive parks make this a very livable part of the city. The *Tico Times* classified section frequently lists homes and condos for sale or rent in Pavas and Rohrmoser. Typically, rents for condos start around $400, and homes can go as high as $1,500 a month for a super-nice place. Still farther out, toward the airport, is Cariari, a luxury area with a golf course and country club.

Directly across the valley, the towns of Escazú and Bello Horizonte match Rohrmoser for elegance and expensive housing. Just to the east of downtown San José, Barrio Escalante is an affordable neighborhood of stately older homes. This used to be the "in" place for wealthy Ticos years ago and is now in the process of adapting to middle-class families. Still farther out on the eastern edge of the city, Los Yoses and San Pedro provide moderate to expensive housing. San Pedro provides a university atmosphere with rentals beginning from $300 a month for an apartment to $600 for a house.

By shopping around, you can usually find places that are even more reasonable, and you must remember that ads in the *Tico Times* are directed toward North Americans who can afford to pay more. For less expensive places, check the classified ads in *La Nación*; that's where Ticos find their rentals. San José has several apartment complexes renting furnished places by the day or week that make excellent "base camps" while looking for permanent quarters or when trying out Costa Rica as a place to live.

Finding Your Way

Searching for an address in and around San José and its suburbs can be an exercise in frustration; few buildings have street numbers and no one pays attention to them when they do. Even worse, many streets have no names, or at least no street names posted on the corners. Suppose you are looking for the García residence, whose address is listed as: "From Caballo Blanco 250 mts. West, 300 South." In order to understand where this house is located, you need to know the location of a store called Caballo Blanco, then go two-and-a-half blocks (250 meters) to the west and then three blocks south (300 meters). At that point you need to ask someone which house belongs to the García family.

This confusion isn't restricted to residences; businesses use the same system. On maps, advertisements and business cards, the word "calle" is often abbreviated as "c," "avenida" as "a" and "central" as "ctl." The distance from a point is given in meters (abbreviated with an "m"), although sometimes people give it in *varas* instead of meters, both meaning a long pace or step about a yard long. (A *vara* is a bit shorter than a yard, about 33 inches, an ancient measurement in use before the introduction of the metric system.)

Examples of address insanity: the address of the Hotel Presidente would be "c ctl, av 7-9," which translates "on Calle Central between Avenidas 7 and 9." The address of the bus terminal for Alajuela is "a 2, c 12-14," meaning "facing Avenida 2, between Calles 12 and 14."

Directions and addresses can be vague to the point of impossibility. This is particularly true away from the orderly grid of north-south, east-west streets. An address might be described as, "From the gasoline station, go 100 meters north and 75 *varas* to the east." Which gasoline station? My favorite address is on a real estate agent's business card. It says: "50 *varas* south from where the Mas Por Menos supermarket used to be."

It doesn't do any good to complain; Ticos understand the system perfectly and actually become confused when you use logical addresses. Often, when I take a cab downtown, asking to go to "Avenida Segundo and Calle Primera," the driver responds with a puzzled frown. When I add: "Teatro Nacional," his face lights up with understanding and away we go.

Away from the City: Alajuela

Although many foreigners live in the city of San José, the majority prefer one of the smaller communities surrounding the city. These towns range from expensive to moderately priced places to live. For some mysterious reason, at least six of these towns have the same name—San Isidro—which adds to the confusion of finding your way around! San Antonio is another favorite place name which is scattered about like leaves in the wind.

One of the less expensive, yet pleasant places for foreigners to live is Alajuela. Situated on the western edge of San José, this small city is convenient to the airport and a 20-minute bus ride from downtown San José. Clean, modern buses run every few minutes during the day, stopping at the airport on the way to and from San José. (If you have a small amount of luggage, this is an inexpensive way to get downtown from the airport.)

Your first approach to Alajuela can give a misleading impression. The highway comes in on a higher level than the town, providing an unfortunate panorama of tin roofs in every direction; some new, some rusted, some painted red to resemble tile—but mostly of corrugated iron or aluminum. Now, in the United States, a tin roof usually implies cheap construction, structures such as storage sheds or temporary buildings. But as explained in Chapter Two, this is earthquake country; those picturesque tile roofs can be deadly when they collapse. You may see occasional tile roofs, but you can be reassured that underneath all that pretty tile is a steel-reinforced cement roof. Since the temperature never gets hot or cold, the insulation value of a heavy tile roof is beside the point.

Alajuela's focal point is a large park in the center of town (called the Parque Central, of course), a pleasant place shaded by tall trees, with chess boards built into some of the cement benches that surround the park. If you would like to meet North American retirees to ask information about Alajuela, this is the place to come; sometimes there seems as much English spoken as Spanish. This is the place to find out about housing rentals, who is leaving for the States, who has a car for sale, and who can recommend a gardener or a maid. A reputable money changer sits on a bench across from the bank in case you want to deal with him rather than stand in line. In the evenings, a mixture of classical and pop music can be heard by the park's bandstand where professional musicians entertain a couple of times a week.

Alajuela has several rather attractive neighborhoods, none very expensive, yet all classy in appearance. One area we inspected is called Trinidad, about a 15-minute walk from the park. In 1996, I revisited an American and his Costa Rican wife at their attractive Trinidad home; three bedrooms, two baths, a maid's room and a garage. Three years earlier, he had estimated the value of his home at $35,000. When asked what the home's present-day value might be, the owner, a retired orchardist from Florida said, "Remember, I told you that property here is bound to go up. Today, I figure $47,000 would be a fair price." In similar U.S. neighborhoods, it would cost triple that, at least. Another nice-looking neighborhood is near the local sports stadium, with prices even lower. All these homes have nice landscaping, some with wrought-iron fences.

Housing costs in Alajuela seem to be exceptional bargains, considering the quality of the area. Other places available during my last visit: a two-bedroom, two-bath home for $29,000 and a four-bedroom place for $58,000. An interesting aspect of Alajuela's housing market is that $250 to $500 a month can rent a satisfactory home, one that would sell for between $30,000 and $50,000. This raises the question: is it better to rent or to buy? Some local people are convinced that property will continue going up here, so they advise buying. Who knows?

Heredia

When I first started visiting Costa Rica, Heredia was located way out in the country—a small town with a scattering of nice homes with acreage on the outskirts. Today, the town has expanded toward the sprawl of San José, Alajuela and other nearby communities. The outskirts are still somewhat rural and countrified, but smaller homes have intruded between the large estates, partially filling in the openness of yesterday.

The center of Heredia, like its sister city of Alajuela, features a large, friendly central park complete with weekly band concerts.

This park is shaded by stands of enormous mango trees and has the usual park benches for informal meetings and gossiping. Heredia doesn't attract quite as many foreign retirees and residents as does Alajuela, at least not in the central part of town. The foreign community seems to be scattered in and around the city.

Heredia's famous market is large, featuring quality meats and exceptionally fresh vegetables, fruits and greens of all descriptions. Much of the market's exotic produce is grown by local residents in their backyards. Saturday is market day, and selections are bountiful as well as fresh-picked. People from all over the valley come here for their weekend shopping. The market is near the Parque Central, as is the town's old church, dating from the late 1700s.

From Heredia's northern edge, hills and mountains rise steadily toward the Poás volcano. All along these foothills are winding roads that travel past beautifully maintained homes, alternating with evergreen forests, small farms and verdant pastures. This is one of my favorite parts of the Meseta Central (I almost bought a coffee farm here a few years ago). As the roads climb higher into the mountains, temperatures become progressively cooler, thus allowing prospective home buyers and renters precise adjustment in their environment.

Some foreign residents live on small coffee farms here, with excellent views of the valley, and with orchards of citrus, avocados and tropical fruit supplementing truck gardens for home use and income. When I visited the area in early 1994, coffee prices were extremely depressed and unlikely to rise in the near future (I thought). At that time, coffee-producing property had dropped in price, and it was a good time for locating bargains. However, two years later, in 1996, the situation did a 180-degree turn, with coffee selling at peak prices and the economy rebounding nicely.

Incidentally, those foreigners who own rural parcels and who spend half the year in Costa Rica and the rest of their time in their home country are sometimes anxious to rent their property in their absence to ensure that someone will keep an eye on their place and protect it from vandalism. Some attractive rental deals can be worked out in these instances.

Other Towns and Villages

To the south of Heredia and Alajuela, several smaller towns and open countryside sprinkled with small farms and beautiful homes, draw Ticos and foreigners wanting to escape the city's crush.

The road from Heredia to Turrucares is particularly striking, with lovely, high-quality homes interspersed with small, neatly kept farms and residences. Our taxi driver, who was renting his cab and services by the day, drove us there and proudly pointed out some of the prettier homes along the way. "I was born in this area," he said proudly. And then, with a hint of sadness in his voice, said, "Of course, it is too expensive for me to live here now."

More to the west, Atenas and La Garita are pleasant places which are gaining in popularity, particularly with foreigners who prefer cooler weather. (Some folks are hard to please!) These towns sit along the alternate highway that winds down through Orotina, toward the Pacific beaches. Right now, the traffic through this area is often snarled and frustrating (frightening on Sunday evenings when everybody's returning from Jacó Beach), but when (and if) the superhighway past Ciudad Colón is completed, coast-bound traffic will bypass the Atenas-La Garita area and make it an exceptionally desirable place to live. It's nice here now, even with traffic, lightly settled, with luxury properties interspersed with modest-priced, livable homes. The commercial centers of both towns are particularly neat and attractive. Some friends considered buying a wonderful three-bedroom house on a large lot on the outskirts of Atenas last year for $46,000; if we hadn't already owned more property than we needed, we'd have bought it ourselves.

The town of Grecia sits a few kilometers north of the Pan-American Highway, along a picturesque road that traverses coffee fields and deep valleys. The center of town features a lovely square in front of one of the country's most unique churches, apparently made of sheet iron, probably manufactured by the Eiffel company of France, during the period when they were pre-fabing churches for export around the world. This is a peaceful-looking place with wide streets and prosperous neighborhoods.

Drive another few kilometers and you come upon the famous town of Sarchí. The village and surrounding area is celebrated for its wood products and small furniture factories. More than a dozen stores and outlets display an enticing assortment of quality furniture and decorations made of tropical woods. As far as I know, few North Americans make their homes in Sarchí, although it looks like a pleasant place to live. But many visit there regularly to furnish their homes. Our beach home and our condo near San José are both decorated in contemporary Sarchí.

For those who like to be nearer the big city, but who are so fussy that even Escazú temperatures are too warm, there is a cooler alternative where living is pleasant and heavy exhaust fumes from diesel buses seldom foul the air. This is the Poás area, up on the side of the mountain and volcanic crater of the same name.

To get to Poás, a winding, scenic road takes you past fields of produce and coffee, past comfortable houses with spectacular views. Along the way are roadside stands vending the specialties of the mountainside farms. Strawberries, enormous and sugar-sweet, are year-round treats here, displayed on stands along with homemade cheeses, candies and fresh veggies from backyard gardens. As you gain altitude, the air becomes cooler and slightly crisp. The panorama of the valley in the distance looks impressive indeed. The vegetation becomes even more lush; enormous plants with leaves six feet across hang over the roadside, and flowering trees filter the sunshine overhead.

Finally the road tops a grade and enters the town of Poás. This is a quiet, middle-class town of workers, farmers and, lately, North American *pensionados* and *rentistas*. Its unimposing, no-nonsense business center lacks spiffy boutiques and gourmet restaurants yet maintains a folksy, neighborly atmosphere with adequate commercial conveniences.

The Poás area isn't for everyone, only those who view temperatures over 70 degrees as beastly hot. If any place in the Meseta Central can be described as "the place of eternal spring," it would have to be the area around Poás. I've been told that temperatures almost never rise above 75 degrees, neither do they drop below 60, day or night, summer or winter.

Escazú

For North Americans who prefer the higher elevations, Escazú is the premier retirement and residential location. Only eight kilometers from San José, and 15 minutes or less driving time, depending upon traffic, the town of Escazú is far removed from the city hustle and bustle. Nestled at the base of a magnificent backdrop of ancient volcanic mountains, Escazú has always drawn the affluent and those seeking tranquility away from the city. Somehow this area has managed to preserve remnants of the peace and beauty of its agricultural past, yet provide a modern backdrop for suburban living. As one hotel advertises: "Close to the capital, but worlds away." Of all the suburbs where foreigners choose to live, Escazú is the most popular and is well-stocked with English-speaking expatriates.

Three mountains hover over Escazú. The tallest is Cerro Rabo de Mico at 7,770 feet, and the most spectacular is Pico Blanco at 7,250 feet, with a dramatic, sheer rock face which has challenged the skill of many a mountain climber. Residential streets on the edge of town ascend the mountainside bravely, with each gain in altitude presenting an even better view.

The total population of the Escazú area is said to be 40,000, but it doesn't appear nearly that large. It looks more like a cluster of sprawling villages, with quaint, old adobe buildings painted in a traditional two-color motif. Incidentally, the three-foot, colored stripe you'll see painted along the bottom of a house is believed to ward off evil spirits and witches. It must work, because I encountered few evil spirits or witches during any of my visits.

Escazú is effectively divided into three separate towns: San Miguel de Escazú, San Rafael de Escazú and San Antonio de Escazú, each having its own church and patron saint. The red-domed church in San Miguel de Escazú was constructed in 1799 and has survived numerous earthquakes since.

As San José grew and spread out, artists and those in search of serenity began moving to Escazú. No longer the peaceful retreat of yesterday, the area retains a reputation as an artists' colony as well as a retirement center. Escazú's higher elevations are ideally suited for those who think that San José's climate is too warm. It is also high enough that the occasional light smog that sometimes touches San José remains far below. For these reasons, a large number of North Americans choose Escazú and the surrounding towns as their place of residence. Here is where the United States ambassador's residence is located. Two famous country clubs provide the area with golf, tennis and a focal point for the society set. Escazú is the center of much of Costa Rica's social life.

An odd-sounding place for newcomers to go for orientation and assistance is Escazú's very active American Legion Post. This is the largest such entity outside of the United States and is combined with a VFW post, making it even larger. More than just a veterans' organization, this group reaches out to all foreigners and Costa Ricans, offering "a socially active, bilingual fellowship of warm, interesting, international people." You needn't be a Legion member or even a veteran to be welcome; this may be the only Legion post in the world in that respect. A Lions Club, Rotary Club and several other service organizations also make their headquarters in this picturesque setting. All of these organizations welcome non-member visitors. The clubhouse is a popular stop for newcomers seeking a welcome and introduction to the community of Escazú and the neighboring town of Santa Ana. I always recommend clubs and charity associations as valuable windows of opportunity for making friends and building a network of social contacts.

Escazú (and its environs) has a sophistication that makes it stand out among San José's suburbs as a prestige address. Although it admittedly has some of the more expensive places to live, modestly priced homes and apartments are also available throughout the community. Those who choose to live here say they wouldn't think of settling anywhere else. "We have the best of all worlds," explained a couple who owns a small house on the slope of Pico Blanco. "We live in the country, with a gorgeous view of the city below, yet we are just five minutes away from stores, restaurants, or whatever we need." They pointed out that although they are close to San José, they rarely go there on other than essential business. Well-stocked supermarkets, shops, doctors, dentists and a first-class health clinic serve the community's needs quite well. Restaurants of all descriptions abound, including European, barbecue, Chinese and even a Cajun restaurant for the yuppie trade.

Although new homes are sprouting on the fringes of Escazú, the municipality requires that construction near the town's center conform to colonial or traditional style. Most buildings are one-story, two-story at most, fulfilling a sense of rural, Costa Rican countryside living.

"Property here is probably the most expensive of anywhere in the valley," explained one of Escazú's many real estate agents. "Everyone wants to live here. You can pay $95,000 and more for a nice three-bedroom home that you could buy for $45,000 elsewhere, but this is a quality area." He pointed out that there is no real "foreign colony" in Escazú, because Gringos tend to spread throughout the community, interspersed with Ticos and other foreigners. Although some prefer to live in "sealed-in" developments—compounds with high walls and 24-hour guards—more folks live in ordinary homes or townhouses. A two- or three-bed-room condo in one of the exclusive compounds might start at around $80,000 and go up from there (way up), whereas a similar place in an ordinary building might start at $60,000. Those who choose to pay more for the security feel it is worth it, since they can comfortably leave their places unoccupied for months at a time while they return home for visits. Others rely on neighbors and friends to take care of things while they are gone.

Escazú is a great place to make your headquarters while exploring the Meseta Central. There are several nice hotels here, small and often relatively inexpensive. Several bed-and-breakfasts in Escazú are priced as low as $35 a night. Getting into San José and environs is easy, since bus service is frequent.

accommodations
see p. 47

Rohrmoser

Rohrmoser is at the upper end of the housing market in the immediate San José area, and it is Escazú's main competition for upscale residences. For some folks, there is no competition; Rohrmoser wins hands down. Here, homes and condos consistently command higher rents and sales prices than elsewhere in the metropolitan area. Unlike Escazú, Rohrmoser looks more like a modern city suburb, in that it has sidewalks and boulevards instead of mostly narrow roads and streets with dirt shoulders. (For some that's an advantage, for others it's not charming enough.)

Homes and apartment buildings here are much newer, with some condo development and home building still underway. Started by a German developer, Rohrmoser begins at the end of Sábana Park and runs along both sides of Rohrmoser Boulevard until it reaches the ultra-modern shopping center of Plaza Mayor. From that point west, Rohrmoser is on the northern side of the boulevard, and Pavas is on the eastern side. The U.S. Embassy, incidentally is in Pavas, on Pavas Highway.

Many North Americans live in Rohrmoser, but the largest percentage of your neighbors will be Tico professionals who like the convenience of being close to the business center of the city. A big advantage of locating here is that it is just a ten-minute drive to downtown San José (five minutes by taxi), yet it is quiet and safe feeling. Something that adds to the security is the presence of private guards who are hired by homeowners on the block. With everyone contributing, the cost of 24-hour security is affordable and comforting.

Santa Ana

Another part of the Meseta Central that attracts North Americans to become residents is Santa Ana, a sunny mountain valley just another six kilometers to the west of Escazú. The altitude here is lower than either Escazú or San José, making it slightly warmer and dryer. A number of small rivers cross the rolling valley, and rounded mountains provide a scenic backdrop.

Santa Ana's setting is also more rural than Escazú, with crops such as sugar cane, rice, beans and coffee growing all around this town of 20,000 residents. Roadside stands sell braids of garlic and onions, garden-fresh vegetables and jars of rich local honey. (Despite Africanized bees' nasty reputations, they produce high-quality honey and more of it than ordinary bees.) All roads converge upon a central area, giving Santa Ana the feeling of a downtown center, rural, yet sophisticated. High above the town, on the mountain Cerro Pacacua, is a 20,000-acre forest preserve and bird sanctuary, keeping nature ever-present in the local ambience.

A few generations ago—before it became an easy thing to drive to the beach for vacations—San José's wealthy families maintained summer homes in Santa Ana. This was the place to spend weekends and school vacations, a place for the upper crust to host parties and entertain lavishly. This old tradition left its traces on today's community, with nice homes scattered about the area. Some rather nice developments, complete with swimming pools, gardens and 24-hour security, are found here. This is the place for polo matches and international equestrian competitions. Seasonal festivals bring an impressive parade of horseback riders, who ride their high-stepping steeds along the streets to the central plaza where the main celebration is underway. (Don't try to drive along the parade route on festival day; horses have the right-of-way.)

Santa Ana has a deserved reputation as a working artists' colony, with a number of writers and amateur artists present as well. The town is famous for ceramics, and production of excellent pieces is a major industry, with almost 30 workshops and 150 local people engaged in the art. Excellent restaurants, a first-class supermarket and shopping of all descriptions are at hand, eliminating the need to go to the crowded world of downtown San José for odds and ends. Yet, when necessary, it's but an easy 10-mile drive along one of the country's few stretches of superhighway. One of the largest and most elegant shopping malls in the country is found between Santa Ana and Escazú on this highway: the Multi-Plaza. It's worth a visit.

Of all the Meseta Central retirement locations, I suspect that communities from Santa Ana west to the town of Ciudad Colón may have the best potential for development and property appreciation. The reason for my belief is a planned extension of the divided highway from San José through Ciudad Colón that will someday hook up with the Pacific Coast Highway 34. This highway, by the way, is one of the few made of cement, instead of the usual mixture of asphalt, gravel and brown sugar (or whatever they mix with asphalt to make a dissolvable road surface). It's lasted without damage—not even a tiny pothole—for about 15 years. Surely, the government transportation bosses will someday realize the value of cement highway construction as opposed to disappearing asphalt surfaces.

Anyway, traffic moves right along on this highway, zipping back and forth to San José with surprising ease. (Surprising for Costa Rica.) When the highway is extended to the Pacific, this will dramatically cut the driving time to the popular beach communities of Jacó and Quepos. With Pacific beaches just an hour's drive from Santa Ana, the convenience will make the area even more attractive as a place to live, and real estate could become a good investment. When I mention this possibility to my Tico friends, they shrug their shoulders and say, "Don't count on that highway in the near future. We'd be delighted if they'd just fill the potholes on the roads we have!"

San Isidro del General

At first glance, this town would seem to be a rather unusual place for North Americans to choose as a place for residence or retirement. There is nothing spectacular about San Isidro del General; it is an ordinary, small Costa Rican city. It's neat and orderly, with the ubiquitous mountain views common to most of the country. Few vacationers visit San Isidro, and those who have passed through the town may get it mixed up with one of the other half-dozen San Isidros in the mountains. But those North Americans who have discovered San Isidro's secrets love living here. The climate is considerably warmer than San José, which suits some folks just fine, and the pace far slower.

Located on a wide ridge, not far from the high peak of Cerro Chirripó, a continuous breeze keeps the air clear and aromatic with flower blossom perfume. Daytime temperatures are pleasantly warm for my tastes (maybe hot for some folks), and evenings are tempered by cool air flowing down from Chirripó Peak. Although not as peaceful and idyllic as some other Costa Rican towns, once you are away from the main square—and the inevitable cars, motorcycles and trucks circling the square in search of a parking space—the pace slackens to a very peaceful stride.

Like most older Costa Rican towns, San Isidro features a main square in its center, the usual well-kept park. Since the park is the social gathering place for local residents, it isn't surprising that the North American community uses it as their social focal point as well. The open-air restaurant of Hotel Chirripó faces the park, and at any given time, you can count on at least some of the tables being occupied by English-speaking patrons.

Real estate and rentals are exceptionally inexpensive here. Since it is off the ordinary tourist routes, with no beaches and lacking in discos and other flashy attractions, San Isidro is likely to remain inexpensive. On one visit, I talked with an American who had just completed building a small, two-bedroom home and was anxious to find a tenant. He was offering to rent it for almost nothing just to have someone in there to take care of it while he returned home.

Several North Americans have taken advantage of the climate and low-cost real estate, living on small farms on the outskirts of town, or along the highway toward the beach at Dominical. The views along this road are absolutely spectacular, with neat, prosperous-looking farms and picturesque homes in the mountain valleys below looking like toys along a model train set. At the time of my last visit, one American from Texas, who was married to a Tica lady, operated a motel, restaurant and bar on the highway, midway between San Isidro and the ocean.

Lake Arenal District

The northern portion of the Cordillera mountain chain, until recently ignored by North Americans, has one of the best potentials for growth of any place in Costa Rica. Certainly that's my opinion and one shared by many other North Americans who are buying property around Lake Arenal as quickly (and quietly) as they can. Those who know about Lake Arenal would love to keep it a secret, but truth will out! The character of this region is so different from other parts of Costa Rica that it's difficult to believe you are in the same country.

The Lake Arenal district is in the upper end of the same mountain chain, but that's as far as the similarity with other highland areas goes. As I understand it, the mountains dip lower at this position in the chain to form a low break or window in the Cordillera. This interruption in the mountain ridges permits a reversal of wind patterns, allowing strong easterly winds to bring moist air off the Caribbean with an abundance of rain. There is no such thing as a dry season in the Arenal area; it's a year-round wonderland of greenness and lush vegetation. When I asked one long-time resident how much it rained, she replied, "On the average, about 14 months out of the year."

Before the government started work to build a dam to create the wonderfully scenic lake, very few people lived here. The project required several thousand workers and support people and 16 years to complete. Roads were cut into the area, opening it up to Costa Rican settlers who started farms and small villages. After the lake was created, many workers elected to stay on in the company housing that was built during the construction stages. The population here is still very scanty, but it is growing daily, particularly in the numbers of foreigners who have "discovered" Lake Arenal.

To get there via paved road, the quickest way is by turning off the Pan-American Highway at Cañas, an extremely hot and dusty place during the dry season. Were it not for the ample irrigation water coming from Lake Arenal, Cañas would be more like a desert than a rich agricultural region. An air-conditioned auto and lightweight clothing are necessities here. Yet just 18 kilometers away by a tortuously winding road, the air conditioner is shut off and car windows rolled down to take advantage of the delightful fresh air.

Tilarán

By the time you reach the little town of Tilarán, only 23 kilometers from Cañas, a sweater might feel comfortable when the sky happens to be overcast. The countryside changes from pool table-flat to steep-sided hills, from dusty dry to bright green. The road climbs gently now, as the fields seem to become greener with every curve, past fat cattle grazing fetlock-deep in richly grassed pastures and—where land hasn't been cleared for cattle or agriculture—some astonishingly heavy stands of tropical forest. Just about every imaginable kind of tropical tree or crop thrives here, from bananas to macadamia nuts.

A surprisingly non-tropical-looking town—with wide streets, neatly maintain homes and prosperous businesses—Tilarán has become the home base of a number of expatriates. The climate is temperate and springlike, due to a continuous eastern wind which drops moisture on Tilarán even during the dry season. This keeps the town green year round, but with less moisture and wind velocity than nearby Arenal. Local residents publish their own newspaper, partly in English, which promotes ecology and recycling projects for the nation.

A few miles east of Tilarán the view of Lake Arenal bursts upon you, one of the prettiest lakes in the world. The fact that it is artificial is something that fades in importance when the overall effect is considered. Windsurfers claim this is the second-best place in all the world to enjoy their sport. What the first place is for windsurfers, I don't know, but it surely can't be any more beautiful than Lake Arenal.

Almost all residents in this area live on or near the drive that skirts Lake Arenal. The paved portion of the road has a scattering of European-type homes, chalets and an occasional commercial unit such as a pulpería, those community store-tavern combinations so common in rural Costa Rica. Most homes are obviously recently constructed, giving evidence of their newness in a developing land.

This area somehow doesn't seem like Costa Rica. Were it not for the colorful bougainvilleas, flowering oaks and luscious yellow Cortez trees, this countryside would look like an exaggerated version of the Tennessee or Kentucky hill country, or perhaps the lower elevations of Switzerland in the summer. Of course, the banana plants and broad-leaved philodendrons quickly dispel this notion.

A few neat, prosperous-looking villages are spaced along the highway, which has a surprisingly good paved surface. However, once you drive past the town of Arenal, the road turns into graded clay and occasional pavement—slow, with astonishing potholes the size of bathtubs rather than pots—but entirely passable in an ordinary rental car. If and when the government gets around to paving this stretch of road, the Arenal district will be quickly accessed from the Meseta Central, and should grow at an even faster rate. For those living or working in San José, this could be a wonderful site for a weekend getaway.

Nuevo Arenal

The town on the lake is called Nuevo Arenal or, quite often, simply Arenal. This is a surprisingly prosperous-looking place, with neat little houses interspersed with expensive-looking ones. The town sits high on the sloping bank of Lake Arenal, with most homes and businesses situated with a lake view in mind. Streets are well-paved, and more are in the process of being paved in anticipation of a population explosion. Parts of town have an oddly unfinished look, with newly paved streets and vacant lots interspersed with an occasional house. The center of town has the inevitable soccer field, but with spectator benches curiously pointed towards the street, away from the field, as if the soccer team is so bad that locals would rather watch the traffic, scarce as it is.

Arenal obviously was a development planned by the government during the dam's construction phase. Many of today's homes here are left over from that era. Unlike the traditional Latin American residential style—built close together and against the sidewalk to allocate space for interior patios—Arenal homes have real lawns, reminiscent of small-town U.S.A. This adds to Arenal's strange, non-Latin American look.

Because of the area's beauty, the temperate-tropical combination climate and the low cost of real estate, the Lake Arenal region is undergoing a buying frenzy. Buyers from Canada, the United States and Europe are furtively looking at property and investing. Germans, Swiss and Italians appear to be the biggest sharks, biting off chunks of the land as quickly as they can. They try not to appear eager as they snap up bargains, and they do their best to keep this place a secret, lest hordes of other foreigners descend upon paradise and ruin their plans of being the only ones there.

Prices have risen appreciably since my first visit, just as I predicted. At that time, a livable three-bedroom place, built of reinforced cement and stucco, could be bought for as little as $7,800; you'd pay five times that amount today—or more. That's still not bad. In early 1994, we could have purchased a three-hectare coffee farm with a house and all utilities for $62,000. Surely, it would sell for more today.

It's not surprising that prices are going up on property around Arenal. It's a very desirable area. Still, it's hard to conceive that inflation could be anything like that along the beaches. But in the meantime, this is one of the few places where inexpensive waterfront property is still available. Another favorable circumstance: since this is lakefront property, it doesn't fall under the complicated and restrictive laws that regulate ownership and construction by the ocean. Here waterfront property is owned outright instead of leasing it from the municipality. You can build pretty much what you like and wherever you care to without fear that someday in the future the government will begin enforcing the coastal building laws more rigorously. However, be aware that the water level in the lake fluctuates from dry season to wet season, as water is drawn off for irrigation and hydroelectric power. Your waterfront lot could end up with a deep frontage of dry land in the dry season.

Something sure to increase the development of tourism, business and residential growth is the lake's world-famous windsurfing. The best is on the western end of the lake, near Tilarán. Aficionados from all over the world come here to brave the steady winds, choppy waves and icy water. "This is the cleanest water in the world," said one sportsman from Montreal. "You can drink it right out of the lake with no worries."

Because of the lake's growing fame, a large number of surfers come here in search of adventure, but find accommodations scarce. This creates a good climate for business opportunities and investment. Several North Americans operate windsurfing rental enterprises, and I understand others are planning to construct a hotel, catering specially to windsurfers.

Arenal Volcano and Fortuna

No trip to Costa Rica can be considered complete until you've visited the Arenal Volcano. Active continuously over several centuries, the volcano's north slope exploded about 15 years ago, destroying a village and killing over 60 people. (A geologist had tried to warn them of an impending eruption, but nobody believed him.) The nearest and best place to observe the activity is in the hot pools of Tabacón, a resort wedged into a steaming-hot river canyon at the volcano's base. You can sit on underwater stools by the bar and sip piña coladas while you listen to the thunder-like explosions accompanied by puffs of smoke and red-hot boulders coughing from the volcano's vent.

The volcano has done marvels for tourism hereabouts. The nearby town of Fortuna has become prosperous, serving the needs of the hordes of sightseers. New hotels, restaurants and stores are appearing each season. Fortuna is an exceptionally neat and pleasant community, one which could well make a good place for retirement. With a new road going through San Ramón, San José is only a couple hours' drive. Surprisingly, not many North Americans have settled in Fortuna at the time of our last visit. However, this could be a place for you to look at—should you like a quiet, neat town with great potential and friendly Tico neighbors.

ATLANTIC
the caribbean
is mainly African
Jamaican

Pacific is
Latin
EUROPEAN

Chapter Four

The Caribbean Coast

The same mountain chain that creates the delightful weather in Costa Rica's highlands further separates the country into eastern and western tropical zones. Because of this separation, the Caribbean and the Pacific zones have distinct personalities. The differences are not only in weather patterns, animals, plants and marine life, but there are marked cultural dissimilarities as well. The Caribbean is Jamaican/African; the Pacific is Latin/European.

"Tropics" implies long stretches of deserted beaches, with thick jungle hovering at the edge of the sand. It means monkeys jostling branches in the strangler fig trees while parrots, macaws and a thousand other birds screech, twitter and sing lyrically in the sunset. Costa Rica's tropics have all of this and much more.

The Caribbean coast has two distinct regions. Its southern portion, which is lightly populated, reflects Jamaican and African influences, blended with Costa Rican and Spanish personalities. The northern half of the coast is almost uninhabited, visited mostly by fishing fanatics, tourists and ecology students. (Incidentally, Costa Ricans often refer to this coast as the "Atlantic" rather than the "Caribbean.")

The northern inland lagoons and waterways are famous for world-class fishing of all kinds. Record-size tarpon and snook are routinely hooked in these scenic jungle rivers and inlets. The best snook angling is usually from the shore, around river mouths, with 20- to 30-pounders not uncommon. Fishermen also bring in jacks, mackerel, barracuda, snapper and other species when fishing the Caribbean coast. While waiting for exciting action, you are treated to the sight of monkeys frolicking in the trees, an occasional parrot or toucan darting among the branches, and sometimes a crocodile lurking along the shoreline. The Tortuguero area is known as an important nesting place of the endangered green sea turtle.

No roads enter this northern region; the only way to get here is by airplane or motor launch. My belief is that the area is far too isolated and the climate too humid for development other than ecotourism projects.

Limón Coast

The southern Caribbean coast attracts surfers, snorkelers and reggae enthusiasts, as well as ordinary tourists and ecology buffs, who want to savor the unique tropical environment. Weather patterns here are unpredictable, with no sharp distinction between winter and summer. Rain can fall at any time, and usually does. Winds often blow down from the north, sometimes causing the Caribbean coast to duplicate Miami's weather. The plus side of the Caribbean weather is that things stay green and lush year round, unlike the Pacific coast. The down side is that it is always more humid, and insects tend to grow healthy and robust on this edge of the continent.

The city of Limón, a two-and-a-half-hour drive from San José, is where Columbus sighted the American mainland for the first time, back in 1502. Apparently he thought it was another island and didn't bother going ashore himself. (If Limón was as depressing back then as it is today, I understand why.) At best, Limón has always been a ramshackle affair--a tropical banana port, too large to have the charm of a village, yet too small to offer the amenities of a real city. To make matters worse, Limón still hasn't completely recovered from the big earthquake of 1991. Several damaged buildings are simply being ignored and probably never will be repaired. To be truthful, many of Limón's buildings look ready to fall if someone should slam the door too hard.

Cahuita and Puerto Viejo

To find real charm along this shore, you must travel farther south along the paved highway that heads for the Panamanian border at Sixaola. As is the case all along the Caribbean shores, from Belize to Panama, many inhabitants are descendants of ex-slaves from the island of Jamaica. Their ancestors came to Costa Rica in the latter 1800s, as construction workers on the railroad from Limón to San José. Isolated from the European culture of the Meseta Central--partly because of the difficulty in traveling between the areas, and partly because of malaria and yellow fever quarantines--the coastal black people developed a unique Afro-Carribe culture, a combination of British Jamaica, Spanish Costa Rica and deepest Africa. Because English is the area's first language (spoken with a delightful British-Jamaican lilt), this area is favored by tourists and visitors who don't want to bother learning another language during their stay.

From San José, three-and-a-half hours of scenic driving brings you to the village of Cahuita. (It's about four hours by bus.) The village has a picture-book quality in its tropical Afro-Caribbean setting. Many houses stand on stilts to discourage insects, some buildings are painted bright colors similar to the style in Jamaica. Women and girls carry bundles on their heads with grace and enviable posture.

The main road follows the shore, past black sand beaches and coral reefs to the north, and past more coral and beaches of yellow sand to the south. Along the yellow sand beach is Cahuita National Park, a 13-kilometer stretch of jungle complete with howler monkeys (which the Costa Ricans call congos), feisty parrots and wildlife of all descriptions. A foot trail parallels the beach through a thick tangle of tropical trees, vines and orchids. Butterflies, orange and purple land crabs and iguanas keep you company on the hike.

Many North Americans and Europeans live here year round, some operating successful businesses. Others regularly arrive in November and head home by May. I had the good fortune to meet a young California couple who invited me to visit their winter quarters in Cahuita. They lived in a picturesque, thatch-roofed cabin perched next to a coral reef and shaded by graceful coconut trees. Their house was very rustic, with minimal furniture, but they enjoyed their winter home immensely. The surf washed at their front door, spilling into a small depression of smooth black rocks where their children played, as if in their own private saltwater swimming pool.

The Limón coast is particularly attractive for the younger set. A special emphasis is placed on youthful activities, with reggae music thumping loudly from tropical bars, and surfboards, snorkel gear and brief swimsuits the order of the day. People who love Cahuita or Puerto Viejo--Cahuita's sister village a few miles south--will tell you that the rest of Costa Rica is too tame for them. They prefer this movie-set tropical setting--romantic, picturesque and inexpensive. One bar in the very center of Cahuita features extraordinarily powerful loudspeakers on the front porch which blare Jamaican rock music day and night. The volume is such that it rattles windows a block away and peels the paint off of passing automobiles. I love to visit here, but for long-term living in the tropics, my personal preference would be the Pacific coast.

dryer winters (handwritten)

The Pacific Coast

This side of the country is characterized by dryer winters, regular surf from the open ocean and a much larger population of foreigners. Although most come from North America, a large number of Europeans are moving into the area. Many come from Germany, Switzerland and Italy, but other nationalities are well-represented, too. Some operate successful hotels, restaurants and other tourist-oriented ventures which the business-friendly Costa Rican government makes possible.

3 areas (handwritten)

The West Coast can be divided into three basic geographical sections: the Guanacaste-Nicoya Peninsula area in the north, the beaches from Jacó to Uvita in the center, and the Golfo Dulce-Osa Peninsula area to the south. Each area has its boosters who will assure you that there is no place in all of Central America as nice as their favorite location. I've seen them all, and I can say that making a choice among them would be difficult indeed.

A nice feature of all these tropical beach areas is that they are accessible from the Meseta Central, within a few hours' drive by bus or automobile, and almost no time at all by airplane. Some locations require longer driving times than others, but as pavement replaces gravel roads, travel times will decrease.

Certain areas are highly developed, focusing on tourism, with discos, restaurants and boutiques as well as expensive hotels and homes. Other places are oriented toward permanent and semipermanent residents, especially retirees. Still other locations are almost totally deserted, offering no facilities other than what you carry with you. Bring camping equipment if you care to; camping is permitted on all of Costa Rica's beaches except for parks and residential areas. The law considers the first 50 meters of beach land public property. Costa Ricans take full advantage of camping, and during the traditional summer vacation period (January and February), you'll see a multitude of tents lining the beaches, as Tico families enjoy economical vacations.

Eastward from the ocean's surf, rolling hills of forest and farmland spread inland and up the mountain slopes, becoming steeper and more picturesque with each kilometer. Much of this land is wilderness, traversed by occasional dirt roads that become quagmires in the rainy season. Despite isolation and transportation difficulties, foreigners find these rustic sections exceptionally desirable places to live. As the government gradually paves the roads along the coast and into the interior, more and more settlers will surely swell the ranks of North Americans and Europeans who live here and operate businesses. With easy access, property values ought to increase dramatically.

Guanacaste's Pacific Coast

A number of important beach locations on the northern coast attract Costa Ricans and foreigners alike for vacations, retirement or business opportunities. These beaches are easily reached from San José in three to five hours by car. The main highway is paved and in generally good condition (if you discount the ever-present potholes), but can be agonizingly slow when you are stacked up behind a string of slow trucks on their way to or from the Pacific docks. Relax, go with the flow and enjoy the sights and the ever-changing scenery from the Meseta Central to the Pacific coast.

Rainfall is lower here than anywhere else in the country. Unlike most of Costa Rica, the dry season here is truly dry, with almost no rain falling during the months of December, January or February. Grass turns parched and yellow; most trees lose their leaves, which are often replaced with a gorgeous display of colorful blossoms. Around homes or along inhabited beaches, you'll see more evergreen, leafy trees because they've been deliberately planted.

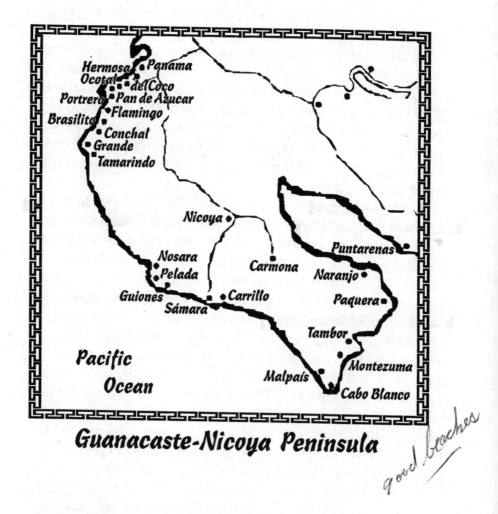

Hermosa • Panama
Ocotal •
Portrero • del Coco
• Pan de Azucar
Brasilito • Flamingo
• Conchal
• Grande
• Tamarindo

Nicoya •

Nosara
• Pelada
Guiones
Sámara • Carrillo

Carmona
Naranjo •

Puntarenas •

Paquera •

Tambor

Pacific

Ocean

Malpais
Montezuma

Cabo Blanco

Guanacaste-Nicoya Peninsula

good beaches

Playas del Coco Area

A quickly developing complex of *playas* (beaches) begins at Playa Panama, and stretches south through Playa Hermosa, Playas del Coco and ending at Playa Ocotal. A nice beach in this complex, and one with development potential is Playa Hermosa. "Hermosa" means "beautiful" in Spanish, and Playa Hermosa lives up to its name. This is a lovely place, with a curving shoreline of clean sand and a peninsula which shields it from the open ocean and dangerous riptides.

Development in Hermosa lags way behind nearby Playas del Coco, the most commercially developed of these beach communities. Since the pavement ends in the center of El Coco, tourists tend to stay here rather than braving annoying stretches of washboard gravel roads to get to nearby beaches. In contrast with neighboring communities, which are sleepy and tranquil, Playas del Coco restaurants, bars and discos stay open late on weekends, with happy people singing and shouting in exuberance all night long. (At least it seemed that way to me one weekend when I was trying to catch up on my sleep!)

Playas del Coco is a fun place to be, with potential for investment opportunities. At least 60 North Americans live here, some with viable businesses. But for retirement or long-term vacations, I might choose one of the quieter, nearby places. A number of foreigners own homes along the fringes of the less populated beaches. I understand that several North American families live in Hermosa Beach and more are in the planning stages of building. Italians and Germans are represented here as well.

One resident, a retired Air Force sergeant, related his reasons for settling here. First of all, he bought ten acres (by mail) before he retired from the military. Then, before he had the chance to visit the property, he received a letter offering to trade the ten acres for one-and-one-half acres of jojoba bean property. This seemed to be a good deal, so he signed the papers for a trade, again, all by mail. When he finally retired and arrived in Costa Rica to claim his jojoba bean plantation, he discovered that jojoba beans don't grow in this area, and furthermore, the property was not only inaccessible by automobile, it had a Nicaraguan family living on it who were not inclined to move simply because the owner wanted them to. While he was looking for a way to visit his jojoba bean farm, he fell in love with a Costa Rican lady and got married. He forgot about his agricultural fiasco and settled down in his wife's village. "Now I have a seven-year-old daughter, a house in a village where I am the only Gringo, and I have a good life. My army pension is only $855 a month, but I live like a king." He took a part-time job at a tourist hotel as night watchman to supplement his pension. "The only thing I don't like about being a night watchman," he said plaintively, "is weekends, when guests party all night; they make so much noise I can't sleep." He was right; they kept me awake too.

There can be no question about Coco's potential for business, retirement or long-term living. Several very successful, American-owned enterprises operate here, and more are on the way. But if I don't sound particularly enthusiastic about the place, it's probably because this is where I locked my keys in my rental car and struggled for two hours in the hot sun before figuring out a way to get inside without breaking a window. A good car thief could have done it in less than 20 seconds. (One of the most horrible sights in the world is a set of ignition keys hanging in a locked rental car.)

A few kilometers to the south is Playa Ocotal, a place that maintains a village atmosphere despite also having a deluxe tourist resort. The accommodations are tasteful, blending in with the natural surroundings, although I've heard complaints about service. The village is on the shore of Bahía Pez Vela (Sailfish Bay), and the fishing is said to live up to the name.

Flamingo Beach

The next beach complex is just a few kilometers south as the crow flies. But since there is no connecting road, unless you can fly like a crow you must return to the paved road and make a wide loop on paved and dirt roads—a 65- or 70-kilometer drive. This array of beaches starts with Playa Pan de Azucar and continues south to Playa Tamarindo, including the beaches of La Penca, Potrero, Flamingo, Brasilito, Conchal, Playa Grande, Tamarindo and Langosta, in that order.

By far, the prettiest is Playa Flamingo. A wide, curving beach of white sand, with startling blue waves that turn to white-capped rollers before crashing loudly against the shore, creates one of the prettiest scenes imaginable. Hotels here cater to affluent tourists who can afford to fly in from San José and spend $150 a day for rooms. Ordinary budget tourists will find few (if any) reasonably priced rooms. Ongoing building activity may change all of this.

As you might imagine, foreigners have taken over this beach and have built some very spiffy places. Some private homes offer rooms for rent and probably do well, for there were absolutely no vacancies in town when I last visited here. Most of the non-developed beachfront is also owned by foreigners. However, local authorities have done well in keeping the first 50 meters open, affording the public unlimited access.

The beach adjacent to Flamingo is Brasilito. At this time, it's an inexpensive place for Ticos to come and enjoy themselves on the beach. It's also a place to look for an inexpensive *cabina* or a room, although few foreigners seem to do so. The beach isn't bad at all; I'm surprised there isn't more commercial development.

The next village is at Playa Conchal. The Spanish word "Conchal" refers to the shells on the beach. In fact, the entire beach is composed of tiny, water-worn shells instead of sand. Although very undeveloped today, a planned 5,000-room resort could change all of that, should it really happen!

Turtles and Tourists

An excellent example of how tourism and conservation can work hand in hand is found to the south of the Flamingo beach complex. Starting at Playa Grande and continuing south past Playa Tamarindo, a broad, sandy beach serves as nesting grounds for endangered Leatherback turtles. It used to be that local residents awaited the arrival of these huge, prehistoric survivors and collected the eggs in buckets as they were being deposited, selling the harvest to bars and restaurants all over the country.

Alarmed by the possibility of the turtles' extinction, the Costa Rican government instituted a model conservation program. Local people are enlisted to help protect the nesting grounds. Guarding the beaches and guiding tourists through the nesting grounds put local people to work. Hotels and restaurants have opened to accommodate the ever-increasing number of tourists. Jobs are created for even more local residents. This boom has only begun; future development seems inevitable.

Conservationists have expressed mixed feelings about this program. While they praise the protection of the nesting grounds, they point out that the extra tourist foot traffic causes damage by visitors inadvertently stepping on the hatchlings. On the other hand, the number of baby turtles killed in this manner is nothing when compared with the ones which used to end up as a tasty *boca* in some San José bar.

Playa Grande

Turtles need a wide, sandy beach with ample portions not touched by high tide; Playa Grande fills these requirements admirably. It's long and unpopulated, with few human footprints to disturb the solitude. A few homes and one or two small hotels have sprung up along the northern part, but nothing like the construction underway on other West Coast beaches. As a part of the Tamarindo Refuge, the area will always be somewhat restricted in tourist development, even though the natural beauty and wildness of the area is bound to attract more people in the future.

I looked at a small development (about a half-dozen luxury homes) on beachfront lots which are supposedly "grandfathered," or titled before restrictions were placed on the beach. One place was for sale, a large, tastefully constructed home with a neatly manicured lawn ending at a beach wall marking the 50-meter boundary. The owner half-apologized for the home's isolation and lack of anything to do, adding, "The hope of this little community is that things won't change. What we offer here is location, nothing else." He indicated the broad expanse of beach visible through a stand of coconut trees and said, "The whole idea here is to fit into the ecology without disturbing things, particularly not the nesting turtles and their life cycle." The house's window frames were made of wood instead of the more practical aluminum, "because metal frames reflect moonlight and confuse the hatchling Leatherbacks. We don't allow any lights from our homes to escape at night. For bright lights and nightlife you have to go to Tamarindo."

Playa Tamarindo

Tamarindo Beach begins where Playa Grande ends, a picturesque estuary separating the two. Tamarindo is where turtle-watchers find hotels. Launches begin ferrying passengers across the estuary around midnight. Tourists tiptoe quietly along the beach and pause to observe the huge turtles as they awkwardly pull themselves up on the beach to bury their eggs six feet deep in the sand. This is an unforgettable sight; some of these turtles are more than 12 feet across and weigh up to 1,500 pounds! The one I watched laying eggs must have been a pygmy; she was barely eight feet wide. Our guide claimed that during the peak of the season as many as 350 turtles can be on the beach in a single night.

The village of Tamarindo is a perfect example of foreign development. Almost every business—restaurants, hotels, shops, bars and so forth—appears to be owned by Canadians, Americans, Italians, or Swiss. The influx of foreign money and the resulting buying frenzy has pushed the price of most properties into the range of the ridiculous. According to local Ticos, the asking price for a lot (not a hectare, but a quarter-acre lot) can top $50,000! There seems to be no end to the buying and selling, constantly jacking up prices.

The emphasis here in Tamarindo is strictly on foreign tourism. I find this a little disturbing; native Costa Ricans are being left out of the picture. Few Tico families can afford to pay the $60 a night and up that hotels demand, and the price of real estate makes property ownership impossible. Several local people expressed a concern over this trend, saying, "We keep selling our land and moving farther back into the hills. We end up working for foreigners on land we once owned. Before long, we won't be able to afford to live in our own village any more!"

Several real estate developments are either underway or completed in this area, plus there are some private houses for sale. Personally, I wouldn't be interested in owning a house here. But you need to visit, see for yourself and make your own decisions. My guess is that property here has more appreciation left in it.

Beaches of Nosara

About 80 kilometers south of the Tamarindo-Flamingo region is an area with a different developmental emphasis: the beaches of Nosara. Starting at the Nosara River, two lovely beaches and a wildlife reserve extend south—from Playa Pelada to Playa Guiones. Property owners here are attempting to keep this portion of the coast residential and natural as they struggle to shun commercial development as much as possible.

It all began about 25 years ago when an American investor purchased a huge tract of forest and beach and decided to develop the property in such a way as to preserve its natural beauty and wildlife resources. He did a marvelous job, developing each lot with its own part of the wilderness. Almost all buyers were from the United States or Canada; they loved the isolation and the idea of preserving beaches, forest and animals.

Things were going well until a few years later, when the original developer unexpectedly dropped out of the picture. Residents feared the area could turn commercial like Tamarindo or Sámara (farther to the south), so they formed a property owners' organization, totally committed to protecting their surroundings. They've convinced the government to dedicate portions of the land to wildlife and nature reserves and are offering to donate even more land. The association provides housing and pays the salary for a government ranger to keep an eye on forest and wildlife conservation. It has spent a good deal of money for legal fees, even taking a case to the Supreme Court, in an effort to keep large developers from turning Nosara into a new Miami Beach. So far they've been successful, limiting new business to small, low-impact, family-operated enterprises.

"One major problem we have is that newcomers aren't as ecologically conscious as the original owners," the association manager said. "Over the past 20 years many of the original owners have died, grown old or lost interest. So we try to educate newcomers about the treasures we have here, about the importance of not cutting down the trees or destroying our animals' habitat." He explained how the monkeys have regular "trails" through the treetops that they use daily to go from one feeding area to another. When the trail is broken by clearing some of the trees, the monkeys are forced to move away.

Because development in Nosara is still in its infancy, property prices haven't skyrocketed as they have in Tamarindo Beach and other places along the coast. At any given time, about 50 lots are up for resale as well as many homes. But, as with all prices along the Pacific coast, asking prices are climbing steadily. View lots start at $35,000; lots without views, but close to the beach, begin at

$10,000. Several local contractors build quality homes at reasonable prices.

The gravel/dirt roads around here make access to medical care a bit difficult; the nearest hospital is in Nicoya, an hour and 15 minutes away. However, an emergency Cruz Roja station in the village of Nosara has a four-wheel-drive ambulance ready for the trip to the hospital. A flight to major San José hospitals takes 20 minutes from the local airstrip.

It's interesting to compare this area with the resort area of Sámara, just 25 kilometers to the south. There, the natural vegetation has been stripped away to make room for commercial projects. What is left is burned off every dry season to make room for new plant cover the following rainy season. Native plants, those specially adapted to this climate, no longer exist; they've been crowded out by plants whose natural winter state is to lie dormant or by those whose seeds resist fire. None of this is to say that Sámara isn't a beautiful place—with its gorgeous beach, it can't miss—but it's different from Nosara, a contrast in attitudes toward conservation.

In Nosara, tall native trees and shrubbery shade the ground, helping to conserve water during the dry season. This keeps vegetation greener the year around. Unlike Playa Sámara, Nosara's landscape is covered with native grasses, bushes and vines, all uniquely adapted and suited to this environment.

North of Nosara, several small-scale developments are underway near the town of San Juanillo, an isolated area with a gorgeous beach and protected cove. Like the other beach communities along the Pacific coast, the major obstacle to full-scale development is the lack of a paved costal highway. Driving can be slow along the bumpy gravel and dirt roads, particularly during the rainy season. The government has plans to pave the main road, but when that will happen is a big question. Estimates run between two and five years.

Sámara and Carrillo

When the government manages to build a bridge across the Tempisque River to replace the bottleneck ferry, this central Nicoya Peninsula area will be an hour closer to the Meseta Central. When this happens, I expect the beach communities here to boom. The last of the easily accessible beaches along this stretch of coast are the twin bays of Sámara and Carrillo. Each curves in a semi-circle of magnificent white sand beach, backed by steep hills that provide breath-taking vistas of the coast. Playa Sámara is well developed, with numerous small hotels, restaurants and other tourist-oriented businesses. The recently completed pavement makes visiting here a relatively simple matter, compared with the old gravel-and-mud road that previously accessed the local beaches.

For some reason, other than business owners, the number of foreign residents in the area is not as large as one might expect. Possibly Sámara's bustling commercial atmosphere has something to do with this, but Puerto Carrillo has even fewer foreigners living there. This is certain to change, for Playa Carrillo is one of the most beautiful beaches in a country of lovely beaches. I have a friend who claims that "Puerto Carrillo has the best and safest beach between Los Angeles and Tierra del Fuego." Development here has scarcely scratched the surface of its full potential. Almost the entire beach is flanked by a wide road, fringed with coconut palms and freely accessible to all. Except at the southern end, almost no development of any kind mars the unblemished shoreline. Like Sámara, several hillside developments offer view lots that suggest future appreciation.

Cabo Blanco

On the southern tip of the Nicoya Peninsula, a string of beaches with tremendous potential is undergoing development. It runs from Naranjo, on the Gulf of Nicoya side, to Cabo Blanco at the very tip of the peninsula and then up along the coast via unpassable roads toward Puerto Carillo. Most investors agree that the developmental potential between Cabo Velas and Cabo Blanco is among the best in the country.

Getting to this area from the northern part of the peninsula has always been a problem. The paved highway abruptly ends at the little town of Carmona, presenting about a 30-kilometer stretch of dirt road to the coast. The road paralleling the Pacific coast dwindles to a trail from time to time, and you have to ford several good-size streams. Even rugged four-wheel-drives avoid the coast route. An easier way is to take a ferry from Puntarenas to Playa Naranjo or Paquera, which shortens the drive considerably.

Conditions are changing. For better or worse, progress arrived on the southern peninsula in the form of a huge construction project—a 1,500-room hotel—at Playa Tambor. To encourage the development, the Costa Rican government agreed to install a new ferry terminal to bring tourists from Puntarenas, to pave the road to the hotel and to provide housing for construction workers who are building the project and who later will be employed by the resort.

I say for better or worse, because construction crews immediately began filling in the mangrove wildlife preserves and leveling a mountaintop. Ecologists claim the builders are destroying the natural wonderland that they came to exploit. At the time of writing, half-hearted legal proceedings are underway against the project, and complaints have been lodged against local authorities for not enforcing regulations more strictly.

Regardless of whether the Tambor project is successful, the rest of the area is ready for less ambitious development. Costa Rica doesn't have more enthusiastic or optimistic supporters than those property owners on this part of the Nicoya Peninsula. The communities of Montezuma and Malpaís are growing and bringing in foreign residents at a respectable clip. I feel it's worth a trip here for the prospective property buyer.

Mid-Pacific Coast

If there is any place in Costa Rica that's bound to bloom with foreign investors and retirees, it would have to be that stretch of beachfront from Jacó to Dominical.

Although pretty beaches line both sides of Costa Rica, these are particularly accessible for residents of the populous Meseta Central. A short drive or bus ride makes this coast practical for overnight sojourns. A weekend home here is convenient and usable by family and friends, whereas one that requires a five-hour drive over horrible roads might sit vacant most of the year. When

Central Coast & Osa Peninsula

the main route has been paved and time-saving shortcuts completed, a drive from Escazú or other suburbs will take as little as an hour to Jacó, or two hours to Dominical.

Playa Jacó and Playa Herradura

Because they are the easiest to reach from the San José area, the most popular places for ocean swimming and weekends at the beach are at Jacó or Herradura. It's entirely possible to drive down in the morning, enjoy the surf and be home for supper.

Playa Herradura is smaller than Jacó, enjoys gentler surf and has more shade trees. Five minutes farther down the coast highway, Jacó offers more amenities and places to stay than Herradura, but with sometimes dangerous surf. Unless you are used to handling riptides, you should be cautious here. Neither of these places are loaded with glamour or elegance, but I'm predicting that in the future they will be. In the meantime, Jacó and Herradura offer economical tourist hotels and weekend homes for highland residents. Many lots within walking distance of the beach are for sale, and construction is booming. An upscale development, known as Los Sueños, is underway at Playa Herradura, by Braemar Group of Southern California. It promises to have a large-scale marina and luxury homes and condos.

Manuel Antonio

It was the middle of February, and I was sitting with a group of friends in a restaurant overlooking the Pacific. A long, palm-fringed beach stretched out into the distance as far as we could see. Behind us loomed mountains covered with rain forest, sweeping down to accent the beach with its azure-blue water and sparkling surf. The sun was at its zenith, beating directly down with dazzling strength. Two members of our group were complaining about the heat. We consulted a thermometer and found that the temperature was 85 degrees. Suddenly they broke into laughter as they realized that Baltimore, their home town, was buried under four inches of sleet and snow. Two weeks of Costa Rica's idyllic weather had turned them into indignant complainers over an ordinary 85-degree day at the beach! We all ordered a cold beer served over ice cubes (a summer tradition here) and looked out over the panorama with renewed appreciation for where we were: Costa Rica's famous Playa Manuel Antonio.

Doesn't that seem to be an odd name for a beach? According to legend, a husband, worried about his pregnant wife, placed her in a dugout canoe and headed north for Puntarenas, hoping to find a doctor to deliver the baby. But before they could go very far, the wife went into labor and they paddled ashore to camp in the shelter of the protected beach. She gave birth to a healthy child whom they named Manuel Antonio, and the beach has been called that ever since.

Travelers who have visited beaches all over the world swear that Manuel Antonio is the most beautiful of all. The coastline north of Manuel Antonio is a long shore of golden sand that catches the full force of the Pacific's waves as they roll in from China. Then at Manuel Antonio Park, a narrow peninsula juts out into the ocean, curving about to form two protected coves on either side of the land. Here the waves suddenly become gentle. You'll often find a sailboat or two anchored here, gently swaying, resting on the way to the Panama Canal or the big voyage north to Acapulco.

Originally United Fruit Company banana property, the area was made into a national park in 1972 with almost 700 hectares of land, partially expropriated, partially donated. The park contains three beaches, each with its own character. The first is Playa Espadilla Norte which sees occasional riptides—although many people swim here anyway. Next is Playa Espadilla Sur and then Playa Manuel Antonio, both quite safe for swimming and snorkeling. From the beginning, the emphasis has been on preserving the natural beauty and protecting wildlife. White-face Capuchin monkeys frolic in the trees, competing with arboreal iguanas for food. A tropical storm in 1993 ripped up some of the trees, causing the sloth population to go elsewhere, but other than that, the damage was minimal.

One of the earlier tourist developments, Manuel Antonio soon became a popular place for retirement and vacation homes, hotels and restaurants. To protect the area from total development, the government demands that new construction must be connected with tourism in some manner. Buildings cannot be over three stories high and must provide a minimum of three times the square footage of green space for each foot of building. To satisfy the requirement that development be tourist-related, several North Americans have built homes with rooms or apartments which can be rented out to tourists; they keep part of the house as living quarters.

Since Manuel Antonio's fame makes it an almost obligatory part of a tourist's itinerary, a bed-and-breakfast or room rentals can be a very viable business. Rooms will likely be rented solidly through the summer (December, January and February) and have low vacancy rates during the rest of the year. During a recent trip, we rented an apartment from a lady who came from Florida 18 years ago to build a small house for herself. She added a couple of rooms for extra income during the tourist season. As the volume of tourism during the off season increased, she added more rooms, until she now has a pleasant 10-room hotel plus two apartments across the road, all with a splendid view of the ocean. "I hadn't considered becoming a hotel owner when I came here," she explained, "it just happened to work out that way."

The biggest hindrance to optimum development at Manuel Antonio is the present condition of the highway. The stretch north to Parrita is 25 kilometers of teeth-rattling gravel-and-washboard. The next 50 kilometers north to Jacó beach is paved, but with some of the deepest craters this side of the moon. Purists might think this is a fine arrangement; it keeps people away. But local residents are so highly incensed at their isolation that they staged a strike in 1993, preventing tourists from entering or leaving Quepos until the government agreed to begin long-overdue road repairs. When (and if) smooth pavement reaches Manuel Antonio, the retiree-investor may expect gratifying appreciation on investments. On the other hand, we'd all hate to see such a lovely setting marred by a Miami Beach type of development.

Any North American thinking about investing in Manuel Antonio (or anywhere in Costa Rica, for that matter) would be well-advised to speak with Roger Connor, affectionately known as Don Rogelio by local residents. His development, the Plinio Hotel and Restaurant, could be considered a model for non-obtrusive construction in ecologically sensitive areas. Buildings cling to the side of the hill, with minimal disruption of the forest and accompanying wildlife. Nature trails wind several kilometers through Roger's 20 acres and adjacent lands to give guests an in-depth appreciation of the area. Don Rogelio's place is on the Manuel Antonio road, near Quepos.

Dominical

South of Quepos and Manuel Antonio—over 45 more kilometers of gravel surface—is another of those "undiscovered" places I feel has great potential for retirement and/or investment. First of all, plans are in the works to complete the pavement from Jacó Beach all the way to Palmar Norte, thus opening this section to traffic from three directions. This route will take considerable pressure off the present Pan-American Highway. Buses travel this route now, and it's not a bad drive in a rental car; they keep it graded, and the trip is flat.

Once paved roads are in place, you are going to see a steady stream of traffic cruising along the beach—tourists looking for rooms and retirees buying property. The village of Dominical and its surrounding communities can't help but flourish. As you might guess, many foreign residents prefer things the way they are; they dread the thought of developments and tourists destroying the peace and tranquility that has been theirs for so long. But road crews are already at work; it is too late for anything but anguish. As one man said, "It will seem funny to think that in a few years we'll be looking back fondly to the time when there were no traffic lights here."

If you want to drive on pavement all the way to Dominical, travel south on the Pan-American Highway and turn toward the Pacific at San Isidro del General, then just follow the signs through town. Because of San Isidro's system of one-way streets, you may have to ask directions by pointing in whichever direction you are going and asking "Dominical?" Someone will steer you right.

In its own way, this road is one of the more scenic in all of Costa Rica. The narrow pavement traverses rich farming country, up somewhat steep grades, running along ridges with breathtaking views on both sides of the road, looking into deep valleys where the farm houses are so distant they seem like toys. Even during the dry season, the countryside is lushly green, plants heavy with foliage and banana trees shading the roadside. Although the drive is less than 25 miles, it takes about 45 minutes. That's the way it should be, because the scenery is so spectacular that you might miss something if you could whiz along at 100 kph. Also, the pavement has a way of disappearing from time to time, turning into stretches of gravel road where construction crews are still at work. The problem is not serious; just slow down and relax.

The paved highway ends at the gravel-and-cobblestone coastal road at the Barú River, a picturesque mountain stream which empties into a lagoon at this point. A turn to the left, over the river's new cement bridge and you find Dominical. Take the first right turn past the bridge. This is not a town—even though it may appear as such on the map—it's a collection of *cabinas*, private homes and a handful of restaurants, sometimes almost hidden behind tropical vegetation.

Dominical's main street (there are only a couple of streets here) follows the river past several rental cabins and businesses. It ends at the beach, where another road follows the shore down to Punta Banda, also known as Roque Azul. Camping beneath a grove of shade trees is free on the edge of the broad, sandy beach of Playa Dominical. Restrooms and showers are strategically spaced along the beach. For the most part, campers are Tico families and backpackers, but all are welcome.

The surf is spectacular, booming in on the sand and making swimming occasionally hazardous, with riptides to harass those not used to handling them. "You usually don't realize what is happening," said Richard Dale, a longtime resident here and the owner of the cabinas on the river where we were staying. "It seems as if you are staying still in the water, but the beach is moving away from you. We lose a couple of tourists every year to these tides, and it isn't necessary. Instead of frantically trying to swim against the current, the best thing to do is to relax and leisurely swim parallel to the beach, until the shore stops moving away. The current is only a few feet wide. Then, work your way back to shore, pausing to float on your back and rest. The water is so warm and so salty that you can float all day long and never get tired. There is no reason for anyone to drown in a riptide."

Serenity and calm at Playa Dominical and Playa Barú make this a great place to spend the winter, away from the ice and snow of northern climes. Many people do just that. Prices are particularly affordable if one doesn't need an ocean view. A visitor from the Yukon, a man who has been coming here for several years, was very excited as he described the house he was buying in a nearby village. It was a brand new, two-bedroom place on three hectares of land. "To make sure everything is all right, I agreed to rent it for two months. At the end of that time, if the house is satisfactory, I'll go ahead and buy it."

Several local businesses are owned by North Americans. A deep-sea diver from Rhode Island, who worked and traveled all over the world, decided Dominical was the place to settle down. He set to work building a combination bakery, deli and coffee shop, which turned out to be a success with Ticos and Gringos

RIP TIDES

alike. It's called the Deli Del Río and is known for brick-oven pizzas, turning out 40 to 50 a night.

Next door is the Auberge Willdale, a small motel owned and operated by Richard and Ann Dale and their son Will. In their absence, the business is managed by Joe Goodman, a resident massage therapist who has lived in Costa Rica for 25 years. A Californian from San Clemente bought a restaurant-bar and named it the San Clemente, after his home town; he also has a set of *cabinas* near the beach called San Clemente. Two couples—one from Brazil the other from Italy—built an impressive building which houses a store, real estate office, salad and juice bar and one of the finest restaurants I've encountered in Costa Rica. (Normally this book doesn't recommend restaurants, but this one, the Manigordo, is special, with a combination of Italian and Brazilian cuisine.)

Every night a couple of bar-restaurants break the tranquility with loud stereo music as they try to attract customers. Since local surfing is reputed to be the second best in Costa Rica, there are always a few sunburned, salt-soaked revelers to join the more sedate patrons of these "night clubs" in hoisting a cold *cerveza*. The music doesn't last long, however, since early-to-bed is the norm here.

A couple of retired North Americans expressed surprise that Dominical hasn't attracted a larger retirement community. "The views from here south to Escaleras and beyond are spectacular," said one.

Dominical and surrounding villages sit right on the water's edge, and rainfall is about the same as in other coastal towns to the north or the south. Logically, Dominical's climate should also be similar: hot days and warm evenings. But this is not exactly the case. Mornings and evenings are much cooler, and even during the middle of the day pleasant breezes come in from across the ocean. At night temperatures drop into a delightful range, making it possible to sleep without an air conditioner.

Don't misunderstand, the climate here isn't like the Meseta Central, but it is noticeably cooler than many parts of the coast. This is due to an odd juxtaposition of geographical features. Not far from the beach, mountain slopes start climbing sharply from the flat shelf of land that borders the ocean. They swoop higher and higher until they reach Costa Rica's highest point: Chirripó peak. During daylight hours, the sun beats down on that narrow strip of land between the ocean and the mountain slopes, heating the air, causing it to rise. As the warm air flows upward along the mountain's face, cooler air is continuously pulled in from the ocean. Then in the evening, when the sun's heating action stops, cool air from the high peaks descends (cool being heavier than warm), reversing the direction of the breeze and pushing the humid, muggy air out to sea.

Uvita

South of Dominical, as far as the village of Uvita (18 kilometers distant), numerous beaches face the ocean, some with houses or tiny farms, places which will someday become villages. One of the prettiest on this part of the coast is called Punta Dominical. A high point juts out into the ocean with cliffs and surf reminiscent of California's Big Sur or Spain's Costa Brava. Below a small hotel, cliffs and rocks catch the full force of the ocean's strength as waves crash and send cascades of white foam flying high in the air.

Most property along this coast seems to be owned exclusively by foreigners, many of whom don't appear to be particularly anxious to sell and, when they do, not at bargain prices. Occasionally a beachfront property can be found, but at highly inflated prices. Affordable property is found away from the beach, where Ticos have land for sale. I looked at one parcel in Uvita, about a kilometer from the beach, five hectares of land (12 acres) with a comfortable house for half of what it would cost near Dominical. There were many fruit trees and enough pasture for keeping a horse or two. (By the way, horses are a very practical form of transportation, with the roads in their present condition.)

A longtime resident named Lillian said, "We looked all over Costa Rica before settling on Uvita. We found a ten-hectare plot up on the mountainside. Not only do we have a gorgeous view, but there are six beautiful waterfalls on the property. For me it's like having my own national park." She added, "We are holding it in trust for our two granddaughters, as a future for them."

A difficulty with a small community like Uvita is that there aren't enough residents to form a central community organization. Local people hold informal meetings, but not enough attend to get much done. Most foreign-owned land is in the hands of absentee owners, with nothing built on the properties. Nowadays, the road south connects with paved roads at Palmar, on the Pan-American Highway. As the road improves and eventually becomes paved, property values should soar and even more property will become available for development. When this happens, a property-owners' association would be a logical move.

Finally, one problem with isolated areas like Dominical or Uvita is the lack of sophisticated medical care. Often, a resident doctor in the village can handle emergencies, but for serious problems the nearest emergency clinic in this region is in Platanillo, about 13 kilometers from Dominical, or the hospital in San Isidro, some 45 kilometers distant. Uvita's medical needs are taken care of in Palmar Norte.

This problem of medical care was brought home to me on a recent trip. As I was driving from Dominical to San Isidro, a *campesino* ran out into the road and flagged me down. His hand was bleeding from an accident, and he needed to get to the hospital. I had to act as an ambulance driver, not knowing whether to go top speed and risk killing us both or to slow down while my patient bled to death. He was the calm one, as he insisted on trying to show me his wound and describing in minute detail what had happened. Fortunately, we both lived.

Golfito Area

For years, I had heard people speak of Golfito and the Osa Peninsula. The area sounded like a place of adventure—panning for gold in forest streams, fishing for trophy sailfish or hiking rainforest trails. In order to complete research for this book, I resolved to spend some time around Golfito to collect information. But when I asked folks around San José, who either owned property or regularly visited here, I found their answers short and vague, always skirting the subject as if trying to draw my attention elsewhere. When I spoke with a man who owned property on Zancudo Beach, his face burned angrily as he said, "Zancudo is my special place, and I don't want any damned travel writers drawing attention to it! It would destroy things for all of us!"

Obviously, our interview was over, but now I knew I had to go! I rented a car and was soon on my way to Golfito, the jumping-off place for the Pavones-Zancudo Beach areas. The drive south on the Pan-American Highway is gorgeous. One unbelievable view after another invites a pause wherever the car can be parked safely off the pavement. Ordinarily, the trip takes six hours, but by the time I stopped several times to sample pork *chicharones*, marvel over the views and take a nap in the shade of a banana tree, the trip stretched into an eight-hour day. If and when truck traffic is diverted along the proposed new coast highway, you'll be able to make the trip in five hours.

Golfito is an often-neglected part of Costa Rica, with scanty information provided by most tourist guides. The only complete description I found was in *The New Key to Costa Rica*. The town began its existence as a banana port for United Fruit Company, but was abandoned when the company decided that the operation had became unprofitable. As a banana port, there was no incentive to develop it as a tourist attraction, although today the area is trying hard to do so.

Sitting on a bay of Golfo Dulce, Golfito's water scene is absolutely gorgeous, reminiscent of the San Juan Islands in Puget Sound. The coastline and islands jut steeply from the water, green and matted with trees, vines and thick brush. The water is so calm at times that it is hard to realize that this is not a lake, but a protected little bay of the Pacific Ocean. From the slope, a rainforest watches over the town as fishing boats ply the calm waters of the Golfo Dulce. During the town's banana shipping days, the company wisely kept these mountain slopes as a wildlife preserve and watershed, assuring Golfito a relatively pure water supply.

The town itself can hardly be described as anything but picturesque. It looks like a cliche movie set of a banana shipping port. Just a few blocks wide, the town follows the water's edge, with some houses actually standing over the water on stilts, others clinging to the cliffs and hanging out into empty space. A couple of excellent hotels accommodate the growing number of curious tourists, but most lodgings are rather rustic.

A surprising number of North Americans live in or around Golfito. One place to meet them is at Louis Brenis Restaurant, which sits across from *la bomba* (the gasoline station). The Costa Rica Surf bar is another local Gringo hangout. The main commercial street, looking ramshackle, climbs a hill paralleling the highway and waterfront. Foreign residents patronize a couple of open-air restaurants here, as well as hardware stores, shops selling tackle and boating supplies and several red-light bars.

Bargain Property

Because of special circumstances, some of Costa Rica's better property bargains can be found around Golfito. A local resident explained, "When the United Fruit Company pulled out it left us without our biggest employer." Workers started moving away, selling property for what they could. Next, a disease called the "Panamanian Blight" hit the cacao crop, which was the second line of defense for farmers here.

Property became a drug on the market. Sellers were plentiful, but buyers scarce. This buyer's-market situation is still in effect to some extent, but demand by foreign purchasers continually pushes beach property prices upward.

The government is working hard to find a solution, trying to attract new businesses to fill the niche that United Fruit left when it abandoned the economy. Starting new types of agriculture is not a good option, because the chemicals and pesticides used to grow bananas have made it difficult to grow anything else afterwards. One project that helps local commerce is a Free Trade Zone, a special place for manufacturing and exporting by Costa Rican and foreign businesses. Those operating within the zone's coverage are exempt from some taxes and customs on importation of raw materials, components and parts. This should attract investors who would like to take advantage of the tax breaks and the availability of good local workers.

Buses from San José take seven hours to Golfito, leaving San José from Calle 4 at Avenida 18. Spectacular scenery makes the trip enjoyable. For the impatient, daily flights, either on SANSA or

Travelair, will take you there, but expect to pay a lot more than for a bus.

Playa Zancudo

Although Golfito is the central focus of the area, most North Americans do not actually live here, their homes and business interests are in nearby communities or on isolated bays around the Golfo Dulce. Playa Zancudo is one community that attracts many foreigners and is especially popular with North Americans. Those who live here are more than usually convinced theirs is the best place on the entire coast.

A long, black sand beach with widely spaced homes, small hotels and cabin rentals, Playa Zancudo promises someday to be the largest traditional tourist development of the Golfito area. Unlike Pavones, the famous surfing beach just to the south, Zancudo's beaches are very swimmable and its land ownership free of the legal nightmares that plague Pavones.

Property isn't cheap here, not by any means, but not exorbitant either. When I was last there, the going rate for Zancudo beach-front property was around $50,000 for a 100-foot lot with a house, and $35,000 for undeveloped property—up many percentage points from my visit in the early '90s. In the case of one property I inspected, this included a generous stretch of beachfront, with perhaps 150 feet of land between the high tide level and the road, as well as land on the other side of the road, ending at a small river. Along the beach the usual coconut and strangler fig trees concealed the property from view of swimmers and surfers. The rest of the property was in varied tropical trees, shrubs and flowers.

Several bars and restaurants serve as social centers, with occasional weekend dances. A stop at Susy's bar-restaurant will usually find a table or two of North Americans or Europeans discussing local news and making plans for the development of their properties. Paving the road is a common topic. Those who own homes along the beach shudder in horror at the image of the throngs of tourists, property-buyers and developers a paved highway will surely bring. They feel that since they have discovered this part of Costa Rica, it is rightly theirs, and it would be downright rude for others to crowd in. On the other hand, those who have businesses, who depend on tourists and new residents to make their enterprises grow, eagerly look forward to the road and the increased prosperity it will bring.

Several folks I spoke with routinely come here for three months and longer every year. A cabin, with a small kitchen, right on the beach can often be found for as little as $350 a month during the off season. Others are available from $500 to $900. By all means, stay for a couple of months before deciding to invest or build.

Bob and Monica Hara, who moved here from San Francisco some years ago, recently completed a pleasant and comfortable facility, the Cabinas Sol y Mar. The restaurant, as all of the other buildings, is absolutely immaculate, with an employee constantly cleaning, sweeping and mopping. This may be the only restaurant in Costa Rica where you're asked to take off your shoes before entering; no sand on those polished floors, please!

"Everyone wants to come here in the winter months," Bob remarked, referring to winter and summer in the North American sense. "People seem to think that summer is a total monsoon. But the weather is wonderful then. It's actually a little cooler during June, July and August. Every morning is sunny and at least part of the afternoon is usually rain-free. Often it doesn't rain at all." The hottest month of the year is March, according to local residents. This is just before the rainy season gets started.

Another Zancudo booster is Susan Robertson, an artist who lives nearby and who handles rental cabins. Boats to Golfito can be arranged by Susan and her husband Andrew. They also offer jungle, river and beach excursions. Originally from England, Susan fell in love with this part of the country and decided to become a permanent resident. When speaking about Zancudo's potential as a tourist development, she said, "Something people overlook is that our waves are excellent for surfing. When the surf is right, our beach is almost as good as Pavones. The waves aren't as long, of course, but fine surf just the same."

Buses and stake-bed trucks bring families from nearby towns on weekends, loaded with children eager to enjoy the beach. The waves are gentle, the water warm, and kids are in no danger of anything worse than sunburn. An easier way to get here is by water-taxi from Golfito. Schedules vary with the tides.

The shortest way to the beach is a two-hour drive over a gravel and sometimes rocky trail. This same road splits off and goes to Zancudo's sister beach to the south, Pavones. During rainy season, this route requires a four-wheel-drive, and it's not all that great in the summer. Maps don't help much in finding either Zancudo or Pavones. I have three different maps; for all practical purposes they might as well have been of three different countries, because each has a different version of the road system, none approaching reality. It's best to stop often and make inquiries.

The road is paved from where you turn from the Golfito highway (10 km from Río Claro) until you come to a quaint little ferry across the Coto River. On my last trip, the old automobile engine that powers the ferry wasn't working, so they used a canoe with an outboard motor to move! If nobody's around, honk your horn, and the operators will come running. (It takes two: one to manage the ferry, one to work the canoe.)

A longer route to Zancudo—which offers much smoother roads and is easier on your rental car—takes about the same time and is usually passable during the rainy season. Follow the Pan-American highway all the way to the border town of Canoas, then along a paved road (one side Panama, the other Costa Rica) to the town of Laurel, and from there a gravel road north to the village of Conte and on to Zancudo.

Pavones

Located in the most southern region of Costa Rica, near the mouth of the Golfo Dulce, the last bit of Costa Rica before the coast becomes Panama, Pavones at one time attracted attention as a possible place for investment and/or residency. Reputed to be the longest surfing beach left in the world, Pavones is well-known among surfboard enthusiasts who pilgrimage here from all corners of the world.

However, in 1991, unfavorable publicity cooled the public's interest, at least for the time being. Squabbling over property rights escalated into armed conflict between foreigners and local Ticos. A tense, anti-Gringo atmosphere prevails. The conflicts continue today, with squatters organized into a union-like organization. Until things settle down, investment here is hardly recommended.

The problems originated a few years ago when a United States citizen bought up about 15 miles of beach and began selling parcels to other Americans, who established homes and small farms on their properties. Unfortunately, the original owner-developer was accused of narcotics dealings (which had nothing to do with the land) and ended up in jail in the United States. Suddenly, the status of his property was in question. Who was authorized to sell it? Who could guarantee title?

To further complicate matters, a group of *precaistas*, or squatters, moved in, attempting to establish their right to the land. Their position was that the original owner didn't legally own anything because he was a criminal. In a wild west showdown between land owners and squatters, an intruder was killed by a guard protecting an American's property. The government, in an attempt to bring peace and order here, established a police outpost to separate quarreling factions. The situation is so complicated that most people are leery of investing, at least until the situation clarifies.

Perhaps a dozen foreign families still live along the beachfront road, mostly North Americans, mostly young (if you consider anyone under 55 young, as I do). Of course surfers continue to visit in numbers unabated, blissfully unmindful of any worldly problem that doesn't involve the height and angle of today's waves. In the local cantina, waves seem to dominate most conversations. A road parallels the beach for several miles just north of Pavones, with only an occasional ranch house or cabin observable from the road or the beach. Farm clearings alternate with tracts of virgin forest, with lovely stands of native trees, tangles of vines and a profusion of birds and animals. Until the government establishes just who owns what and whether the squatters have any rights, things will remain confused.

Buying Beach Property

When considering beachfront property, always bear in mind my warnings about having a good lawyer and not taking sellers at face value. The pertinent legalities are discussed in detail in

Chapter Eighteen. If nothing else, remember you don't actually own the first 200 meters of land; that belongs to the municipality. You lease it, on renewable periods, usually from five to twenty years, and in some cases, up to 99 years.

Chapter Six

Why Choose Costa Rica?

When traveling in Costa Rica, every once in a while I meet someone who, after hearing my name, says: "Oh, yeah. You're the guy who wrote that book about retirement in Costa Rica, aren't you? Well, I don't think this is such a great place to retire. Hotel prices aren't much less than they are back home, and restaurant meals aren't cheap, either!"

Although I have a hard time imagining a quality place in the United States or Canada that could make Costa Rica look expensive, my routine reply is: "Well, if rock-bottom prices are your priority, maybe you're right. Many places in the world offer cheaper living than Costa Rica. But is the quality of life the same? Is the weather as nice? Are the people as friendly? Besides, it isn't fair to judge a country's retirement potential by the cost of luxury hotels or restaurant meals."

The hotels we residents patronize in Costa Rica usually range from $25 to $60 a night for a couple, including breakfast. These aren't luxury establishments by any definition, but they clearly offer far more than budget hotels in the U.S. or Canada for the same price. Yes, some Costa Rican hotels charge $80 to $120, but similar hotels in many parts of the United States or Canada will easily eclipse that.

Restaurant meals? Go to just about any good restaurant in Costa Rica and check the menu. Few entrees are priced over $9. A juicy steak goes for about $7.50, and if the item is over $13, you're probably ordering lobster or jumbo shrimp. (For some reason, while regular-size shrimp are inexpensive in Costa Rica, jumbo size are costly.) If you're into *tipico* Costa Rican food, you can order a *casado* for about $2.50, which consists of a huge plate of beans, rice, fried banana or yucca, salad and your choice of chicken, fish or a pork chop. All for less than a hamburger back home.

Cost Comparisons

Let's forget about hotel prices and restaurant costs; they don't figure heavily in most long-term residents' budgets. More important is comparing the cost of everyday living here with the lifestyle the same amount of money provides elsewhere. You would be hard pressed to find a place with so much to offer, for such a reasonable outlay. Let's start with housing prices.

In many foreign countries North American residents feel they must live in certain "safe" areas, for which they pay premium costs. Because Costa Rica is not a stratified society, North Americans feel comfortable living in just about any neighborhood. This means a wide selection of rents and housing prices. While you can pay $1,200 a month for rent in a luxury section of Escazú, you also can often find a nice place for $600 a month in the same neighborhood or for $300 in a very livable area like Alajuela. All three locations are just a few minutes away from shopping and conveniences, and all offer quality living with superb climates. If you're content with less sumptuous digs, your rental costs can be even less.

Utilities, a significant part of most budgets, seem almost free in Costa Rica when compared with the United States or Canada. Our last telephone bill (with unlimited local calls) was $6.40, and that included a $1.67 long-distance call to Oregon. (That's not to say that some areas of Costa Rica don't have much higher rates, just as regional rates vary in other countries.)

Water and garbage service would cost about $4, but they are included in our monthly condo fee. Homes on the Meseta Central have neither furnaces nor air conditioners to drain money from budgets. Electric bills for our condominium in Rohrmoser averaged $13 a month, a fifth of what we pay back in California. At our Costa Rican Pacific Coast home, electric bills are considerably higher, but almost free compared with our bills back on the coast of California.

We have friends in the Midwest U.S. who spend more to heat or cool their homes than most Costa Ricans earn! Compare these bills with those in your own home town and then tell me Costa Rica is expensive.

Food is affordable too, with tropical fruits and veggies not only at giveaway prices, but also deliciously fresh. Costa Rica produces tasty grass-fed beef; a filet mignon in a San José supermarket costs about the same as round steak in a Baltimore supermarket. Some new residents here report spending a third less on their food budget than they did at home. The key is to buy local foods and avoid imported goods, which carry heavy import duties.

Property taxes are almost nothing, at least for North Americans accustomed to forking out big money for taxes. According to people we interviewed for this book, an average middle-class home—with three bedrooms and two baths—is taxed at the rate of $150 to $200 a year. Most U.S. communities collect more taxes than that every month. Tax reform laws passed in 1996 boosted some property taxes, but they were basically aimed at collecting from those who've evaded taxes altogether.

Besides affordable housing, utilities, taxes and food costs, what other bargains does Costa Rica offer? Oh yes—servants. A house-keeper-cook will clean your house, wash and iron clothes for $220 a month, including benefits such as Social Security and Christmas bonus. (See Chapter Eleven for further details.) We pay our gardener/handyman $1.50 an hour for part-time work, and that's well above minimum wage. We have a delightful cleaning lady who comes in one half-day each week. She washes clothes, changes bed linens, mops and disinfects floors and toilets, and waxes the veranda deck—also for $1.50 an hour.

Is everything inexpensive in Costa Rica? Of course not. Clothing prices will probably be the same as where you came from. Gasoline costs about the same, sometimes a little more: ranging from about $1.10 to $1.48 a gallon, depending on the current world price of crude oil and whether the government needs more tax revenue. Still, gasoline prices in Costa Rica are the cheapest in Central America.

Also, since the bulk of Costa Rica's governmental income comes from customs duties, obviously anything imported will be pricey. Cameras, TVs, electrical goods and other imported items will cost much more because of high tariffs. Tropical countries aren't suited to wine production, so drinkable wines must be imported from Chile, Europe or California. Since almost anything from Europe or North America is expensive, local consumers solve this problem simply by making do with goods made in Costa Rica or other Central American countries. They drink excellent Costa Rican beer instead of Napa Valley wine.

Automobiles are expensive. New-car sticker-shock will knock your socks off, with import duties of 100 percent of list price, plus a hefty sales tax. The cost of a Japanese import with a small engine is about $26,000. The same car might sell for $12,000 in Oregon! Something with a larger price tag—say a Mercedes that would sell for $45,000 back home—will set you back over $100,000 in Costa Rica. The government tried to do something about this by lowering the tariff on used cars, but soon restored the tax when the already overcrowded streets of San José were flooded with cheap used imports! High import taxes are a way of life in almost all Latin countries.

Fortunately, public transportation is excellent and inexpensive. A family car is not the absolute necessity it is back home. Buses travel all over the Meseta Central, at frequent intervals, for as little as 35 colones, more for longer distances. Taxis are plentiful and inexpensive.

Quality of Life

No, I've never promoted the idea of retirement in Costa Rica on the basis of cheap living. The attraction here is quality living— an adventurous, interesting life in a superb climate and exotic tropical surroundings. A bonus is affordable cost. As I said before, there are places in the United States where you can live inexpensively, but what about the quality of life?

When asked why they decided to live in Costa Rica, most people begin by describing the gorgeous weather and magical tropical surroundings. They'll rave on about favorite beaches, mountain retreats and rain forests, and of course they'll mention the affordable cost of living. But oddly enough, when you ask them to pinpoint the most important factor in making the decision to move, most people will agree that lovely surroundings are only part of it. There's something else involved, because after a while, pretty, exotic scenery becomes like new wallpaper: you get used to it.

When you pin most people down, they'll say: "We like the friends we've made and our social life here." It turns out that North Americans who live in a foreign country behave in an interesting manner. They tend to cling together, to form close social groups, to reach out to draw newly arrived English-speakers into their midst. In large part, this is partly because they feel isolated from non-English-speaking neighbors; they crave all the friends they can possibly attract. And because the pool of English-speakers is limited, each addition to the circle of friends is valuable. People with almost nothing in common—who wouldn't even nod at each other back home as they passed on the street—become great pals in a foreign setting.

This is true, no matter which non-English-speaking foreign country you look at. In my travels, whenever I ask, people always respond: "Everyone is so friendly here! I have more friends and companions than I ever had when I was back home working. There, I barely knew my neighbors, and my friends were mostly people I worked with." Only as an afterthought, did they mention the exotic surroundings. Friendship and social activities almost always headed the list of reasons.

Think about it: let's say you're moving from Syracuse to Scottsdale. You know you'll enter the neighborhood as total strangers. If you want friends, you must start over. That's not easy; it takes a certain personality type to successfully cultivate a compatible circle of friends from a field of aloof strangers.

This doesn't mean that you don't have to do any work at making friends in Costa Rica. You must go half way. If you wait for expatriates to knock down your door and drag you out to dinner, you may give the impression of wanting to be a hermit.

But what about making friends with Ticos? That's another bonus about living here: Ticos are also friendly and approachable. As you travel through Central America, or any Latin country for that matter, you'll note definite national personalities. I see Mexico and Chile, for example, as having introspective, formal and quiet personalities, while other countries, such as Costa Rica and Argentina, exhibit gregarious, exuberant, personalities.

Unlike Costa Rica's Central American neighbors, there's a fierce sense of equality here. Social classes aren't very well defined, simply because there isn't such a wide gap between rich, middle class and poor. Instead of meeting foreigners with an awestruck bowing of the head, a Tico will look a stranger in the eye, shake his hand and invite the stranger to visit his home. That would seldom happen in other foreign countries—probably not in your home town either.

Even if your Spanish is far from fluent, communication flows. Most Ticos have learned about as much English as you've learned Spanish. So, all sides have lots of fun talking, learning new phrases in the other's language, and being friends. For many people, that's enough; they can be satisfied with a circle of Tico friends. But most North Americans need a circle of English speakers as well. They find that, even though the communication is good, many common elements of understanding are lacking. After a while there's a craving to talk politics, to discuss movies or reminisce over the "good old days." You'll receive blank stares from your Tico friends. In short, the average newcomer to Costa Rica needs both Gringo and Tico friends. Happily, this is possible here! Newcomers are attacked with friendliness.

Clubs and Activities

There's no excuse for being lonely in Costa Rica. There's too much to do, too many people to meet, too many places to go. Take some Spanish classes, attend a meeting of Republicans Abroad or Democrats Abroad, do some volunteer work, learn to play tennis or bridge. You'll meet more friends than you've dreamed of, and you'll live the rich life you moved to Costa Rica to find.

The biggest mistake some make is not keeping active. Some newcomers will take a drink or two when things get too quiet for them, and the next thing they know, they're drinking too much. If you haven't already acquired interests to keep you busy in your

Costa Rican Scenes (including the author supervising construction of his dream house)

Photos by: Alan Cohen, John Howells, Don Merwin, Charles Pastor

new location, open the *Tico Times* to the Club Directory section and look at the broad range of invitations. (If you can't find a group of friends who are involved in your favorite activity, chances are your favorite activity is illegal or immoral!) Volunteer work is another satisfying way to make friends and become involved in fun activities. This can be much more satisfying than sitting around a bar talking to losers all day.

An excellent example of a volunteer project in which we're currently involved is the establishment of a library for a village primary school in Guanacaste. Local expatriates are contributing funds to purchase several shelves of reference material as well as books that are fun to read and that will enhance the kids' interest in education. When enough money is donated, we plan to expand the library by renting a building separate from the school and open the facility to adults as well as children. Eventual plans include an art program for children, a computer room for teaching marketable skills to teenagers and adults, plus fiction and nonfiction shelves in both Spanish and English for Gringos and Ticos. Those interested in participating in this project are urged to throw a few children's Spanish books into their luggage for their next trip, and either drop them off at Rancho Tico restaurant in Nosara, or at the Chispas Books store in San José, on Calle 7 between Avenida Central and Avenida 1.

Latin Lovers

Single women visitors find that most Costa Rican men they'll meet fancy themselves prototypes of the "Latin lover." It's as a Latin friend once explained, "When I was a young man, my father one day took me aside to tell me the facts of life. He said, 'My son, in this world you must understand one thing: you cannot expect to go to bed with every woman you meet. But, of course, you must try!'"

This attitude often is expressed in the form of *piropos*, or flirtatious, double-entendre remarks emitted as a lady strolls past a group of "Latin lovers" on the street corner. The remarks are intended to be humorous asides to draw laughs and approval from the man's companions. The woman isn't expected to respond. Unlike in some countries, the remarks here are rarely blatantly obscene, so a lady can safely smile as she continues on her way. Costa Rican ladies take it all in stride, either pretending they heard nothing, or smiling if the *piropo* was particularly flattering. But American women, unused to this unwanted attention, sometimes take offense. Showing anger is a mistake, because your indignation simply amuses the offender and the bystanders. Although you may disapprove of this social absurdity, *piropos* are a fact of life in Costa Rica. When you, as an outsider, single-handedly try to change cultural behavior, you could end up making a fool of yourself. If you absolutely cannot ignore the remark, a simple curling of the lip as an expression of disgust, as you continue on your way, is ample. You've put him down as repugnant instead of his being clever enough to get under your skin.

It's perfectly acceptable for single women to enter higher-class bars, restaurants or nightclubs. Here they'll rarely be bothered by *piropos*, because this behavior is suitable only for street corners, and most bartenders won't stand for it. But since the bar will be full of "Latin lovers" you can be sure that before too long some feisty man will be testing his luck and charm by professing his undying love. Curiously, according to the foreign ladies I've talked to, every one of the men who tried to date them in bars was either "single" or "divorced." Now, isn't that convenient? The fact is, while divorce in Costa Rica is not common, a married man pretending he's single or divorced is quite common! Before you consider marriage, check out your intended rather closely. Remember that the custom of having a mistress is a socially accepted custom here, as in most Latin countries.

What About Single Men?

"After the divorce, the first thing I thought about was coming here to get away for a while. There's something romantic about the name 'Costa Rica,' and I needed something to cheer me up after all my problems. I just knew this would be a great adventure." This was a typical reply when I would ask a single man why he was visiting here. A common follow-up statement was, "Actually, I only planned to stay for one month, but before I knew it, I met this pretty young lady, and now I'm married again!"

I've known a dozen or more fellow countrymen who married Costa Rican women, but just a few American women who married Costa Rican men. Why? I asked an ex-New Jersyite who married a Tica lady almost five ago. "Why? Because Costa Rica women are different in many ways. It's not just that they are pretty and young. That's not what it's all about. We come here looking for something we think we lost somewhere back along the years. What we find is a pretty young thing who treats us as if we were special and 20 years younger. They don't complain; they do whatever they can to make us feel at home and wanted. It turns out to be a pretty fair arrangement; she agrees to treat me like a king until I kick off; in the meantime, she and her kids from her first marriage have financial security, plus my pension after I'm gone."

What's the downside of this kind of relationship? "When you marry a Costa Rican, you marry her whole damned family! I'm expected to buy a new refrigerator for Mami when it goes out, and new false teeth for Papi whether he needs them or not. When cousin Raúl needs a transmission for his car, guess who he 'borrows' the money from? I have to attend every family function from birthdays of third cousins to funerals of great-aunts-once-re-moved. And I can't understand a thing anybody's saying!"

Single North Americans tend to congregate in an area I call Gringo Gulch, around the odd-numbered Avenidas and odd-num-bered Calles, on the edge of downtown San José, where a number of inexpensive hotels and singles bars attract a large number of male fugitives from the northern climes. They hang out in small bars, where they console each other over bottles of Pilsen beer, or visit spacious, romantic night clubs—which feature droves of glamorous, $100-a-night prostitutes—as well as tiny bars where $25 will rent a lovely for the evening. (Prostitution is legal in Costa Rica, with women undergoing mandatory testing on a regular basis.) Many North American habitues of Gringo Gulch are di-vorced, widowed or confirmed bachelors. The majority are of Social Security age, looking for that one last go-round. Surprisingly enough, some actually find it. Many ladies in these bars aren't hookers—amateurs sometimes—they're really hoping to meet a financially-fixed foreigner to marry, someone to take them away from all of this. An older Gringo with a decent pension will do just fine. After all, Mami needs a new refrigerator, and Papi needs new false teeth.

One word of caution to would-be Don Juans: be cautious after dark, and especially avoid the *zona roja* (red-light zone) in the opposite corner of downtown as it gets later in the evening. Some street girls here are fairly good thieves. Your wallet can disappear quickly while basking in sweet talk from a pretty young thing. In any part of downtown, particularly near the Gringo bars, beware of girls working in groups of three. Their scam is pretending to be overwhelmed by a man's sex appeal. Two of them distract while the third goes through his pockets. Then again, if a 60-year-old thinks his sex appeal is so overwhelming to 16-year-old Ticas, maybe he deserves to be scammed.

Gambling Casinos

For those addicted to the sound of a roulette ball bouncing along the wheel, or to the riffling sound of cards being shuffled, you'll find no lack of action in Costa Rica. There are numerous gambling casinos scattered about the country. Many large hotels have casinos, sometimes in the lobby, as if this were a miniature Las Vegas. Some gambling casinos are found upstairs over night clubs or restaurants.

While I sometimes like to gamble, I also like to have a chance of winning. I have the distinct feeling that gaming in the average Costa Rican casino is not really gambling, merely donating to the profitability of the establishment. House rules make it highly unlikely that you will break even, much less win. The games aren't standard ones which can be easily understood—even though they seem similar to poker or blackjack. Play is similar to Las Vegas or Reno, but the rules and payoffs are different, sometimes confusing, stacking the odds in favor of the house.

Another disquieting thing about gambling in Costa Rica is that there is almost no government regulation as there is in Las Vegas or Atlantic City. I doubt very much if the house cheats; it doesn't have to cheat, since the odds are so much in its favor, but there is little or nothing to prevent cheating from happening.

Chapter Seven

Living in Costa Rica

A long-time resident once said, "I don't consider Costa Rica a third-world nation. I'd call it a 'second-world' nation—if there were such a thing. After all, it's a place where you can drink the water and eat the food, where your conscience isn't continually assaulted by beggars and abject poverty. Furthermore, it's a place where the government isn't run by a bunch of military thugs." For these reasons, North Americans find adjusting to Costa Rican everyday living conditions rather easy. Of course there are differences in lifestyles, but instead of being traumatic, in most instances the variations are charming.

However, whether you thoroughly enjoy living in Costa Rica depends on your approach to life. If you expect people to conform to your ideals, if you want conditions to be exactly as they are in your home town—you are bound to be disappointed. Costa Rica is, after a foreign country—and that's exactly why most of us choose to live here. In this chapter, we'll look at some everyday living conditions that make Costa Rica different.

Latin American Time

A most difficult thing to understand is the way Latin Americans view time. When invited to a social event in the United States or Canada, it's considered ill-mannered to arrive late. Not so in most parts of Latin America. Should you receive an invitation for dinner, say at 7 p.m., and you actually arrive at that time, you are likely to embarrass the hosts. She is probably in the shower, and he is still at the office. Guests are expected to arrive late. It doesn't matter, because the 7 o'clock dinner isn't served until 8 or 9 o'clock anyway. When keeping appointments with business people, you can arrive at the office a few minutes late without worrying about it. You'll have time to catch up with the latest goings-on in the world by reading *Newsweek* and *El Nación* while waiting for your appointment. Still, even after several decades of exposure to Latin American time, I've never understood it, nor will I ever. When invited for a social gathering at 8 p.m., I always ask, "Is that 8 o'clock Tico time or 8 o'clock Gringo time?" The reply is usually a grin and, "Better make that 9 o'clock." Most Costa Ricans share this cavalier view of time, however not to the extremes found in Mexico or Argentina.

On the other hand, my personal experience with my Costa Rican employees is that they're usually on time. I'm always surprised to see them arrive at my house early, start to work on time, and—after a morning and afternoon break—go home on time. Maybe this is because I pay more than the going wage scales, but I suspect that the Costa Rican work ethic is unusually positive, at least for Latin America.

Courtesy and Custom

Costa Rican social behavior is a curious mixture of old-world, European formality and a special Tico style of relaxed interaction. You shake hands politely when being introduced or when meeting an acquaintance on the street, women as well as men. Women also may greet other women friends with a kiss on the cheek; with close friends a lady may do the same with a man, but only if they know each other well. Exaggerated hugging and kissing—common in the U.S.—is not approved here. Men, when greeting truly close friends, will give an *abrazo*—a quick hug and pat on the back—or perhaps lightly clasp the friend's wrist or forearm instead of shaking hands.

"Getting down to business," as we North Americans are apt to do, without any preliminary greeting and small talk is considered somewhat rude in Costa Rica, but not terribly so. Costa Ricans know how we North Americans are, so they never make a big deal out of it; they realize that "business" is the custom in our countries. To be polite, you might spend a few moments inquiring about someone's children or spouse, or perhaps give a compliment about their clothing, the weather, or anything else you might think to say before talking business. It gets things off to a smoother start.

Costa Ricans have a delightful habit of issuing off-the-cuff invitations to visit them at their homes, for dinner or for cocktails, but you should always wait for the invitation and not just drop in. An exception to this is when someone moves into the neighborhood, or when you move into a new home. Then it's considered polite to knock on the door and introduce yourselves. When invited to someone's house for the first time, it's customary to bring flowers or some small gift.

A very important point to remember: in social or in business transactions, Ticos just cannot handle confrontation. Unlike some countries—where arguing, shouting and mock displays of anger or emotion are the accepted norm—Costa Ricans are appalled at such behavior. It's not only considered rude, it's also humiliating and degrading. Confrontation is foreign to the culture.

I know a New Yorker who lost an excellent gardener when he briefly lost his temper because the worker had planted some flowers in the wrong place. As usual when making a point, Chuck raised his voice and waved his hands in the air to signify his displeasure. "No, no! Not here! I wanted them over there!" The astounded gardener loaded his tools in his wheelbarrow and left the property, never to return, despite pleas from the homeowner's wife, who tried to explain, "That's just Chuck's way—he doesn't mean anything by shouting."

The Post Office

Although Costa Rican mail service is pretty good when compared with some Latin American countries, it's hardly up to the standards we expect at home. (Such as they are.) In a country where streets rarely have names, and houses lack street numbers, home mail delivery can hardly be expected to be reliable. I waited six months in vain for my first bank checking account statements. Then one day out of the blue, they all appeared at the same time. Instead of complaining, I was astonished that the mail carrier actually found my house. The address on the envelopes read: "300 meters north from Amistad Park, 100 meters to the east, and 25 meters to the south." (But which house?) The poor guy probably carried these bank statements with him every day for months, just in case he deciphered those directions and figured out which house I lived in. Unfortunately, the statements arrived after we'd sold the house and closed our checking account—having decided that having a checking account wasn't all that convenient.

That's why most folks rely on post office boxes, known as *apartados*. This means a trip to the post office every couple of days, but at least you are fairly certain your mail will be waiting for you. My post office box in the village near our Guanacaste home costs $7.50 a year. I understand the cost is considerably higher at the downtown San José post office.

For the last couple of years, there's been a problem with mail being stolen by employees within the post office system. My impression is that most thefts occur in the main post office in San José rather than in the smaller substations around the country. Postal officials are working on the problem, and they seem to have stopped most of the thefts. At least newspapers haven't reported recent problems with mail, and our letters have been getting through okay. But never send cash. It's preferable to send checks or postal money orders via certified mail, which seems to get through okay. The substation holds a certified letter until the recipient identifies himself and signs for it.

Air mail between Costa Rica and the U.S.A. or Canada involves ten days each way. That means at best, a 20-day turnaround between the time you send a letter and when you receive the reply. A practical way to avoid this delay is by fax machine. Seems like everybody's got 'em here. A fax to or from the United States or Canada costs about $1.65, but the turnaround for an important letter or document is a matter of minutes instead of weeks. Internet service is also available in Costa Rica, with the government hookup costing about $30 a month for access. Internet e-mail messages zip off anywhere in the world for nothing.

Another way to beat the system is with one of several Miami-San José P.O. Box services that offer same-day delivery by air courier to and from Costa Rica. One I'm familiar with, a company called Star Box, charges $22 for up to five kilos of mail, magazines, catalogues, samples, etc., with $3.25 for each kilo thereafter. Call 221-9029 in San Jose, or write Star Box, 5177 N.W. 74th Ave., Miami, FL 33166. Other similar services are: AAA Express, 233-4993; Aero Casillas, 255-4567; and Interlink, 232-2544. Ask your neighbors for recommendations.

Telephone Service

Sometimes, when a government manages the telephone system, you'll find absolute chaos. In many countries you expect to be on a waiting list for a new phone for several years. When you finally get one, it may not work, and you get on another waiting list for repair. Costa Rica must be doing something right, because the system actually works, and works well! When the phone in our condo in Rohrmoser went on vacation, we had a repairman out in a matter of hours instead of weeks, as in many Latin American countries. Yes, there is a waiting list for new telephone installations, but in many areas of the country the wait is only measured in weeks or months, not years, as in many other countries. Should you be impatient for a new phone installation, check the classified ads in *La Nación* for people who want to sell their phone lines.

Cellular phones are invading the country and more are on the way; that should help out of the way places where phone lines are scarce or impossible. You can call 257-2527 to see about one from the government phone company. An American company, Millicom, is trying to obtain franchises to install their equipment. If successful, this might spur the government monopoly to rush lines to distant, phone-starved parts of the country in order to head Millicom off at the pass.

Making a pay-telephone call in a foreign country can be difficult and frustrating. You don't know how many coins to use, what kind to use, or when to drop in the money. The apparatus often makes strange noises: whoops, wails and whistles, all having meaning to someone who knows the system, but a total mystery to those of us who don't. Sometimes, after you finally get through to your party, the call terminates before you can begin talking.

Thankfully, Costa Rica's phone system isn't at all difficult to use, and it is surprisingly efficient even though it does send out mysterious signals at times. Phone calls to anywhere in the country go through very quickly. Even when dialing from a tiny village from one end of Costa Rica to the other, connections are as clear as if it were just across the street. Tolls are surprisingly low. A five-colón piece (about 2-1/2 cents) will place a call anywhere in the country. The length of time allowed for a five-colón coin depends upon the distance, but the time allocated per coin is always generous. You can speak for about a minute from as far away from San José as you can get and still be in Costa Rica.

Public pay phones operate differently from those we are used to. Hotel phones usually only accept a ten-colón coin, whereas public phones located on the streets or public squares accept five-, ten- or 20-colón pieces. With hotel phones, you must be ready to drop in another coin when you hear a funny noise or beeping sound on the line, a sound that indicates the call will be terminated unless you quickly insert another coin.

Public pay phones have a kind of rack at the top where coins go. To make a call you line some coins in this rack—more if you are making a long call or a long-distance call—and then start punching in your number as soon as you receive a high-pitched tone that indicates the phone is ready. When your party answers, the phone automatically swallows a coin, permitting the other coins to roll down and be in position to drop if you go over the limit for that particular coin.

To reach an AT&T international operator, you dial 0-800-0-114-114, no coin needed. An English-speaking operator will accept your credit card number or place the call collect. Other long-distance operators are: Telcom Canada, 161; British Telcom, 167; U.S. Sprint, 163; and MCI, 162. Compared to other countries, where it takes hours of waiting around a telephone office to get a call through, this is a miracle. If you have a phone in your home, direct dialing is not only easy, but it's the most inexpensive way to place an international call. The telephone directory lists codes for each country. You dial the country code, wait for the connection and then dial the number you wish to reach. For example, to dial the United States from Costa Rica, first dial 001. To call Costa Rica from the United States, the prefix is 011.

Emergency calls can be made by dialing 911—just as you do back home. The fire department is 118; highway police, 117; the Rural Guard, 127; and an ambulance (Cruz Roja) is 128. To report a problem with your telephone, dial 119. For electrical problems dial 126, and water, 223-5555.

Costa Rican Delicacies

A delightful custom in Costa Rica is the serving of *bocas*, or free appetizers, with drinks in bars—they may be fried shrimp, a chicken dish, barbecue or some more exotic specialty. They aren't served as frequently as they used to be, especially in bars mostly patronized by Gringos, since we don't expect them. But Tico bars usually sustain this custom, so when you see someone else being served a treat, don't hesitate to ask. You may have the chance to sample a raw turtle egg—bars are just about the only place where you can legally find them.

One time I found a bar-restaurant that was still serving a variety bocas with drinks, and they were exceptionally good. I told the owner that next time, I was going to bring my wife to sample them. He was so delighted when I brought her in that he presented us with the delicacy of the house: a raw turtle egg apiece. Not wishing to hurt the restaurant-owner's feelings, I managed to down mine in one gulp. But my wife's expression told me that I would have to somehow dispose of her raw egg as well. When the owner turned his head momentarily, I grabbed the other turtle egg, closed my eyes, performed the heroic deed, and quickly replaced the empty dish in front of my wife. The owner was so pleased that we enjoyed his treats he set us up with two more! As I recall, my appetite never returned that evening.

Dining Out

It's difficult to look at any particular restaurant menu and point out many dishes that could be described as typically Costa Rican. Curiously, for a country with so many unusual ingredients available, restaurant cuisine tends to be rather ordinary. Steaks, fried chicken or shrimp seem to be almost obligatory on every menu; they taste fine, but after a while one gets very tired of fried chicken or steak. One of the most common complaints tourists have about Costa Rica is the large number of boring restaurants.

On one research trip, I stumbled across a new restaurant that advertised "good old-fashioned American cooking." Since it was operated by an American from Los Angeles, I anticipated tasty "California cuisine." I ordered the featured dish of the evening: a specially prepared beef tenderloin. The owner assured me this was not at all like the normal Costa Rican fare. It wasn't. It turned out to be an over-cooked slab of dry sirloin, topped with a slice of Velveeta cheese and doused with canned mushroom sauce. The veggies were canned string beans and carrots. So much for good old-fashioned American cooking. The last time I was in that neighborhood, I noticed the restaurant was closed, presumably due to lawsuits by outraged gourmets who object to Velveeta cheese on their steaks.

Not that there aren't some wonderful dining establishments around. It's just that you'll encounter more of the ordinary variety. Around the San José area you can find interesting dining places, ranging from elegant French restaurants to superb pizzerias. Some excellent Chinese restaurants will surprise you with dishes that are quite different from the oriental cuisine you are used to back home. Their style of cooking is a cross between traditional oriental and tropical American. Also, some terribly mediocre Chinese restaurants are to be found (ask friends for recommendations).

One very common Costa Rican food—served everywhere, sometimes for every meal—is *gallo pinto*, which inexplicably translates as "spotted rooster." This is a mixture of cooked rice and black beans—sometimes mixed with cilantro and chopped onions—which are fried together until the rice turns a purple color. Mixed with eggs and topped with salsa Inglesa or salsa Lizano, it makes a filling breakfast, nutritious, but boring when served at every meal.

In small restaurants away from the city, a typical menu item is a *casado*—a kind of lunch plate with beans, rice, fried *plátano* (a green cooking banana) with some sort of meat, chicken or egg. ("Casado" means "married man"; why the meal is called this is a mystery.) Olla de carne is a tasty meat stew with vegetables such as *chayote*, squash, yucca or *plátano*. *Arroz con pollo*, chicken with rice, is one of my favorites when properly done and not too dry. *Sopa negra* is a soup made of puréed black beans with an egg poached in it, topped with green onions and cheese or sour cream. Another favorite is *empanadas*: fried dumplings filled with meat or cheese, often sold by children who carry them around in galvanized buckets. A tortilla in Costa Rica is properly defined as an omelet made with chopped potatoes or yucca root. Mexican-style corn tortillas are popular in the countryside and are also called tortillas; these are far more common than the egg-and-yucca variety.

Great Coffee!

A big plus for Costa Rican cuisine is the coffee. Some of the best coffee in the world grows on shaded mountain slopes in Costa Rica. These exceptionally rich-tasting beans are used by coffee merchants around the world to add flavor to otherwise bland Brazilian or African varieties. In Costa Rica, you can brew your coffee from 100 percent flavorful beans. We sometimes purchase coffee beans direct from the roaster, and take them home while they are still hot. The use of instant coffee (a barbarous practice) hasn't caught on here. A *café con leche* with just a dash of sugar makes a wonderful starter for breakfast and is useful for washing down mouthfuls of *gallo pinto*.

Costa Ricans have an interesting way of making coffee here which gives characteristically a rich flavor to the brew. Instead of using a percolator or an automatic coffee maker, Ticos use a wire or wooden stand holding a cloth strainer bag that hangs over a waiting cup. They place two teaspoons of coffee into the bag and pour boiling water over the grounds letting it drain into the coffee cup below. Then, for each additional cup of coffee, another teaspoon of ground coffee is added. The result is a flavorful, velvety drink that grows richer with each cup made. The grounds aren't discarded until the sack is full of grounds or until end of the day—whichever happens first. "The aroma and essence of the coffee is much better if it isn't boiled," explained a Tico. "We call our coffee-making system a *chorreador*. It brings out the flavor without acid bitterness. This method requires more coffee grounds, but since coffee is inexpensive here, we use nothing but the best."

Cooking at Home

For those staying for longer than a vacation, an apartment or house with a kitchen is a wonderful way of enjoying Costa Rican cooking and experimenting with the unusual tropical ingredients available in the markets. Around the San José area, every neighborhood has at least one supermarket, supplemented by weekend *ferias* or open-air markets. Every neighborhood also has its little *pulpería* or convenience store where you can buy items you forgot at the other markets.

Major supermarket chains are: Auto Mercado, Periféricos, Pali and Mas X Menos. The "X" in Mas X Menos is pronounced "por," which means "for" in Spanish, making the store's literal name "More for Less" markets. Open-air markets are held on weekends, the major ones being: Saturday in Escazú, on the south side of the main square; Saturday in Pavas, about five blocks from the main shopping center; and Sunday in Zapote, next to the Bull Ring. Heredia's farmers' market, also on Saturday, is perhaps the best known of all, with local families selling produce raised in their backyards. Heredia's main market, open every day of the week, is a wonderful place to browse for food, clothing, tools, furniture, whatever you can imagine.

Costa Rica's selection of fruits and vegetables are sometimes bewildering for us North Americans. In addition to delicious pineapples, strawberries, melons and other things we are used to, you'll find *chayotes, pejibayes, palmitos, plátanos* and other strange-looking items which will soon become standard parts of your menu. A common substitute for potatoes, the yucca root, in my opinion, tastes much better than ordinary spuds. Exotic tropical fruits such as *guayabas, tamarindo* or *carambolas* are exciting to experiment with, and make delicious *refrescos*, blended drinks. One of my favorite *refrescos* is made by blending fresh cacao nuts (the source of chocolate) with *horchata* (a rice flour and sugar drink). My wife prefers a *batida* of fresh papaya, milk and ice, whipped to a milkshake-like consistency.

Some fruits are so exotic they border on fantastic—with shells, spines and barbs—looking like something from a science fiction book cover. Especially interesting is the *marañón* fruit, the source of the common cashew nut. The nut itself grows at the end of an edible orange or yellow fruit that can be eaten raw or, more often, made into a refresco by blending with sugar and ice cubes. But the cashew nut itself is encased in a rubbery shell which is primed with cyanide, making it bitter and extremely poisonous. I have to marvel over the wonderful way nature designed this fruit as a way to disperse its seeds. In the wild, monkeys, parrots and other creatures pluck the fruit and carry it away to be consumed. When they finish eating the sweet fruit, the bitter-tasting seed is discarded, dropped on the ground to produce another tree.

Since Costa Rica is a cattle-growing country, steaks and roasts are quite tasty, with the flavor that only grass-fed beef can have, and they're inexpensive. You might be surprised to discover that pork and chicken are sometimes priced higher than filet mignon. One reason is that pigs and chickens require large amounts of protein in their diets, which isn't available in bananas or other cheap tropical foods, so imported protein supplements bring prices up. Still, the quality of pork and chicken here is very good. Eggs are delicious, having a brighter-colored yolk and a better flavor than we're used to up north, with our mass-produced egg farms.

With an ocean on both sides, of course Costa Rica enjoys a wide selection of seafood. And since shipping distances from either ocean involve just a few short hours, the sea harvest arrives fresh. Almost any kind of fish and shellfish you can imagine is available, plus some you can't imagine. You might want to try some of the shellfish and conch that only thrives around the Costa Rican shores.

Imported foods are expensive. Partly because of shipping costs and partly because of foreign exchange differentials, North American and European products can be prohibitively costly. Central American substitutes are often as good and locally grown—fresh foods are always much better than something canned or packaged.

Furnishing Your Home

It used to be, when foreign residents received their papers they had the right to import household goods duty-free. This was a valuable consideration, since electrical appliances, televisions, video recorders and the like are expensive in Costa Rica because of high import duties. The rules were, after the goods had been in your possession for three years, you could legally sell them, possibly turn a profit on the transaction, and then buy new ones.

To the dismay of incoming *pensionados*, this benefit was repealed in April of 1992. The anguish and wailing over the loss of these privileges rocked the North American resident community to its heels. But after a series of appeals, the new laws were not applied to those who already had their *pensionado* status or those whose applications were pending.

Even though tax breaks are a thing of the past, we should be aware that duty-free imports on household goods aren't nearly as important as they once were. At one time, demand for furniture outstripped the capacity to produce it. It was cheaper and more convenient to ship your used stuff from Miami than wait several months for the factory to fill your order at exorbitant prices.

Today, supply has caught up with demand; you'll have no problem finding a wide variety of furniture at reasonable prices— usually less than you'd pay back home. The amount of money you'd have to pay to have that bedroom suite and living room furniture shipped from Des Moines, Detroit, Denver or wherever would go a long way towards furnishing your new home in Costa Rica. Furniture stores have great selections, and you can visit small, family-operated factories and have pieces custom made for about what you'd expect to pay retail. Earlier, I mentioned the town of Sarchí as a place for furniture made with tropical woods. You can visit a factory there and have your pieces made to order. The chances are you'll also find a woodworking shop near your home where you can have furniture custom-made, at prices even less than at Sarchí.

Household appliances such as refrigerators, washing machines or TVs can be purchased from a local dealer without waiting for months, as was the situation before. But these prices will include very high import taxes. For example: a few months ago we purchased a popular U.S. make washer and dryer; we paid over $600 for the washer and $525 for the dryer. We could have bought them for 40. percent less in a United States appliance store. Our Tico neighbors, by the way, were astounded that we would waste money on a dryer when we could simply hang the wash on a line and let the sunshine dry it in an hour for free! But being spoiled Gringos—too impatient to wait for the sunshine, and too often forgetting about the drying wash until after the next shower wet the clothes down again—we felt we couldn't live without an electric dryer.

Yes, it hurts not to be entitled to *pensionado* discounts, but Costa Ricans have been paying full price for years. What's so terribly unfair about having to pay the same for goods as your Costa Rican neighbors? You can be sure this special treatment was a source of irritation and resentment among the Costa Rican community. Perhaps they didn't blame foreigners for paying less, but they did fault their government for taxing them more.

Household Servants

The notion of housemaids and gardeners seem a bit wild for most of us when we first move to Costa Rica. (The last time we hired a cleaning lady in the U.S., she charged $14 an hour and wouldn't do windows.) But in Costa Rica, servants are affordable. With the minimum wage for domestic servants starting at $220 a month—this figure includes the additional costs of fringe benefits such as Social Security and a Christmas bonus—it makes sense to hire a housemaid and a gardener, at least on a part-time basis. Ticos are generally hard working and honest, and if you can afford it, you can have someone working around the house who won't complain about doing windows.

Most North Americans report that they pay more than minimum wages; it makes their employees happy and loyal. However, while servants are affordable, you must be aware of the laws covering their benefits. By law, not by custom, you are responsible for things like vacations, Christmas bonus, social security and severance pay. Wages are indexed twice a year, according to inflation. You are responsible for knowing about the benefits and paying them on time. These rules are discussed thoroughly in Chapter Eleven. Don't hire a servant until you've read the rules!

Television and Other Media

A few years ago, in order to watch baseball or football games you had to wait for a video cassette to be mailed from the 'States. Today there are six cable TV services just in the San José area, plus numerous private satellite dishes throughout the country. Costa Rica's modern television system offers six channels, some of which can be received in some remarkably out-of-the-way places. On our San José cable system we enjoyed abundant programming direct from the United States: two TV stations from Denver, one from Atlanta and one from Chicago. Several international channels delivered programs coming from South America, France and Germany as well. We found that watching CNN, CBS and NBC nightly news on our cable TV made up for not having a daily newspaper delivered to our door.

Note that I described our TV cable system in the past tense; where we live now, on the Pacific Coast, our reception is two weak channels. That's the price you pay for not living near the big city. Still, video rental stores routinely stock the latest offerings from Hollywood. You'll find them in every neighborhood. The farther you are from the bigger population centers, it seems the more video stores—understandable, because cable TV doesn't reach far into the countryside.

In San José and most of the surrounding cities, you'll find stores selling English-language paperback books and magazines. In addition to the essential *Tico Times*, you can buy daily editions of the *Miami Herald Latin American Edition*, the *New York Times*, *Washington Post*, and the *Wall Street Journal*. These papers are a bit expensive—they arrive by airplane—but there are times when North Americans become absolutely starved for a big-city daily newspaper.

In San José, a dozen theaters show first-run and recent English-language films—mostly from Hollywood. Tickets cost about a third of what they cost back home: from $2.00 to $2.50. The dialogue is almost exclusively English, and Spanish subtitles are printed over the lower part of the screen. This provides an opportunity to improve your Spanish skills by reading Spanish and listening to English at the same time. In many countries where almost no one understands English, the sound is turned down to a whisper, and the audience chatters away, making comments about the movie or whatever. But in Costa Rican theaters the soundtrack runs at a normal volume so the many Ticos who know English can listen. They enjoy sharpening their English by listening and using the subtitles to clarify the meaning. The end result is that Tico audiences are as polite as you could hope for and everyone enjoys the movies.

San José boasts nine legitimate theaters, mostly in Spanish, offering entertainment for those who are well along in their study of the language. One ongoing production is about the history of coffee in Costa Rica, tracing its arrival from Arabia, plus legends and beliefs about the wondrous substance. It is half in English and half in Spanish, with discounts for Costa Rican citizens and *pensionados.* Two little theater groups produce plays in English.

Two *folklorico* troupes regularly present traditions from various parts of the republic, one at the Herradura Hotel and another at the Melico Salazar Theater. Also there are regular concerts by the National Symphony Orchestra. Sponsored by the government Ministry of Culture, Youth and Sports, many visiting musicians from other countries add to the quality of the presentations.

Gratuities

Restaurants, by law, add a 10-percent service charge to the bill, then it's up to the customers if they care to leave something extra. I find that a five percent tip is greatly appreciated and leads to extra special service the next time. Barber shops and beauty salons expect a 15- to 20-percent tip. My last haircut cost 600 colones ($3) and I tipped 100 colones (50 cents).

At Christmas time it's customary to give something to the newsboy, supermarket attendants and garbage collectors, and by law you give a yearly Christmas bonus to the maid, gardener and any other employees. Since this Christmas bonus is not a gift or a tip, but is required by law, an extra Christmas present would be considered thoughtful.

If you are a guest in someone's home where there are servants, it isn't necessary to tip them, not unless they've done something special for you, such as laundry, ironing or running errands. If a friend lends you the services of her maid, it's customary to tip and to pay for her taxi or bus fare home. Hotel chambermaids like to be tipped just as they do back home. I try to carry a few solar-powered calculators which I hand out as special gifts for those·who go out of their way for me. Gifts of this nature will be accepted as presents, while giving a cash tip might be demeaning to someone who doesn't work for tips. Items like calculators can be purchased inexpensively back home; in Costa Rica they are costly because of import duties.

Money Matters

Costa Rica's currency is the colón. Like many foreign currencies, the colón's value fluctuates against the dollar according to supply and demand. For years, rates have remained fairly stable, rising with inflation, and the currency has not been over- or under-valued. For example, in 1992, the rate was 138 to the dollar; four years later, in the spring of 1996, the colón's value was 200. That's an inflation rate of about 10 percent a year—not much, when banks pay as much as 25 percent interest on colón certificate of deposit accounts. Most financial experts predict that the colón will remain stable, with devaluations paralleling inflation.

Some people feel uneasy when inflation continually deflates a nation's currency. The important point is whether the exchange rate between Costa Rican colones and U.S. or Canadian dollars are in line with reality and not overly managed by the government (which has led to disaster in other Latin countries). Many people, even some economists, tend to assume that when the exchange rate is stable, inflation is under control and all is well. Ain't necessarily so. When exchange rates are steady—yet prices of goods and services rise in the host country—your dollar loses value every day! Just because a currency holds its own against the dollar isn't necessarily a sign of a healthy economy; it could be an artificial manipulation of currencies that masks serious problems. Therefore, do not confuse inflation rates with currency exchange rates!

Yes, a mild inflation has been going on in Costa Rica for decades, but the colón adjusts for this inflation as prices and wages rise, so there's no appreciable change for those who own dollars. For example: prices and wages in Costa Rica today are twice as high as six years ago. Yet, we North Americans receive twice as many colones for our dollars as we did six years ago. So it's a wash. There's no foreseeable reason to expect that exchange rates will vary in any significant way in the future other than a steady adjustment to world currencies, totally in line with reality.

Dealing in Dollars

A big business in Costa Rica is buying and selling dollars. As you walk along the streets, money-changers badger you, offering to buy or sell dollars. A word of caution: street currency exchange is illegal—although the police seldom enforce the law—and some money-changers are con men and short-change artists. You might end up with a handful of Colombian-printed counterfeit bills; 5,000-colón notes are the favorite fakes. Also, because of a worldwide glut of counterfeit currency, avoid accepting $100-dollar bills from street money changers or gambling casinos. The few extra colones per dollar you make by dealing with street people isn't worth the risk. Play it safe and cash your money in banks, *casa de cambios* or in your hotel, where it's legal and safe. By the way, some hotels don't give good rates; check with the desk before changing your dollars.

Interest Rates

In early 1996, a nice rate of interest was being paid on time deposits of colones, over 25 percent at non-government banks. (Dollar accounts pay about the same as CD rates in New York.) While 25 percent sounds like a terrific return on your investment, you must consider the inevitability of the colón losing value against the dollar. You are gambling that the colón will devaluate less than expected, in which case you come out way ahead. If the rates fall at the expected rate, you'll do fine. But if, for some reason, the colón's value falls more quickly than the expected 10 percent, you could lose money. My guess (and it's only a guess) is that deflation of the colón will be slow and steady, as in the past. The reason I say this is that Costa Rica has plenty of foreign reserves, placing the government in a strong position to control currency fluctuations. Furthermore, in January of 1996, for the first time in years, the country had a positive balance of payments—something the United States can only dream of. Again, my prediction of stability is only a guess. Also, remember that non-government banks sometimes don't have good track records, and it's difficult to discern which do. Personally, I don't bother myself by speculating in currency. I have too many other places to spend my money.

Banking

In many ways Costa Rica is a modern and efficient country, but for some inexplicable reason, a visit to the bank is an Alice-in-Wonderland experience. It takes forever to do a simple transaction such as changing dollars or travelers' checks into colones. Although each bank handles things a little differently, it usually involves standing in two or three lines while the clerk checks your passport, examines the bills or checks, fills out forms in triplicate, and pounds everything in sight with a rubber stamp. Then you move to another line and wait until a second clerk fills out more forms in quadruplicate and does more rubber stamping. The money is counted at least three times, then counted again as the clerk finally surrenders the colones to the customer. I fully expect, some day, to receive a rubber stamp in the middle of my forehead, just to make the transaction completely official.

Banks are also where you pay traffic tickets and utility bills and make Social Security payments for your maid and gardener. Since each transaction requires a flurry of forms, rubber stamps and calculations, you can count on spending a lot of time in Costa Rican banks. Because of the time-consuming process of dealing with banks and government bureaucracy, some Ticos make their living by standing in line for you, by knowing who to contact and when. They are called *tramitadores* (from the verb "tramitar" to transact, to take legal steps). Your friends and neighbors can recommend a reliable tramitador to make your life easier.

Criticize the banking system as I do, the fact is government banks are financially sound. Not long ago, one went under.

BancoAnglo, one of the big three of Costa Rican banks, was forced to close its doors because of mismanagement and reckless speculation. The situation closely paralleled the savings and loan debacle in the United States. Costa Rican investors didn't panic; they simply took their passbooks to one of the other national banks and exchanged them for new passbooks from that bank. Nobody lost a nickel; contrast that with the U.S. savings-and-loan shenanigans. By the way, the Costa Rican bank officials responsible were immediately arrested. Now, just consider how many U.S. savings-and-loan wheeler dealers were even scolded, much less shown the inside of a well-deserved jail cell.

Not all banks are government-owned. Many private banks deal with the public, usually in a much more efficient manner, at least as far as the amount of time you spend in line in front of a teller's cage. But there are two problems with private banks. One is that deposits are backed only by the bank's reserves; no government funds are available in case of default. And the second problem is that some private banks have been known to be fraudulent, the reserves siphoned into private accounts in the Bahamas. Before you invest in a private bank, investigate its past performance and talk to your neighbors about its reliability. If the bank just opened last March, and the main office is a post office box in Haiti, you just might be suspicious.

Until 1996, only nationalized government banks were permitted to offer checking accounts in both dollars and colones. Now private banks have equal status with government institutions in this respect.

Local residents and business owners recommended a private bank to me: Banco Internacional de Costa Rica (BICSA). It has a branch office in Miami and operates under Florida's laws and regulations. I haven't used it yet, but this seems to be the most convenient way to transfer or wire funds from the U.S. and Canada. If it makes you more secure, you can keep most of your money in a dollar account and transfer dollars to the colón account to write checks and cover bills.

Bank accounts can be in either colones or dollars. But an unpleasant bank practice is holding dollar checks from foreign banks for 30 days or more before crediting them to your account.

(This is supposed to change as a result of the bank reform laws of 1996, but it's not clear yet how many days banks will be allowed to hold checks before cashing them.) Another quirk is that they often do not have enough dollars on hand to cash a large check. You have to take a cashier's check instead. This is okay if you are making a local purchase with the money, since the party to whom you are giving the cash will probably deposit it in his account anyway. But when you need cash for a trip home, better plan ahead.

Bringing Your Pets

Those who cannot stand the thought of going anywhere without their pets will be happy to know there is no legal problem in bringing them to Costa Rica. It does, however, require a bit of paperwork. To get a doggy or kitty passport, you must write to: Jefe del Departamento de Zoonosis, Ministerio de Salud, Apartado 10123, San José, and request a *permiso de importación* (import permit). Complete the form and send it to the ministry with the fee and documents.

You will need a health certificate for your pet, signed by a registered veterinarian, which must be certified by a Costa Rican consul. Your hometown veterinarian should be able to handle all the paperwork, which must state that the animal is parasite-free, has all current vaccinations against rabies, distemper, hepatitis, parvovirus and leptosporosis. The rabies shots must be at least three months old, but less than three years. Canine or feline fingerprints are not necessary. Your pet then becomes a legal *residente* with full rights of litterbox use or guard duty, however without voting privileges.

To leave the country, your pet needs an exit permit, just like human *residentes*. You'll need a health certificate from a Costa Rican veterinarian, complete with vaccination records. You take this document to the Ministry of Health to obtain a stamp, then to the Banco Central for a *permiso de exportación* and more stamps. Unlike a human *residente*, your pet doesn't need a certificate of good conduct to leave, so that time Fifi attacked the mailman's leg doesn't count.

Costa Ricans love their pets but they tend to keep them on leashes or in their yards more than do some North Americans. Your free-wandering pooch or kitty could be at the not-so-tender mercy of the big watchdogs that swagger about the neighborhood, always ready to bully. Contrary to some Latin American countries, pet food is readily available at most Costa Rican supermarkets and sometimes in the local *pulpería*. Veterinarians are numerous, at least half a dozen practicing in the San José area. There's even one who makes house calls!

Crime and Personal Safety

I'm always surprised when friends visit us in Costa Rica and express dismay when they see wrought-iron bars on our windows. "Is crime so bad here," they ask, "that people must live behind bars?"

This question surprises me because bars on Costa Rican windows seem as logical and natural as window screens in Miami or storm windows in Cleveland. Maybe that's because my family moved to Mexico City when I was a youth, a place where homes traditionally have bars on their windows, so I suppose I grew up with the custom. The fact is, in every Latin-American country, from the Río Grande to Tierra de Fuego, a home isn't considered complete without a set of decorative wrought-iron bars. To me, a Latin-American home looks naked without them, like a Cape Cod home without shutters or a Southern mansion without a portico and tall columns. When the first Spanish colonists came here five centuries ago, they brought iron bars with them. Roman settlers brought window bars to Spain 2,000 years ago; for all I know, the Romans picked up the custom from the Greeks, or maybe Egyptians.

Do window bars deter professional burglars? Not really; not any more than window locks keep out burglars back home. Bars and locks simply keep out honest people. But I think they make the house look finished—plus, they discourage amateur burglars and remove temptation from neighborhood kids.

Like any place in the world, Costa Rica has crime. And without question, crime rates have been increasing over the past few years. That shouldn't surprise anyone coming from the United States, a place where crime and personal safety has become the number one concern of the country. Take a look at some U.S. neighborhoods. The bars you see on windows and doors clearly aren't meant to be decorative. They are grim attempts to protect occupants from runaway, violent crime. The alternative to bigger and stronger bars is moving to a safer place with lower crime rates, perhaps rural Kansas or small-town Costa Rica (that's my solution).

I personally see crime as another one of those annoyances I have to put up with if I want to live here—an annoyance like potholes. To avoid destroying my car I have to drive carefully to avoid potholes. That's an annoyance. To avoid crime, I have to be careful where I park my car and where I keep my wallet. That's an annoyance. So far, I haven't been affected by crime, but potholes have eaten several of my tires.

Of course there's crime in Costa Rica; but it's of a different nature than in the United States. It doesn't seem fair to compare the two places in the same paragraph. The difference is a growing incidence of petty crime in Costa Rica compared with a booming growth of brutal crimes in the United States. Criminals don't just rob up north, they savage and maim as well.

One big difference is the lack of rampant drug addiction among Costa Ricans. You won't find an army of desperate addicts who are forced to steal several hundred dollars each day to support a habit. The law provides a jail sentence of eight to 20 years for anyone involved in drug dealing. Drug use is considered extremely serious, and mere possession of drugs can be interpreted as evidence of drug dealing. By the way, these laws apply equally to native Costa Ricans and Gringos.

Recently, the downtown section of San José was bothered by the appearance of *chapulines*, gangs of street urchins who robbed pedestrians by grabbing wallets and jewelry. ("Chapulines" literally means "grasshoppers," describing the way the kids jump on a victim and keep him off balance while one of them goes for the wallet.) I personally believe that incidents of this nature have been somewhat overstated. The fact that each episode made headlines in San José newspapers suggests that such incidents can't be all that common. However, the problem all but disappeared when strict laws were passed, with stiff sentences for juvenile offenders who previously avoided punishment because of loopholes in the law. Recently a San José judge handed out sentences of up to 25 years in prison to a band of chapulines.

It's best to take basic precautions when wandering about the center of San José—or any big city in the world, for that matter. To be fair, having a wallet lifted or a gold chain stolen are crimes that plague tourists, not only in Costa Rica but anywhere in the world tourists go. Furthermore, this kind of crime can usually be avoided by taking reasonable precautions. Residents and long-term visitors infrequently haunt downtown San José, so they are rarely bothered by pickpockets.

The overall rate of burglaries in Costa Rica is much lower than in the United States. But a high percentage of break-ins are performed on foreign-owned homes. Burglars know the average Gringo has a nice VCR, a TV, microwave and maybe a stereo. Here again, a little precaution is in order. Besides a decorative set of bars, it's worthwhile to contribute to the neighborhood *guardia*, the watchman who patrols your neighborhood on foot or by motorcycle. Every block has a couple of them. Because of these guardias, most middle-class neighborhoods are far safer than similar places in the United States, where a police car cruises by once a day—maybe.

If you're going to be gone for some time, perhaps a housesitter may be in order. Costa Rican burglars rarely enter a house when they think somebody might be home. Making friends with your neighbors is a great insurance policy, since they'll watch out for your vacant home, just as you take care of theirs. And, as in any country, the farther you live from the big city, the lower the crime levels.

Miscellaneous Information

Electricity: The same as in the U.S. or Canada—110 volts alternating current. Short power failures are common. Keep candles and matches in a place where you can find them in the dark.

Time: Costa Rica is on Central Standard Time, but because the length of the days is virtually unchanged over the seasons, Daylight Savings Time is not observed.

Holidays: Sometimes it seems as if every time I go to the bank to conduct business, it's closed for a holiday. Costa Rica celebrates more than a dozen national holidays and uncounted numbers of local celebrations that call for closing the bank. Watch the Tico Times for announcements of upcoming holidays, and plan your official business around those days. The country's biggest celebration starts a couple of days before August 2, when thousands of people walk along the highways in a pilgrimage to Cartago to honor the national saint, the Virgin of Los Angeles. Drive cautiously at this time.

January 1: New Year's Day

March 19: St. Joseph's Day (patron saint of San José)

Easter Week: Thursday through Sunday

April 11: Juan Santamaria's Day (national hero)

May 1: Labor Day

June 29: St. Peter and St. Paul's Day

July 25: Anniversary of Annexation of Province of Guanacaste

August 2: Virgin of Los Angeles Day (patron saint of Costa Rica)

August 15: Mother's Day

September 15: Independence Day

October 12: Columbus Day

December 8: Feast of the Immaculate Conception

December 24 and 25: Christmas Eve and Christmas

Religion: Although the country is predominately Catholic, it isn't fanatically so. All religions are accepted with tolerance and good will. You can find English services in just about any denomination of church or synagogue you can think of, including Yoga, Mormon and Rev. Moon's Unification Church.

Chapter Eight

A Healthy Country

Costa Rica is a healthy place to live. The United Nations recently noted that Costa Rica is in first place in Latin America for development of preventive and curative medicine, ranking with the United States and Canada among the 20 best in the world. Infant mortality is lower in Costa Rica than in the United States, and the average life expectancy is longer. This is not happenstance; the Costa Rican government spends a great deal of money on health care.

For example, in many third-world countries you play a game of Russian roulette when choosing a restaurant. A dining room can look wonderful, with white tablecloths, gleaming silverware and tuxedo-attired waiters, but the kitchen can be a virtual cesspool. Not so in Costa Rica. If a restaurant looks good, then its kitchen will probably be just as nice. I've found very few places where I would hesitate to eat, and I've never been served spoiled food. (I can't say that about some United States restaurants.) This is due in some measure to the high standards of the underground water supply, but also to the Ticos' natural inclination toward neatness and order. The level of cleanliness of Costa Rican restaurants is remarkable.

Another factor in restaurant safety is the relative scarcity of houseflies in Costa Rica. Since this is the tropics, you might expect to see more insects than you would in the temperate zones of North America, and you do, but in balance. Yet, you'll see remarkably few houseflies, true villains in spreading disease. In San José and other towns on the Central Plateau, you can eat outside at a sidewalk cafe without sharing your lunch with flies. This seems strange to visitors from North America's Midwest, where the fly population blooms in the summer to a plague. Yes, an occasional fly might drift past, curious as to what you are having for lunch and hoping to join you, but nothing like you expect back home in the summer.

The same thing goes for mosquitoes; in the dry season, they are as scarce as houseflies, and even in the wet season they aren't so plentiful as to require screens on windows in many areas. Still, mosquito repellent is essential, for the little critters can carry Dengue fever, a flu-like illness which has also appeared in the Southeastern United States. So far, it's only affected a few parts of Costa Rica. A concentrated campaign to wipe out the particular mosquito that carries the virus is underway, and the incidence of the disease is fading.

You Can Drink the Water!

As a part of its commitment to serving the public, the Costa Rican government has spent large sums of money on water and sewage treatment. Unlike in most Mexican and Central American cities, you can drink the water in San José and other major towns around the country. Most smaller towns have excellent quality water, as do most hotels, where drinking water comes from safe wells. The government strictly monitors these water systems, even those private ones used by a handful of people. Every two months, at a minimum, tests are made for purity.

There are, however, a few places with questionable water supplies, where ordinary precautions should be observed. In some areas, amoebas and giardia are not unknown, but local people know about this and will warn you. Escazú, a ritzy suburb of San José, is an example of a place where drinking water has been known to be unsatisfactory in the past. The problem is intermittent, so if you are renting a place here, check with neighbors and follow their example.

By and large, you don't have to worry about drinking water or brushing your teeth when living in the Meseta Central. However, should you come down with something resembling "travelers' disease," with symptoms of diarrhea and nausea, you should take a stool sample to a local laboratory and have it analyzed for a small fee. The lab doctor or a pharmacist can tell you what kind of medicine you'll need. By the way, prescriptions are generally unnecessary in Costa Rica except for addictive or dangerous drugs.

Medical Care

The United States' irrational health-care system, with its exclusion of nearly 40 million citizens from the ranks of medically insured, is a major reason some folks think favorably about living in a country where health care is not only available, but affordable. Although there's been frivolous talk of reform in the United States, the problem only promises to get worse. In a typical U.S. hospital, patients with Medicare coverage usually pay more—just for the deductible share of an operation—than the total surgical and hospital bill would cost in Costa Rica! To make matters worse, U.S. Congressmen (who receive free medical care, bless their hearts) have increased Medicare premiums, reduced future medical benefits and are considering even more drastic cuts.

In the United States, should you visit an emergency room, the first thing they demand is your hospitalization plan or credit card. If you have neither, you could be told to get lost. If you have Medicare, you will find many doctors who won't accept it. In Costa Rica, when going to an emergency room in any government hospital, there is no charge for resident, visitor or even someone in the country illegally! This affordable medical system is another of the benefits Costa Rica enjoys because there is no military to absorb resources. Statistics show that the general level of care is equal to or superior to the United States—and it's available to all citizens, not just those who can afford premiums.

Why is quality health care inexpensive in Costa Rica? A prominent physician (in private practice in San José) explained it this way: "Here, our government considers medical care a public service and obligation, just as it considers education and highways a public responsibility. The government builds hospitals and trains medical specialists to serve the people, not as a business. But in the United States, medical care is a profit-making industry, a big business where profits are maximized to the highest point people can pay. Here, a doctor working for a government clinic earns between $800 and $2,000 a month. In the U.S.A., where doctors work for profit, $20,000 a month is more common. Some heart surgeons in the United States will schedule five heart-bypass operations the same day; this assembly-line technique raises the surgeon's income by a quarter of a million dollars for one day's work!"

The doctor went on to say, "Where there is no competition, medical specialists can charge what they like. But here in Costa Rica, we have competition between our free, public hospitals and private clinics staffed with private doctors such as mine. We private doctors must keep our fees in line, or we lose our patients to free clinics."

Health Tourism

In 1996, the Tourism Institute (ICT) announced a government-sponsored Health Tourism Project, the only project of its kind in the world. The idea is to maximize the use of government hospital operating rooms and equipment (which are idle a good portion of the time) by "renting" the facilities to qualified private physicians. By combining modern surgery with pleasant tourist surroundings for recuperation, the joint government-medical project is expected to boost tourism. Part of the plan includes the use of bed-and-breakfast rooms for pre- and post-operative care.

Doctor Longino Soto Pacheco, the Health Tourism Project's director said, "Here we can do the same surgery on the very same type [of] operating tables, with medical equipment of the same quality you will find in the States, and with surgeons trained in the same medical schools." (From "Business Costa Rica," December, 1995.)

In the United States, a typical heart bypass operation is currently $50,000—just for the surgeon—plus big bucks for the hospital room, anesthesiologist, medication and other medical fringe benefits. However, in Costa Rica, the total cost of a heart bypass operation is currently $15,000—that's "out the door," for everything. In other words, the complete process—including pre- and post-operative expenses—could be about what you pay in deductibles on a typical major medical policy in the United States. Currently, Medicare won't cover out-of-the-country care, but the Tourist Institute will try to show the U.S. government how taking advantage of Health Tourism will save large sums of money. Expected services will include a full range of surgical procedures, including a kidney transplant center operated by a world-renowned surgeon specializing in renal transplants.

Medical Bills

In San José, a routine visit to a private physician's office costs between $17 and $35. As of spring 1996, a day in a first-class private hospital was only $90! (Hospital food is excellent, by the way, not the skimpy, tasteless food we're used to in U.S. hospitals, but delicious and usually more than you can eat.) That $90 rate is at the country's most expensive hospital—for a private room, private bath, color television, plus an extra bed and meals for an *acompañate* or companion. (It's customary for a family member or friend to spend the night in your room after an operation or when you are in serious condition, at no extra charge.)

If you are willing to put up with sharing a bath with the room next door and can do without your own private phone, the cost drops to almost half. And for a shared room and shared bath, you'll pay less than $40 a day. As you can see, a first-class hospital in Costa Rica charges about the same as a moderate hotel for a room! Compare these prices to those in your community. In the United States if you can get out of a hospital for less than $1,500 a day, just for the room, consider yourself lucky.

Choosing a Doctor

Foreign residents can "buy into" the Social Security system ("Caja," as it's called in Costa Rica) by paying a fee from $40 to $50 a month and then going to government hospitals for treatment. However, since medical care is free, it isn't surprising to find the public system well-used and crowded. When people don't feel quite up to snuff, they traipse off to the hospital to see a doctor. Of course, for emergency treatment, there is no problem—you are seen immediately—but for an ordinary office visit with a government doctor, you could find yourself standing in line or sitting in the waiting room for a long while. For elective surgery, you can expect a wait of several months for your turn.

However, there is a better way: choose a family doctor who is in both public and private practice. See him as your private doctor, in his office, for minor problems. Then, for something serious, he can fit you into the public system. A resident of Heredia told of his strategy for choosing a family doctor. He said, "I joined the Social Security plan by paying about $40 a month. Then I visited a free clinic a few times until I found a doctor I liked. I made an appointment to see him in his private practice. Now, as my regular doctor, I can see him any time simply by making an appointment and paying for an office visit. But if something expensive ever comes up, such as a major operation, he'll check me into the government hospital for free treatment—by the same doctor!"

Even if a patient chooses a private doctor and uses a private hospital, costs are ridiculously low compared to the United States. For example: in San José, the typical bill for a gall bladder operation is $2,500, and for an appendectomy $1,200 to $1,800.

Again, for those with Medicare, be aware that it is not valid outside of the United States. However, for those under 70 years of age, there is a Costa Rican government insurance company, the National Insurance Institute (INS), which offers a policy similar to Medicare for $170 a year for adults and $110 for dependents under 24. This policy pays 80 percent of hospitalization (private room), post-operative care, medicines, lab tests, X-rays, CAT scans, cardio-grams, therapy, home care and support systems. For surgical fees, the policy pays 100 percent, up to a maximum set level. Doctor visits are also covered to the limit of the schedule. The limits of the policy are said to be generous, taking into account the low medical costs in Costa Rica.

All retirees we interviewed swear by the quality of Costa Rican medical care. I can tell you my personal experience: I went to a doctor with a bad case of the flu, severe back and neck pains, and a fear that I had pneumonia. The doctor decided that I was going to be okay, but he suggested that I go to the hospital for a checkup and a rest. I asked for a shared room, but since the hospital wasn't full, they didn't put another patient in with me; essentially I received a private room for a two-bed ward rate. After three days of tests, medication and tender loving care (plus great meals), I was presented a bill which made me feel even better. The entire cost of three days in the hospital, including electrocardiogram, blood tests and x-rays, was less than if I had stayed in a moderately-priced hotel and dined in ordinary restaurants for those three days!

Dual System

Many Costa Rican doctors, after graduating from medical school, go to universities in the United States for further study and to do residencies. This is particularly true for specialists; since Costa Rica is such a small country, there aren't enough patients with the same problem to allow a doctor the opportunity of seeing the wide variety of patients needed to get the experience in his specialty.

I asked a physician from the United States who had retired in Costa Rica some years ago, "Why would a Costa Rican doctor, who does a residency in the United States or Canada, return here to work for Costa Rican medical earnings?"

"You have to understand," he replied, "most doctors only work half time for the government. The rest of the time they work for themselves. Take the case of a cardiologist who charges $50 an office visit. If he sees five patients a day on his own, that's $250 a day or about $50,000 a year, plus his salary from the government. When you consider that income taxes and the cost of living is far less here, and that high malpractice premiums aren't necessary, a huge percentage of the doctor's earnings is available for savings or investment. Even though Costa Rican doctors earn a fraction of what U.S. doctors do, they live here just as well or better, and they can live in Escazú instead of Kalamazoo!"

Hospitals in San José

Three large Social Security system hospitals provide San José with round-the-clock emergency care—with regular hours for laboratories, X-rays, pharmacies and doctor's appointments. These are the Calderón Guardia, San Juan de Dios and Mexico. Some private hospitals are Clinica Santa Rita, Clinica Biblica and Clinica

Catolica, all excellent hospitals—the Clinica Biblica being the newest and most modern—offering the same services as the government hospitals, but with no waiting for elective medical care. Note that "clinica" usually indicates private hospitals or clinics, available to anyone.

Next to the Clinica Biblica is the Clinica Americana, an office complex with a group of English-speaking doctors, most of whom did residency in prestigious U.S. university hospitals. The KOP Medical Clinic in Escazú specializes in treating foreigners, with a staff that speaks English, French, Spanish and Japanese. They offer a wide range of services, including obstetrics, gynecology, pediatrics and dermatology.

Some emergency rooms specialize; for example, Hospital Mexico specializes in heart problems, and San Juan de Dios has a burn center. All towns of any size will have a hospital, and those that are too tiny often still have a doctor or paramedic and emergency equipment.

Rest Homes

Care for infirm elderly patients is excellent in Costa Rica, with the cost paid for by the government. However, I believe that this is something available only to long-term residents who become infirm after becoming *pensionados* or *rentistas.* In order to receive residency permission, one needs to pass a health examination, and I cannot imagine a doctor giving an Alzheimer's patient, for example, a clean bill of health. However, if you develop Alzheimer's or some other condition that requires long-term care after you have been living in Costa Rica as a resident, that's a different story.

Still, a government facility may not be suitable for a foreigner because of language and communication problems. But there are several private full-care facilities who are able to address the needs of non-Spanish speakers. (At least one of these offers specialized care for Alzheimer's patients: Golden Valley Hacienda in Alajuela; also in Alajuela is the Villa Confort Geriatric Hotel which specializes in folks who are not bedridden but who need care in everyday living.) The cost is about $1,500 a month for round-the-clock care.

A facility in Los Yoses, the Hogar Retiro San Pedro, has been given high praise recently by an American lady for the care there. Another facility is the Hogar para Ancianos Alfredo y Delia González in Heredia. This one is in the process of starting something new in Costa Rica: a senior citizen residence-development of individual cottages for folks who do not require full care. Housekeeping services and meals will be provided plus recreational facilities and physical therapy services. In addition to medical care it will have recreational, hobby, arts and travel programs for its people. Residents must be over 65 and able to purchase a cottage. A catalog can be obtained by writing to Apdo 138 in Heredia.

Office Visits and Hospital Rooms

The following rates by Costa Rican doctors for office visits were published by the newspaper *La Nación*. Understand the maximum rates are average maximums and depend on the type of clients, location of the doctor's office and the professional standing of the physician. Those practicing in the more expensive areas of the San José area could charge more than the average maximum; those in more isolated areas, less.

Speciality	minimum fee	maximum fee
Gynecology	$18	$35
Pediatrics	$17	$30
General Medicine	$25	$30
Oculist	$25	$30
Cardiology	$25	$35

Below are comparisons between two private hospitals in the San José area, as of early 1996.

Room	Clinica Biblica Rate	Clinica Catolica Rate
2-Bed Ward	$66	$48
3-Bed Ward	—	$40
Intensive Care	$150	—
Small Room	$72	$65
Private Room	$90	$78

Dentists

The University of Costa Rica trains medical specialists of all kinds, including highly skilled dentists, periodontists and orthodontic surgeons. Like medical care, dental care in Costa Rica is also affordable. I go to an English-speaking dentist in Pavas who has a very modern clinic. After he received his degree in Costa Rica, my dentist did post-grad work in the United States.

When asked about Costa Rican dental prices compared to the United States, the dentist replied, "Depending upon where you live in the United States, dental care [there] can be three to six times as expensive. For example, in Costa Rica the standard price for a porcelain cap is $135. In Los Angeles the same work costs from $600 to $700. A bridge typically costs $375 here, but a similar job in Los Angeles would cost at least $1,800. I've had patients who fly here, pay for their hotel, food and airfare, and still save money."

What about quality? "Dental work in Costa Rica is equal to that done in the U.S.A.," he replied. "There is absolutely no difference in the competency of the dentists. However, the quality of dental laboratory work is usually better here in Costa Rica. Don't misunderstand, the U.S.A. also has excellent dental labs, but because they can get the work done cheaper in the Philippines, many dentists routinely send bridgework and dental caps overseas, to low-cost laboratories. The quality just isn't up to the standards of Costa Rican or American labs. If I were to have caps or bridgework done in the U.S.A., I'd certainly insist that my dentist use an American dental laboratory."

The following average rates by Costa Rican dentists were published by the newspaper *La Nación*, from data from the Colegio de Cirujanos Dentistas de Costa Rica. The fees can be higher or lower than shown here, depending on the area and the dentist's clientele. I know of one Dentist in Rohrmoser who charges $60 for cleaning teeth, another dentist in Pavas (ten blocks away) who charges $25, and the other day a dentist in Nicoya charged me only $12.50 for an excellent job of teeth cleaning. The Costa Rican national average is $18.50; my dentist in California charges $80.

Service	average fee
Cleaning	$18.50
X-ray (routine)	$25.00
Full-mouth X-ray	$27.50
Filling, one surface	$12.50
Fillings, three surfaces	$21.00
Crown and metal bridge	$60.00
Dentures, upper	$100.00
Dentures, upper & lower	$200.00

Plastic Surgery

Costa Rica has gained worldwide recognition for another of its medical services: reconstructive surgery, commonly known as plastic surgery. San José is becoming known as "Beverly Hills South" because of the number of people coming here for body renewal. Several excellent surgeons specialize in face lifts, liposuction, breast reconstruction and other corrections of nature's mistakes. Not only are Costa Rican plastic surgeons ranked among the best in the world, their fees are based on Costa Rican medical standards. In a word, inexpensive.

Why would Costa Rica be so popular with those wanting to rid themselves of wrinkles? Besides affordable costs and quality surgery, it turns out that San José is a perfect place to slip away to have an operation because of its climate—never hot, never cold—which makes recuperation faster, safer and more comfortable. Since the healing process takes three or four weeks, many patients find this a great time to learn Spanish in one of the many "total immersion" schools around the city. These schools provide for home-stays with a Costa Rican family and have small classes or even individual instruction if you prefer.

Another attractive thing about Costa Rica as a base for cosmetic surgery is that many folks feel embarrassed about having their friends and family know they are going to have it done. Therefore, a growing number of them vacation in Costa Rica—where they are unlikely to run into acquaintances—have the operation and return home a month later when all traces of the surgeon's handiwork have disappeared.

What does all of this cost? Happily, the cost of a face lift, a breast job or a tummy tuck with liposuction—including surgery, postoperative care and hospital stay—is less than one might pay just for three days in a hospital in the United States! For example, a complete face lift costs from $2,000 to $4,000, plus $900 for operating room and recovery days in the hospital. The same operation in New York or Los Angeles would be $22,000, plus a lot more for the hospital.

San José's leading plastic surgeon is Dr. Arnoldo Fournier, who did his residency in reconstructive surgery at New York's Columbia University and who has the oldest established plastic surgery practice in Costa Rica. Dr. Fournier charges $800 to $1,200 for an eyelid operation when done separately. Nose surgery or liposuction to abdomen and thighs costs about $1,500 to $3,000, compared to U.S. rates of about $10,000 for the same procedures.

How safe is it? Costa Rican hospitals are excellent, with all modern equipment. Personnel are highly trained. Dr. Fournier points out, "Most of my surgery is done under local anesthetic and sedation. The patient is given some pills a couple of hours prior to the operation, and intravenous medication is given by an anesthesiologist during surgery. This is much safer than using a general anesthetic. Some patients just stay one night in the hospital and then check into a bed-and-breakfast for a few days. Others prefer to stay a while, since hospital rooms don't cost any more than a first-class hotel."

For more information, you may write to Dr. Fournier and ask for his free booklet, *A Brief Introduction to Plastic Surgery.* The address is P.O. Box 117-1002, Paseo de los Estudiantes, San José, Costa Rica, Central America. The FAX number is 506-255-4370. This publication explains thoroughly what to expect, illustrates the procedures with detailed drawings and gives preoperative and postoperative advice. For those connected with the Internet, there's a World Wide Web page on plastic surgery at:

http://www.cool.co.cr/usr/fournier/fournier.html

Chapter Nine

The Real Estate Game

Because North Americans in Costa Rica don't feel the need to group together—living in compounds or sealed-off neighborhoods as they do in other foreign countries—housing selection is far more open. Costa Ricans and North Americans are so similar in temperament and personality that most Gringos feel comfortable living just about anywhere in the country. Since juvenile delinquency isn't out of control in residential areas, and because neighborhood kids are generally well-behaved, we North Americans don't feel threatened as we might in some lower-economic areas back home.

Granted, North Americans do tend to congregate in the more expensive areas—nice homes, condominiums and plush housing developments. But not everyone can afford to live in these neighborhoods, and not everyone wants to live in an English-speaking enclave. Therefore, you'll find foreigners scattered all over the Meseta Central and, in fact, all around the country.

One expatriate who has lived here for 12 years with his family of five said: "We live in a Costa Rican barrio with Ticos who are typical of most Costa Ricans I know. They love their family, neighborhood and country, and [we] all work together at watching out for each other....Our home has never been broken into, and we don't live in a fortress. We have no walls, pit bulls, Dobermans or security systems. Five minutes and a crowbar could gain entry."

(Letter to the editor of the *Tico Times* by Steven Corgan, Dec. 15, 1995.)

Another thing that makes living in Tico neighborhoods easy is that even though Spanish is the dominant language, most Ticos have been exposed to English in Costa Rica's excellent school system. (However that doesn't make them fluent in English, any more than your two years of high school Spanish made you fluent.)

Renting

Starting around 1994, rents and housing prices leveled out and have stayed steady since. This is true at least for the Meseta Central. Some hot beach properties will always rent for whatever the market will stand, and rents in these areas fluctuate with the season. A tip: for getting the best dollar value when renting in a beach area, make your deal in September or October—the slowest months of the year—when homeowners are anxious to have tenants through the rainy season. At that time, you have bargaining power.

When you first arrive in Costa Rica you will likely want to rent for a while, to get an idea of where you want to live. Neighborhoods vary greatly in quality of shopping, access to transportation, compatibility of neighbors and, of course, in price. There are some areas where you definitely wouldn't want to live—you can usually detect "bad vibes" quickly—and there are other areas that may look great at first, but later you could be sorry you didn't know about another, more interesting neighborhood.

To get an idea of what you might have to pay to rent a house or an apartment, check the *Tico Times* classifieds for a wide range of rents. The last time I looked—in the Spring of 1996—houses and apartments were offered at rents ranging from $250 to $2,500 a month (and even higher). While the $2,500 place should be spacious and luxurious, chances are the $250-a-month place could be perfectly livable, and just as nice as places back home that rent for twice that amount. Don't rent on price alone, however; check out the neighborhood closely.

For many Costa Rican families, the idea of paying even $250 a month is prohibitive. So, if you are looking for the rock bottom in rents, check the classifieds in the Spanish-language newspaper, *La Nación.* The ads in that paper are read by local people who do not have the ability to pay higher rents.

Apartments by the Week

Most people, when trying out Costa Rica for livability, don't enter into long-term rentals or sign leases until they are absolutely sure they want to settle in for a long time. An ideal way to savor living in the country, particularly on the Meseta Central, is to rent an apartment by the month or by the week. Short-term rentals are particularly useful when determining which neighborhood you'd like to settle in.

San José has several "apartotels," small furnished apartments complete with cable TV, telephone and cooking utensils—in short, everything you need for a trial of Costa Rica living. Several apartment complexes regularly advertise rates of $50 a day or $900 a month for a three-bedroom apartment, others from $225 to $495 a month for a one-bedroom place including telephone, TV and washing machines. You can pay a lot more, but these apartments seem okay by my standards. (Of course, I'm easily satisfied. I do, however, insist on wall-to-wall floors and, preferably, a waterproof ceiling.)

Another excellent way of discovering whether you like a neighborhood or a city is to rent a room in a Costa Rican home. Because of pressure on hotels for tourist rooms a few years back, many private families converted spare bedrooms into rentals for the busy seasons. They're delighted to host North Americans on their visits, to take them into their homes and treat them as part of the family. A bonus to living with a family is the opportunity to perfect your Spanish by total immersion in the language. Most language schools encourage students to stay in private homes and routinely make rental arrangements for the students. Typically, a family will charge from $80 to $150 a week for a room, which includes two meals a day (breakfast and supper) and your laundry.

Don't confuse the private home setup with traditional bed-and-breakfasts. Many B&Bs around the country are similar to small hotels, but with a tasty breakfast thrown in. Bed-and-breakfasts range from cheap, near downtown San José, to expensive, in the suburbs, depending on the luxury of the accommodations. The *Tico Times* lists many renting for about the same as an ordinary hotel.

Buying Real Estate

Many, if not most countries in the world severely restrict the rights of foreigners to buy property. Some absolutely prohibit it. Not Costa Rica; this is one country where you needn't be a citizen or go through all kinds of legal gymnastics in order to own property. If you're big enough to buy it, it's yours.

The standard recommendation to visitors is to wait at least six months before buying property. However, many catch real estate fever within the first few days of their initial visit and end up buying something anyway. At this particular time, the buying spree in Costa Rica has diminished somewhat, but people from all over the world are still plunking down money to buy something—anything—before it's all gone. My guess is that the boom will continue, with predictable cycles of frequent selling followed by slack periods, just before another frenzy of buying and selling.

Although buying property in Costa Rica should be rather straightforward, it can be tricky if not handled carefully. The following are some points to keep in mind. For complete details, see Chapter Eighteen.

The first rule is: **find a competent, English-speaking attorney to handle the deal for you.** This can be a challenge in itself. Inquire around the North American community for recommendations. You can also inquire at your embassy for a list of reputable attorneys. Some claim that attorneys from one of the "old families" are best, because they know a lot of people in the bureaucracy who can make things easier.

You need a lawyer to be sure the person who is selling you the property actually owns it. A lawyer can make sure that liens, mortgages and second deeds aren't attached to the property like warts on a toad.

The second rule: **never count on a verbal contract for anything.** A handshake means nothing. You may think you have a deal, and when you return with the cash, someone else owns the place and is moving in furniture. Get everything in writing, after you are completely satisfied that the property is registered and actually belongs to the seller and that the seller is who he or she claims to be. This seems elementary, but you'd be surprised how often buyers don't bother to check!

An attorney told of a client who insisted on buying a piece of view property against the lawyer's advice. The attorney reluctantly investigated and found that not only was the seller asking twice the value, but he knew the land belonged to someone else, a man who had bought the property 20 years ago and forgot about it. To complicate matters, the real owner had died and his heirs couldn't be located. That land will be vacant for some time.

Since Costa Rica is so small, the government is able to keep land records in one place, at a central title registry called the Registro de la Propiedad. All liens and attachments must be registered here and the books are open to the public. Even though the process of checking out a deed takes a short time, your attorney needs to know how to go about it. If you find nothing registered against the piece of real estate, you can safely transfer it to your name; any outstanding debts or obligations not registered are none of your concern. But don't feel smug until you make sure that your lawyer actually registers your new property and the documents are stashed away in your safe-deposit box.

Rule three: **do not trust the seller or agent just because he is a fellow North American!** There's something about Costa Rica that seems to bring out latent tendencies toward larceny in our compatriots. An astounding number of confidence men come out of the closet the moment they arrive in Costa Rica. Mostly they are rank amateurs, but since they deal with people like you and me—also rank amateurs in business deals—they can cause much damage before they are finally stopped. This leads to rule four: **make sure the lawyer you hire represents only you, and not both parties!** Legally, he can represent both sides; if his first client is a crook—look out.

In Costa Rica, installment sales are not the norm; you need to plop cash on the barrel head for most property transactions. When you consider that interest rates often top 40 percent, you'll understand why. Real estate agents should charge a commission of five percent of the sales price. Be skeptical of those who insist that ten percent is the customary commission. Closing costs can amount to another five to seven percent—customarily split between buyer and seller. The lawyer's fee is about 1.25 percent. Conveniently, prices are usually quoted in (U.S.) dollars.

Brokers and sales personnel aren't regulated in Costa Rica as they are in the U.S. or Canada. As a result, fast-track wheelers and dealers often get into real estate sales. Some have been known to boost the sales price of property by 50 percent over the asking price, keeping for themselves the difference between the owner's asking price and the actual sales price. Ask local property owners for broker recommendations and try to contact the seller personally before closing the deal. When selling property, be wary of a brokerage agreement that doesn't pay you the full sales price less commission!

The fifth rule: **above all, do not be so overwhelmed by the beauty and tranquility of Costa Rica that you pay the first price asked.** Ticos can display irrational streaks of optimism when valuing their properties. Foreigners, bloodthirsty for profit, can be even worse. Determining the actual value of properties is difficult, because there are no "comparables" to gauge value as we are accustomed to back home, where selling prices are a matter of record. In Costa Rica everyone knows how much is asked for a property, but the actual price is always kept a guarded secret because property taxes and transfer fees are based on the selling price. Incidentally, my attorney tells me that although it's customary to fib a little to tax collectors about the sales price of a property, if you get too creative about your fibs, they can arbitrarily assign a value to the property, no matter how much you paid!

Naturally, the farther from the city or ocean, the less expensive the property will be. But that private, isolated, mountain slope location with a gorgeous view of the valley could be an open invitation to thieves whenever you go shopping. Rule six: **if you're buying unimproved land, be sure you can bring electricity and year-round water to the property.** (Some parts of Costa Rica suffer water shortages every dry season.) Make sure the soil is suitable for a septic system. If sewage can't be absorbed, it will sit around, back up and make your new home smell like an open cesspool.

When buying property, if the title is in the name of a Costa Rican corporation, or *sociadad anónima*, that's good. If not, one of the first things you'll want to do is form a corporation. This may sound strange, but there are several advantages. The section on tax havens in Chapter Eighteen explains how corporations are set up and how they are used in buying property. Although offshore corporations are sometimes used for tax avoidance, hiding assets and other marginal activities, there is nothing at all questionable or illegal about using corporations for real estate ownership. The big advantage of property registered in the name of a corporation is the ease of transferring ownership. Instead of going through the expensive procedure of transferring property to your name, you simply purchase the corporation's stock, take over the books and you are now the owner.

Beachfront Property

Real estate is booming along both coasts. Prices in some areas are going wild, although other places still have bargains available. The situation is somewhat murky, because some properties that are being bought and sold have tough building and ownership restrictions which you might not be told about until you're ready to start construction. Foreigners are supposedly limited as to ownership of ocean front property, but they manage to sidestep this law by putting their land into Costa Rican corporations.

Everyone is restricted as to how close to the beach they can build. The most important point to bear in mind is that you cannot actually own beachfront property. It must be leased from the local municipality. Make sure you're comfortable with this concept before deciding on that wonderful stretch of coconut trees and sand.

Chapter Eighteen discusses beachfront property in great detail, but generally, the law goes like this: the first 200 meters ashore, starting halfway between low tide and high tide lines, is the "maritime zone," and it belongs to the municipality. It cannot be sold, but it can be leased. The first 50 meters from the beach is the "public zone," which belongs absolutely to the public, off-limits to construction of any kind.

Construction between the 50- and 200- meter points must have the permission of the municipality. Building permits are sometimes issued only for tourist-related projects. It's also my understanding that permission to build commercially can be withheld from non-citizens until they have five years residency. Therefore, that $35,000 lot on the beach is not an outright purchase; you actually pay that money for the right to renew a lease every five years. It's yours providing you do everything right, make the lease payments, pay taxes on time and obey all the rules.

Caution: a seller may claim that an existing building, which falls within the first 50-meter mark, is legal because it's been "grandfathered." That's possible, but more likely, someone in the past ignored the rules, and the bureaucracy hasn't gotten around to enforcing the laws. The government could force you to dismantle the buildings and restore the property to its original state, when and if it chooses to do so. Check grandfather clauses with a skeptical eye and a good attorney.

Problems with Parachutists

Anyone who has followed the battles between North Americans and squatters in the *Tico Times* is aware of hair-raising stories concerning squatters and legitimate property owners. The popular name for a squatter is a "precaista" or "parachutist," that is, a person who "drops in" on your property and claims it as his own. If you're thinking of buying a piece of rural property, you need to be aware of the squatter problem. The problem is with agricultural land, not residential property.

We've all heard stories of North Americans who purchased lovely tracts of forested land with the intention of building a home someday, then when they returned a few years later, were surprised to find the land cleared and someone farming it.

If the property you are interested in has an extra house and a Tico family living in it, beware. Don't let the seller glibly pass this off as the "caretaker's residence." It could be a squatter's home! "This family takes wonderful care of the place," the seller might exclaim, "they just never leave the property unattended." They should add, "They'll never leave, period!" Make sure you see documents proving that this is indeed a caretaker employee, not a squatter. In order to be an employed caretaker, the employee must receive the legal minimum wage rate, including social security, and all other legal benefits. The papers proving all of this must be up to date. Insist on your lawyer examining the proof.

To most of us, the idea of someone simply moving in on your property is outrageous; it's trespassing; it's theft! Can this really happen in a law-abiding country like Costa Rica? Aren't property owners protected by the law? Isn't all of this illegal?

Well, it turns out that to an extent, it is legal. There are laws to the effect that unowned or abandoned property is open for homesteading, just as it was in the early days of the United States and still is in some Western states. These Costa Rican laws were intended to prevent a few wealthy people from hogging land they don't use and don't need. This is precisely what happened in all the other Central American countries; two or three percent of the people own 90 percent of the land, while the majority goes hungry. One reason Costa Rica is so much better off than her neighbors is that citizens have access to land. The laws are well-intentioned and fair. The problem lies in how these laws are interpreted.

Just when is a piece of land abandoned? One law, which seems clear, states that after property goes unattended for ten years, whoever has been using the land for that period may apply for a title. And, they will be successful unless the original owner has a good lawyer and a valid excuse.

Typically what happens is that someone's unattended property becomes a tempting target for *precaistas*. They'll construct a cabin and plant a crop in hopes they won't be discovered for a year. If the occupancy is less than a year, it's considered trespassing and is handled by the Ministry of Interior and the courts. If the trespass is less than 90 days, you call the local police, and they are obligated to evict the squatters and "present you" with a paper that confirms that you are the true owner of the property. But let it go a full year, and the situation becomes serious. The owner usually has the option of paying the squatter for his expenses and "improvements" or else going to court. ("Improvements" could be cutting down all your beautiful trees and selling them to make a pasture of your forest.) When the bill is too high—you can be sure it will be padded—sometimes it's cheaper to walk away. Understand, these problems seldom occur anywhere but on agricultural land. Land zoned residential doesn't fall into the category of this law.

The solution to this problem is a matter of prevention. While you are out of the country, have a friend or a management agent drop by the property at least once every three months. At this point, a simple complaint to the police is usually enough to boot someone off your land. Be sure to keep records of expenses and improvements to the property; this constitutes proof that you haven't abandoned the land. Having a friend plant a tree or clip some hedges once in a while covers you. Any place where there are a lot of foreign property owners, you'll find someone who watches property as a paid service. However, be absolutely sure you know who is caretaking your property, and keep records that he is being paid. The last thing you want to do is hire a squatter to watch over your property!

Occasionally a problem arises when a foreign resident decides to return to his home country for an extended stay and has to lay off his employees. If he isn't familiar with the laws, and neglects to pay workers' benefits such as severance pay, accrued vacation and year-end bonuses, the employees could feel justified in taking over the land as compensation. Chapter Eleven covers this in detail.

However repugnant the idea of squatting may be to you, it is important to operate within the law. After all, *precaistas* have rights, like it or not. One lady, who had just purchased some property, told me that she was informed that "the only way to deal with squatters is to burn down their houses," and that's what she intended to do if she ever found any on her property. I was horrified to think of someone on a tourist visa, a guest in the country, taking the law into her own hands! This is the way the problems start, and problems of this nature have been known to escalate into gunfire! Sometimes squatters are well-organized and have their own ways of striking back; the best advice is to leave this problem to the law.

Building Your Own Home

When my wife and I first visited Costa Rica back in 1972, like all first-time visitors, we began looking for some excuse to stay, some way to earn a living, and we looked at property with dreamy eyes. We fell in love with a marvelous tract of 10 hectares of coffee trees perched on a mountain slope overlooking San José. It had a modest owner's home of frame construction and a slightly larger adobe house for the caretaker and his family. The price was only $18,000.

By the time we returned to Costa Rica, two years later, the property had been sold and was back on the market for $26,000. Of course, we just knew that the real estate market had topped at a crazy level, so we reluctantly gave up on our dream of owning 10 hectares of coffee. However, every return trip brought us a new conviction that we were foolish for not buying something last time, because the market had to be at an absolute top. "It can't possibly go higher!"

This process continued for over 20 years, until we finally stopped kicking ourselves for not buying last time, and we started seriously looking for property. We found a good deal on a condo near San José, a place with a wonderful view and convenient to everything we needed. But after a while the condo seemed to be frivolous, because we found ourselves spending more time away from there, renting places near the Pacific beaches. So a new search began with an exciting possibility: building our own home!

We faced two choices. The first option: a lovely view of the beach—up on the side of the mountain. But this type of lot was a ten-minute drive to the beach; walking was out of the question. The second option was something within easy walking distance to the beach, where we could hear but not see the surf. The bonus was a low price, one-third the cost of a view lot.

We located a gentleman who had bought a lot near the ocean, in a development that featured a golf course as part of the design. After 20 years of waiting for the golf course, the forest crept up to and encompassed his lot. When the buyer, an avid golfer, realized that a golf course was not in the picture, he lost interest. Fortunately, he was willing to sell at what we considered to be a bargain price.

On the advice of our lawyer, we decided upon a local contractor rather than one from some other part of the country. The reason: local people have their own crews and know who to hire. They also know the local officials and have little trouble cutting through red tape. After interviewing several retirees who had experience with local builders, we asked for bids.

The plans were drawn on napkins while sitting at restaurant tables, and ideas were tossed about as to what would be the best design. To our surprise, all three building estimates came to the exact same amount, about $30 a square foot for a quality home— sitting 28 feet in the air on one end—of reinforced cement, stuccoed concrete block and tile. The bonus was, by perching our home on concrete pillars, we would have an eye-level view of monkeys, parrots and butterflies from our veranda.

When estimating how long it would take to build the house, our contractor wisely said, "I can finish it in three months, *no hay problema*." But, since this is Costa Rica, he promised it would be built in five months. "That way you will be happy if I finish in four months," he said.

A work crew set about cutting just enough trees to lay out the house. I watched over them to make sure they didn't cut too many. They thought this amusing, and I made friends with several of them. They started calling me "don John" (which is a term of friendship and respect accorded to those older and more wrinkled than you). They still do—long after the house has been completed. As I drive to or from the village, someone is always waving at me and saying, "*Hola, don* John!" I've gotten into the habit of waving at everyone, for fear I might hurt someone's feelings at not being recognized.

Watching over the crew is a good idea, by the way. Not because they will loaf, but because when you go away for a few months contractors have a tendency to take their men and go work elsewhere. You can't blame them, because there is a labor shortage from time to time. They figure they can always get back to your house before you return. It doesn't always work that way.

As construction got under way, I discovered we needed some bureaucratic busy work. One required item was a *plano catastral*—a legal description of the property—which was kept at my lawyer's office along with the corporation books for the property. I drove to San José for the required documents. When I announced to the lawyer's secretary that I needed a *plano castrado*, she eyed me with surprise and then explained that I probably wanted a *plano catastral*. It turns out that a *plano castrado* is a "castration plan." I quickly agreed that was not the plan I had in mind! Other requisites were a set of architect's plans and a building permit. *No hay problema*, I was told. What with a little bureaucratic delay, they were delivered to my hands six months after we moved into our house. *No hay problema.*

During the early construction phase, I stayed at a nearby bed-and-breakfast, and arose at dawn to hang around the building site and observe the wildlife that is so bountiful at daybreak. Monkeys, coatimundis, parrots and other animals put on an early morning show.

Hanging around my building site at dawn brought surprises other than wildlife. I discovered something about the Ticos who worked on my project: they not only arrived on time for work, but most were early—quite unlike other Latin countries I can think of. Starting time was 6 a.m., and at exactly 6 o'clock, work commenced in earnest. They worked hard, with regularly scheduled breaks, until 3:30 p.m. (a nine-hour day). The famous *mañana* mentality wasn't apparent on this job. On the other hand, they were well-paid by Central American standards and enjoyed a comparatively high standard of living. I'm not saying all Tico workers are like this; I'm only relating my experience.

A major problem I feared was that the hubbub of workers, pounding hammers and general noise would frighten away the wildlife of the forest. That would essentially destroy the value of our property, since the forest denizens were to be the showcase of our new home. We were pleasantly surprised when that problem didn't materialize. In fact, during the construction phase an unruly gang of howler monkeys congregated in the trees around the building site, spending hours shouting insults and making caustic remarks in monkey language about my work crew's sex habits.

Don't misunderstand, our building experience was not all peaches and cream—all expected problems raised their ugly heads, and a few creative problems joined in the fun. We quickly learned a Spanish lesson: the difference between "*hay un problemcito*" ("there's a little problem"), and "*no hay problema*" ("hey, no problem!"). Essentially, it's as follows: "*hay un problemcito*" means: "We've got a big problem, pal, and it's going to cost *dinero.*" On the other hand, "*no hay problema*" means, "Things are fine now, but just you wait!"

However, after four months—a month earlier than promised—we had our dream house in Costa Rica. Would we do it again? I would. My wife wouldn't.

Chapter Ten

Business Opportunities

Many countries severely restrict foreign business investment. Anxious to develop their own industries, these governments give special tax breaks and favors to local businessmen and throw roadblocks in the way of foreign investors. The rationale behind this practice is that foreign investors only want to take advantage of low wages and slack government controls to generate high profits, which are then spent in the foreigners' home countries. The only benefit to the host country is a number of minimum wage jobs that don't pay workers enough to purchase the products they create. When working people can't earn enough to be consumers, all businesses in the country suffer. Often there's an appalling increase in poverty, with workers toiling 10 to 12 hours a day just to keep food on the table. Merchandise that isn't exported is dumped on the market as cut-rate competition to local businesses and manufacturers.

Costa Rica takes a different attitude toward foreign investment. The government welcomes outside money as a way to spur development, yet it strictly enforces labor laws and keeps wages at a fair level. The average Tico worker has enough disposable income so that stores, shops and businesses flourish.

Any investment that promotes tourism, creates jobs and doesn't harm the environment is considered especially welcome here. Another plus: most foreign investors in Costa Rica live in Costa Rica. For them, the whole point of going into business is to be able to enjoy living in Costa Rica. They spend or reinvest profits in the country, further bolstering the economy.

To attract desirable investments, Costa Rica offers generous incentives and tax breaks. Depending on the type of business, there can be a 12-year exemption from income taxes as well as waivers on import duties. If ecology is concerned—particularly projects involving reforestation—tax exemptions can be forever!

A growing number of businessmen and investors are discovering that Costa Rica, in addition to having a wonderful climate for vacations, also offers a pleasant business climate. Among the things Costa Rica has going for it are political stability, a strategic location, a relatively inexpensive and dependable labor force and an up-to-date infrastructure. Governmental incentives, in addition to tax breaks, include lines of financing for specific industries, elimination of customs duties on importation of primary materials and equipment and a Free Zone program. In recent years, millions of dollars have been invested in Free Zones, of which approximately 65 percent is of U.S. origin.

This Free Trade Zone program was developed for foreign-owned firms for the operation of exporting enterprises and related industries. Generous tax exemptions are granted on all types of equipment, machinery, merchandise and goods needed for operation. Depending upon where the enterprise is located, up to ten years' tax exemptions are granted on property, real estate transfers, net capital and assets. Up to 100 percent exemptions on profits or other taxable income are granted for the first eight years of operation and is at a lower rate for the next four years. Firms operating in Free Zones can also sell up to 40 percent of their production in Costa Rica, with approval of the Ministry of Economy, Industry and Commerce. (Regular customs duty must be paid on these sales.)

Anyone who owns a business is permitted to import many items necessary to operate the business, without the usual import duties. This can be important. For example, while the owner of a motel or other tourist facility is restricted in the importation of an automobile, he is given tax breaks when importing a passenger van, because he needs it to transport clients. The owner of a farm can buy a pickup or four-wheel-drive vehicle at reduced duties, because it's necessary for operation of the farm. However, there's been a crackdown on non-essential use of pickups, and this tax break has become difficult to obtain unless you really qualify for it. In fact, the taxes on pickup trucks went up sharply in 1996.

Investments of $50,000 or more in specially approved projects qualify the investor for residency and eventually, a Costa Rican passport. A popular $50,000 investment is in reforestation projects; some businessmen in Hong Kong are buying these as an insurance policy; should the scheduled takeover by the Chinese Communists become onerous, they can escape to Costa Rica. With $150,000, the investment can be in any enterprise.

Reforestation projects aren't just a matter of deciding to start planting. You need to present detailed plans prepared by an approved forestry technical expert (a member of the Forestry Professionals of the General Forestry Office). The property, once planted, can be resold, as long as the purchaser agrees to continue with the reforestation project. Furthermore, serious questions as to profitability need to be addressed. There's more about reforestation later on.

Going into Business

Before we go into the subject of going into business in Costa Rica, you should ask yourself some important questions. Do you really want to move to a beautiful country and spend your time working at a business? Ask yourself whether you'd be better off bird watching, swimming or tanning on the beach instead of doing bookkeeping, tending bar or changing linens in your bed-and-breakfast. Do you feel up to the challenge of dealing with a quixotic, entangled bureaucracy, in a language you don't entirely understand? And finally, if it's so easy to start the business you have in mind—and make large sums of money from your idea—why hasn't somebody else already filled that niche?

Too often, dreamers feel confident that all that's necessary to become a successful businessman in Costa Rica is to show up and dazzle the country with entrepreneurship. Well, yes, it happens sometimes, but mostly to those who know what they are doing, employing skills and special knowledge gained from business experience in their home country. But if you're one of those who needs to be doing something, and volunteer work doesn't fill the bill, then you might consider joining the numerous foreign business investors already in Costa Rica.

Many North Americans who go into business in Costa Rica don't bother qualifying under the $50,000 or $150,000 investment laws, since tax advantages accrue to any qualifying business and because a Costa Rican passport isn't an enticement to those already holding U.S. or Canadian passports. Residency papers can be easily obtained under the *residente rentista* provisions of the laws (explained in Chapter Twelve).

Since most businesses are registered in the name of a corporation, even a foreigner holding tourist papers can effectively control and manage the enterprise. While it is against the law for a non-citizen to work at an ordinary job without permission, it's perfectly okay to oversee your own business. Discretion is required here, however, since part of the scheme is to create jobs, and if a business owner is doing work that could be performed by a citizen, there could be complaints. I know of one case in which a foreign couple built a small business and managed it entirely by themselves (working very long hours, incidentally). Local government officials hinted that perhaps they should hire some help and were slow in granting permits, as a way of reinforcing the hint, until the couple finally hired much-needed employees.

Some North Americans have done exceptionally well in Costa Rican business ventures. They bring enthusiasm, expertise and imagination, often recreating successful enterprises they operated in their home country. One businessman from Illinois, who started a successful beach resort about ten years ago, said, "It's interesting to see who makes money here and who goes belly-up. The successful ones are those who come here because of the attractive Costa Rican lifestyle and who go into business as a means of staying in Costa Rica. They usually make money despite themselves. The ones who face one disaster after another are those whose main interest is making a pile of money."

Foreigners can be successful in tourist-oriented businesses because they understand the wants and needs of other foreigners who visit Costa Rica. Restaurants and bars are popular ventures. However, as in any business endeavor, you should know what you are doing, particularly in the restaurant or bar business; there's an unusually high failure rate in Costa Rica. Motels, hotels or bed-and-breakfasts fare better, although demand for new rooms has slowed considerably. In some areas, they've over-built. A thorough market analysis is essential before buying or building that little hotel you've always wanted.

Real estate sales and development have created fabulous success stories as well as woeful tales of spectacular flops. Too many wheeler-dealer types start developments that look great on paper, but never get past the fantasy stage. Be cautious about floating your investments on blue-sky fantasies.

You needn't start your own business; numerous in-place enterprises are always available through ads in local newspapers. Of course, just as is the case back home, you need to investigate why the business is for sale. Maybe it's too much work, not enough profit, illness, or perhaps the owner feels it's time to cash in the equity and stash the profit. Don't consider buying a business unless you're competent to handle it and understand exactly why the enterprise is up for sale. What makes you think you can make money at this if someone else failed?

Among the many businesses advertised in the Spring of 1996 were bed-and-breakfasts, car-rental agencies, a pharmacy, travel agencies and lots of bar-restaurants and discos. Apartment buildings, hotels and beach resorts are always on the market, as are teak and palm-oil plantations (often not a good idea, as I'll discuss shortly).

Checking It Out

Newcomers to Costa Rica are tempted by all sorts of "free" seminars to help them get settled and to make decisions on how and where to invest. Unless you were born yesterday, you know that the free lunch went out with the nickel beer. That's not to say that you can't learn something from these free seminars, just as long as you keep in mind that the presentation will be tilted toward selling a particular product. Never let anyone pressure you into parting with your money on the basis of a sales pitch. Always check with independent experts before considering investing, and then check out the experts. To be fair, I must admit that the few free seminars I've attended were quite informative, and I found surprisingly little sales pressure.

Still, it's just as easy to lose money in Costa Rica as it is back home. For a stranger in a foreign land, it's even easier. You must know what you are doing. Business consultant Ray Nelson says, "My best advice is to come here for six months and look around. Study the existing businesses and find out why some are successful and why others fail. Above all, don't jump into a business just for the sake of being in business—particularly a business that you don't know much about."

Because of Costa Rica's liberal attitude toward foreign business ventures and sometimes lax regulation, a surprising number of foreigners feel as though they have complete freedom to operate as they wish and that ordinary laws and ethics don't apply. This is probably why Costa Rica draws more than its share of swindlers, crooks and con artists.

The Costa Rican government does what it can to keep on top of offenders, but it's impossible to do much more than prosecute crooks after the damage has been done. And this rarely happens because the swindler simply skips the country before the trial date. For this reason, look very carefully at any business deal presented to you. All too often, ostensibly honest businessmen surprise everyone by turning out to be swindlers. Make sure you have a good, English-speaking lawyer check with all the proper government agencies and verify the integrity of your deal before risking your hard-earned money.

Popular scams include phony mutual funds, non-existent banks and so-called "tax shelter" investments; gold mines; hotels and resorts that never leave the drawing board; real estate that is sold to several people, property that didn't belong to the seller in the first place; and teak, macadamia and jojoba plantations—all the get-rich-quick schemes you can imagine.

After pointing out all the pitfalls of going into business, I have to admit that many people are having fun doing so. You can feel a dynamic sense of progress and excitement in Costa Rica. This is the country of the entrepreneur, of wide-open opportunity, cheap land, dependable labor and honest government. Modern-day Costa Rica is reminiscent of the old frontier days of the U.S.A. and

Canada, full of success stories about North Americans who've opted to "start all over again. Just be aware there are failure stories as well.

Agriculture as Investment

Because of incredibly rich soil and year-round growing seasons, Costa Rica is an agricultural paradise. The country is checkerboarded with crops of all descriptions. Just about anything grows here, with bumper crops the rule rather than the exception. Rich volcanic soil and a rainy season that coincides with the peak growing season makes farming a dream in Costa Rica. Therefore, agriculture would seem to be one of Costa Rica's best bets for investment. It is, actually, but it can also be Costa Rica's biggest investment disaster for novice farmers and for those who do not understand the ground rules. Just because crops grow well doesn't guarantee you are going to make money.

One long-time agriculturist who has struggled to make a living in Costa Rica says, "Farming is a great way to go broke even if you are an experienced agriculturist. There are too many unknowns and too many marketing problems. If I had invested the same amount in real estate as I spent trying to get an orange grove started, I would be a rich man by now," he said wryly.

Newcomers are bombarded with brochures, advertisements and lecturers, all promising huge profits from oranges, macadamia nuts, black pepper and other such crops. Seminars on teak, mahogany and other exotic woods tempt investors with promises of 30 percent return on the dollar. Most of these promotions feature absentee management; you put up the dough, the company handles the rest. Other investors plan on living on the property and actually doing the growing, harvesting and marketing all by themselves.

Of course, growing and harvesting are the nitty-gritty of agribusiness, but a third factor, marketing, is truly the key. Without a marketing strategy, all your efforts in growing oranges or bananas are in vain and your crops a waste, except for whatever you and your family can eat. One farmer pointed out, "If you don't have a contract, you are banging your head against the wall. What are you going to do with a field full of pineapples without buyers?

Local marketing is the only way to move them, but there is only so much local demand. Bananas are the country's top crop, but a little guy can't compete with the huge multinational corporations. Coffee growing is a small-scale operation, that's true, but world prices fluctuate so much that you often can't make money."

One ex-farmer narrated some problems he encountered trying to farm profitably in Costa Rica. "We had some great orchards, with good production, but we couldn't get marketing contacts. Local markets can absorb only so much citrus fruit, and high export costs kept our products out of range for foreign markets. The only money appeared to be in marketing juice. So a few of us citrus farmers decided to invest in a juice extraction plant. But, before it could be completed, a government plant went into operation, causing our project to go bankrupt."

Next he tried growing starfruit. "We did great at first, because we were the first to put it on the market. But the problem was, a starfruit vine bears a thousand fruit, and each fruit has enough seeds to grow a thousand plants. Before long, starfruit flooded the market and we couldn't give it away. Then we looked toward Europe as a market for starfruit juice. That worked out great for a time, but competition reared its head again. European buyers began demanding concentrate rather than juice, and we couldn't afford to build a concentrate plant."

A long-time Costa Rica resident who dabbles in agriculture for fun advised, "It's a mistake to blindly take the word of promoters and developers who claim huge returns from agricultural projects. If you don't know Spanish and don't understand Costa Rican labor laws or the legal system, you are going to have a tough time under the best of circumstances. If you don't understand the problems of production and marketing, then you have no business trying to be a tropical agriculturist." He added that even if an investor is an expert in these fields, he shouldn't buy a farm unless he is prepared for continuous, personal, hands-on management. "Absentee ownership seldom works," he emphasized.

But what about all of those advertisements for plantations of high-profit crops? Listed here are some problems and questions related to me by farmers:

Black pepper at one time was indeed a profitable crop, but East Indian overproduction has dropped the price. Buyers are insisting on low prices because they use black pepper as a loss leader in their marketing strategies.

Jojoba bean production was once popular, but like many other crops, jojoba wasn't native to this area and a glitch in the climate killed off most of the trees in one season.

Macadamia trees take a long time to produce and then are susceptible to pests; the wrong spray can kill the trees.

Hawaiian papaya is becoming popular for shipment to Japan. But this market is very selective, with buyers hand-picking and accepting only about 30 percent of the crop. Another problem with papaya and other crops is that Japan and other countries usually insist on certification of medfly-free crops. The difficult part is getting medfly-free certification. It's difficult enough in places like California or Florida, and extremely difficult in Costa Rica,.

Teak plantations are getting the biggest push in Costa Rica at the moment. According to promoters, this is a sure-fire venture that will pay huge dividends. One company advertises that a $6,500 investment "will earn almost $300,000 over a ten-year cutting period." I asked an American agriculturist about this. This was his opinion: "First of all, teak isn't native here, and nobody knows what the production will do or what kind of wood it will produce. It takes about 15 to 25 years for the trees to be big enough for harvesting, and we won't know for sure until then. That is a long time to wait for profits." In 1993, the *Tico Times* ran a series of investigative feature articles on teak as an investment. The controversy is ongoing, so before you invest, do some investigation on your own. You'll likely find investors who feel they've made a mistake.

Tourism and Investment

Tourism has become Costa Rica's top industry, bringing in even more cash dollars than the export of coffee or even the number one crop, bananas. Tourism's importance as an economic resource for the country cannot be overstated, neither can its opportunities for foreign investors be overlooked. Most hotels and tourist facilities constructed in the past five years have been financed through outside investment. Since 1989, more than 6,000 hotel rooms have been added to the country's inventory. Every week sees new bed-and-breakfasts opening their doors to tourists. Yet, despite all this action, we still couldn't find vacancies along the Guanacaste coast during Christmas week! Instead of seeing hotel room prices dropping because of increased competition, rates edged upward—not drastically, just enough to prove that there is still room for more tourist businesses, albeit with larger vacancy rates than before. Again, do a careful market analysis before adding new rooms to the inventory.

As pointed out earlier, Costa Rica's environment combines several tourist attractions. Visitors are drawn here to enjoy a unique climate, lovely facilities, gorgeous beaches and Costa Rica's ecological wonderland. Therefore, with a new awakening of environmental awareness on our planet, it's no surprise that Costa Rica attracts large numbers of affluent visitors who insist on seeing these wonders first hand, sights not available anywhere else on the tourist circuit except in a zoo or a greenhouse arboretum. They go out of their way to come here, to enjoy the sensation of walking through a rain forest hoping to catch sight of a quetzal bird, inhale the odor of tropical blossoms, to hear the bizarre calls of howler monkeys.

Accommodations are a secondary consideration for many of these visitors. If they wanted discos, shopping and spiffy beach-front hotels, they wouldn't travel all the way to Costa Rica. Most come here for something special. They pay well for the privilege of viewing tapirs, ocelots, wonderfully colored butterflies and marvelous flowering trees, all in their natural settings. This idea of combining vacations with ecological marvels in a tropical paradise is called "ecotourism."

Ecotourism Investments

Traditional tourist resorts, in order to attract visitors, must invest heavily in great views, tennis courts and golf courses, luxury rooms and first-class restaurants. Then, after they've sunk a fortune into a project, there's always a danger of someone building an even more expensive resort next door to lure away clientele, making the place obsolete. The facility must be top quality and well-maintained to stay even with today's competitive market. Without something special, tourists have little reason to patronize a particular resort.

Ecotourism, however, is a game played in a different league. An intriguing feature is that it doesn't necessarily require an enormous investment in land and accommodations. The point is: ecotourists search out facilities located away from fancy hotels, discos and boutiques. The best nature preserves are located on almost inaccessible mountain tops or hidden away on isolated beach coves far from shopping centers, beauty parlors, miniature golf and other necessities of civilization. It isn't necessary to provide nightlife, gourmet restaurants and deluxe accommodations. In fact, most visitors would be disappointed if they found them.

Land for ecotourism developments can be incredibly inexpensive because it has little commercial or agricultural value, is difficult to reach by automobile, and is of interest only to ecologists and special types of tourists. If visitors have to fight their way over rocky, muddy roads to arrive at their nature accommodations, so much the better. This adds to the feeling of isolation from civilization. If getting there requires an hour's boat trip, having to wade the last 50 yards to get to shore, ecotourists don't complain. It's part of the adventure. Let me hasten to add, it's also less expensive for the investor.

Investment in a successful eco-project can be quite modest, and tourists will still be eager to visit. They're satisfied with small and sparsely furnished rooms, a community bathroom, and meals that consist of rice, beans and fish. At an ecotourism development, they're happy to find space available. Some places put guests in tents, where they sleep on cots, use outdoor showers and wear rubber boots to breakfast. And ecotourists love every minute of it! In ecotourism you have two choices: either you put up with what is available or you don't enjoy the ecological treasures Costa Rica has to share.

Ecotourism dining rooms operate on the same premise. Instead of a fancy menu with a list of gourmet selections, the kitchen serves up one meal for everyone. The food is tasty and well-prepared, that's true, but from the management's position, very efficient and cost-effective. Ecotourists don't complain if *gallo pinto* is served three times a day, if fried yucca and *plantains* replace baked potatoes or if they're served smoked pork chops instead of steak. After working up an appetite slogging through dripping forests, climbing mountain trails in search of elusive butterflies and toucans, they'd probably enjoy your cooking!

In addition to getting into business with the lowest possible investment, ecotourism entrepreneurs derive satisfaction from working toward the preservation of the environment. If they didn't feel that way, they probably would have gone into some other endeavor. Visitors feel they, too, are contributing to a better world by supporting environmental understanding and education. That investors break even and occasionally make money while doing what they enjoy is a pleasant side benefit.

The Costa Rican government welcomes and encourages this type of non-destructive development. Every hectare of cloud forest or primeval beachfront used as a living museum is a hectare saved from chainsaws and cattle grazing. Some ecotourism projects have even gotten off the ground through grants from U.S. government agencies or from conservationist groups.

Investing in Costa Rican Stocks

This is not something I'd recommend, even if I were a competent player in the stock market. I've had my problems with U.S. stocks and bonds and would never encourage someone to jump into something I or they know nothing about.

The Costa Rican stock exchange (known as the Bolsa) has some unique problems. One is that the most successful companies are privately owned, by families, and aren't found on the stock market. Unlike the United States and Canada, Costa Rica doesn't have a watchdog government agency looking over the shoulders of corporation officers to make sure business is conducted in an orderly and competent manner to protect stockholders. My understanding is that reporting to stockholders can be erratic and sometimes fraudulent.

This is not to say that the Bolsa in general is not on the up and up. Many knowledgeable investors have money in the Costa Rican stock market, and they seem to be satisfied. The key word is "knowledgeable." If you know what you are doing, be my guest.

Working in Costa Rica

An often-asked question is: "How can I get a job in Costa Rica?" The answer is: it can be done, but it's not easy. The Costa Rican government discourages foreigners from competing with citizens for work. In order to work legally, you'll need a special permit, which involves proving that you are uniquely qualified for a job that can't be done by a Tico. Foreign companies are entitled to a percentage of non-citizen employees, but in practice they seldom fill this quota. The reason is simple: they can hire all the qualified Tico employees they need, and foreigners don't want to work for Tico wages.

An exception to this non-employment of foreigners is in teaching. A qualified English as a Second Language teacher can usually find work and get a permit. But the wages are so low that most don't feel that it's worthwhile. English-language schools in the San José area often have positions open for qualified high school or elementary school teachers, but you must have credentials or some speciality that makes you valuable. Again, the pay won't be exciting.

This isn't to say that there aren't a large number of foreigners working illegally in the country. Some work in real estate sales, property management and tourism. A few with special skills work in construction—usually on a temporary or emergency basis. Unless the foreigners are obviously taking work from Ticos, their activities are often ignored. But the bottom line is that working without a permit is illegal, and you can be deported for doing so. After you've had your residency for five years, you can apply for a *carta libre*, a permit to work freely, and can then accept any type of work without restriction.

Examples of Business Ventures

In the course of researching business opportunities in Costa Rica, I've met many foreigners who've made the decision to become entrepreneurs. Their experiences vary, as do their levels of enthusiasm for being in business. Here are a few examples.

Night Club/Restaurant. It looked like a good deal; every weekend, as many as 300 people crowded into the Cebolla Verde (the Green Onion) to dance to a rock-and-roll band. They paid 1,000 colones apiece cover charge. The night club/restaurant sat on the road between Escazú and Santa Ana, two of the more affluent areas of the Meseta Central, areas where many North American expatriates reside. With crowds like this, how could you miss?

But after Robert Masek (from California) bought the Cebolla Verde, he and his partner Graham Henshaw (from England) discovered they weren't making money, despite the throngs of patrons and the crowded dance floor. It turned out that the youthful crowd came to dance, not to drink or eat. The cover charge went to the band and the customers bought one soft drink or beer to last the night.

They soon realized that the success of the restaurant depended on food—not entertainment—and in attracting customers who had money to spend. So they fired the rock-and-roll bands and concentrated on meals. Business dropped off, then started building up, but slowly. They needed something special to bring people in. They decided to try spit-roasting a pig every week as well as serving American-style prime rib. This worked, bringing people from all corners of the area to sample this hard-to-find fare. They not only attracted more Gringos, but a large contingency of affluent Ticos are now regular customers.

Graham's advice to anyone wanting to go into business in Costa Rica is, "First: spend at least six months here, looking around and doing market studies. Second: either do something you really know well, or else something you've always wanted to do, but don't have to make a living at doing."

Trout Farm. The Costa Rican government has been encouraging the establishment of fish farms as supplementary income for farm families. A government agency imports eggs and fingerlings from Alaska and Idaho and makes them available at cost. A group of Canadians, Americans, Europeans and Ticos living near San

Isidro de General decided to take advantage of this unique business opportunity.

They leased some land high on the mountainside and raised about $100,000 to build the necessary tanks and equipment. The property is strategically located at the edge of the Chirripó reserve, with cold water cascading down the mountain peaks (Costa Rica's highest) to feed the tanks needed for breeding and hatching fish. "There aren't any farms or homes above us to pollute the water with insecticides or sewage," Chuck Narry, one of the partners pointed out. "And since trout like cold water, they thrive."

The partners' lease is an interesting arrangement. The Tico landowners leased the land with the proviso that they share equally in the enterprise. The Ticos agree to supply the labor, while the foreigners supply experience and capital. The group purchased several thousand hatchlings from the government and started their first crop. The first batch of broiling-size trout sold out immediately in local grocery stores. The dream looked as if it were coming true. At the time I interviewed the entrepreneurs, an order of 175,000 hatchlings was due, and they felt sure they would be getting orders from all over the country, from restaurants, upscale supermarkets, and eventually, for export.

"However, a big problem is, most pieces of equipment we need don't exist here," Chuck Narry said. "We either have to make it ourselves, or order it from the U.S. and pay an enormous duty. We even have to make our own fish feed." One headache they don't have is problems with employees. Since the workers own the land and are part owners of the business, labor relations are ideal.

Bakery. When I met Ron Kozlowski a few years ago, he was in the process of constructing a bakery and learning how to handle Costa Rican workers. The construction stage wasn't easy. "I had good employees, and they worked very hard, but sometimes they drove me wild. One day, I had to go out of town, and when I returned, the workers had built a wall where there wasn't supposed to be a wall. Had to sledgehammer it down and start over." Today, Ron has one of the best-constructed buildings and a thriving business in the village of Dominical.

An ex-Navy Seal, Ron is a deep-sea diver specializing in underwater welding, and he spends half the year working, the other half in Costa Rica. Rather than go into debt, he built the bakery from savings and his paychecks, thus avoiding the horrendous interest rates common in Costa Rica.

"I decided to specialize in Tico-style baguettes and European-style croissants and desserts. Getting quality merchandise for the deli and ingredients for baking and cooking is my biggest problem," said Ron. "For example, the secret to good pizza is the gluten flour for the dough. Then it has to be cooked in a brick oven. Otherwise, the crust comes out like crackers instead of real New York–style pizza." His clientele is about half Ticos and half Gringos, and he is proud of this, "It shows that everybody appreciates my attempts to bring them something different."

Ron's advice for newcomers: "Do your homework and anticipate at least a third over cost." His biggest problem: "Electricity bills. Because I'm on a commercial rate, I pay $1,200 month for the bakery-deli. Yet I have two private homes, with two refrigerators, two stereos and so forth, and the bill is $25 a month!"

Massage Therapy. After Joe Goodman graduated with a degree in political science, he came to Costa Rica in 1975 for a vacation. He decided he wanted to stay and made application for residency. After eight years of managing hotels and agricultural projects, he decided he wanted to do something different. He went back to the States to study physical therapy and returned to take jobs as a therapist and masseur for a health club in a luxury hotel in San José and work with a chiropractic orthopedist.

After a few years Joe became tired of the city and wanted to get away to a small town in the tropical part of the country. So he made a deal with a small motel on the Pacific coast where he could have a room and place to do massage in exchange for managing the motel when the owners aren't around.

About becoming a resident, Joe said, "It's not easy to establish residency, and it never has been cheap. It requires lots of patience. Plan on spending triple the amount of time and money you originally planned on." As for advice for those going into business, he added, "Don't sell the business back home. Rent it, lease it, or let someone else run it while you come down here and look around—get to know the country. Often folks settle in someplace without knowing what's happening elsewhere and are sorry they hadn't seen everything before making a decision."

Rental Cabins. When Richard and Ann Dale retired from a successful retail furniture business, they looked forward to moving from Washington D.C.'s harsh winters. They methodically started exploring Caribbean islands one by one in search of a retirement home. Nothing seemed right.

At that time their oldest son, a post-graduate student in biology at Harvard, had been traveling in Costa Rica. He began telling his parents interesting tales of that country: monkeys, parrots, nice people and so forth. It sounded so nice that Richard and Ann decided to they had to visit, just in case this might be their retirement Eden.

"Everything seemed so natural after the Caribbean Islands," Ann explained. "There everything seemed artificial; even water was often imported." They found a delightful lot on the Barú River—just a few meters from the main road and the beach—and decided to build a two-story home with both a river and ocean view. However, after a busy life of business, they became restless and decided to add a few cabins on the property and rent them out. This was the start of their small motel, now with five rustic cabins that rent for about $30 a night. They added a floating dock and some rental kayaks and inner tubes for their customers' float trips on the Río Barú.

"An interesting part of the construction phase was that the workers weren't familiar with power tools," said Richard. "Machetes and hand saws were their basic implements." After careful instruction and training, and some close calls, the workers learned to handle drills, power saws and electric sanders. It wasn't easy, "Once a worker had a power saw cradled in his lap when he plugged it into the power. Fortunately, it was upside-down, so he wasn't injured. Another time, a power sander sitting on a work bench zipped away at high velocity when the cord was plugged in. But today, they are excellent craftsmen."

Bed-and-Breakfast. Around the turn of the century Barrio Amón was the most elegant residential area in San José. High society families lived in opulent mansions, arguably the Costa Rican equivalent of San Francisco Victorians. But as the wealthy moved to Escazú or Barrio Escalante, Barrio Amón fell into disrepair. Then, a few years ago, the barrio was "rediscovered" by entrepreneurs who acquired the mansions at bargain prices and began restoring them as hotels and bed-and-breakfasts.

Carl Stanley, who had extensive experience restoring Victorians in the Monterey, California, area, decided to try his hand at creating a bed-and-breakfast. His purchase was the 1910 residence that once housed a wealthy coffee-growing family. The 20-room mansion had 14-foot ceilings and a desperate need for refurbishing. "It was in terrible shape," Carl said. "I spent two and a half years in restoration, another year setting it up as a luxury inn." Furniture pieces in each room are exact replicas of those depicted in old photographs taken in the house 70 years ago. He named the bed-and-breakfast Casa Verde de Amón. "Last year, I received an award for the best restoration in Costa Rica," he added proudly.

When asked for advice for folks who are considering coming to Costa Rica to enter business, Carl Stanley said, "If you can be successful in the States, you have a chance at being successful here. The catch is, you'll have to work twice as hard and for less money. You go through a learning curve. You come with great expectations but you go downhill for a couple of years until you become *chispa*, that is, 'street-wise.'"

"You simply cannot come to a third-world country and expect to make money without learning the language, working intensely within the culture, the bureaucracy, with the workers. The problem is, too many foreigners here tend to live in isolation, in their own English-speaking world. Yes, a man may marry a Tica, but she protects him from everything Costa Rican, and together they remain in their isolated world."

Supermarket. Billed as "The Biggest Little Supermarket in Guanacaste," the Pura Vida Market in Garza is operated by Richard and Ginger Powers from Manhattan Beach, California. When asked, "What made you decide to go into the grocery business in Costa Rica?" Richard replied, "Originally, we were thinking of a bed-and-breakfast, but it seemed everyone had the same idea. We hit on the idea of a supermarket when Ginger started complaining about the availability of good food. The markets were dark inside, vegetables old, and things were difficult to find. She said, 'Somebody should put a supermarket in here.' And I said 'Why don't we do it?'" They had never been in the grocery business before, but the more they thought about it, the more obvious it became that a supermarket could be a success. They were correct, for the store made money the first year it was open, something they didn't really expect.

"The best thing about the business is that it makes enough money to provide a living so we can afford to live here. The worst thing is that it doesn't provide enough income to do everything we'd like to." Since their children are enrolled in a private school in San José, they need to rent a home there in addition to the lovely home they built in Garza.

At first, they had problems with employees. "Dependable people were hard to find." Then they found Jorge, an exceptionally good man, so they put him in charge of the store and made him a 10-percent partner to ensure his loyalty. "Each year he works, he receives another five percent," Richard said. "It's nice to be able to spend as much time as we want with the children in San José and know the store will be making money."

Bar and Grill. Bill and Pam Lancaster—who used to have a bar and grill in Key West, Florida—came to visit friends who owned a bar in Nosara. Before they realized what was happening, their friends talked them into taking over the business. Their friends were tired of working and wanted to return to the States, so Bill and Pam found themselves back in the business.

"We had to learn to work with new foods, new liquors, and a totally different way of doing things," Pam said. "At first, language was a problem, but fortunately, many of our customers are English-speakers. They come because of the Florida-style food we serve. Interestingly, that's also why many Ticos come to our place [Bill's Bamboo Bar]. They're curious about American food and often order one dinner to divide between two or three of them, just to try the different cuisine. I make sure they get a huge serving and extra plates so they can make up their own little portions."

When asked about the downside of running a bar-and-grill in Costa Rica, Bill replied, "Well, the margin of profit is so low, you can be sure you'll never get rich. With beer selling at less than a dollar a bottle, it turns out the cheapest form of entertainment is drinking at Bill's Bamboo Bar!" Then he added, "It does provide a living, though...and we didn't expect to get rich in Costa Rica." Pam added, "One good thing, though, is your investment is minimal, at least when compared with the U.S. licenses, insurances, liabilities and business problems."

What advice would they give to someone wanting to go into the bar business in Costa Rica? Pam said, "The best thing would be to find someone who is willing to walk you through the legal steps, explain the lease laws, how to purchase supplies, and on and on. Maybe offer to work in a business for a month in exchange for the experience."

Fishing Charter Service. Tom Cochran loves to fish, but while working as a contractor in the United States, he couldn't find the time to wet a hook. "It only seemed natural to get into the fishing business when I moved to Costa Rica," he said. "I'd be out fishing anyway, so why not make money while I'm having fun?" He bought a small boat, just large enough to carry a few passengers, and he went into the charter business.

"The best part about being a professional fisherman is that I enjoy every moment, and my clients always turn out to be friends. The worst part is that there aren't enough clients. But I go fishing anyway." When asked if he makes a profit, Tom says, "I really haven't figured that out yet. But I'm having lots of fun." To supplement his income, Cochran does some contracting, building homes for newcomers.

Where to Go for Business Help

Listed here are a number of sources for help and advice for those interested in going into business or investing in Costa Rica. These are folks who've been around Costa Rica for a while and who are up on the latest scams. (Note: unless otherwise stated, all phone and fax numbers in this book are in Costa Rica and require that you dial the proper access and country code to reach.)

First, look for the Costa Rican-American Chamber of Commerce's publication, *The Guide to Investing and Doing Business in*

Costa Rica. They also publish a monthly magazine, *Business Costa Rica.* The Chamber's phone number is 220-2200; fax 220-2300; e-mail: **amchamcr@sol.racsa.co.cr**

The Canadian Chamber of Commerce plans to hold meetings every other month to advise countrymen; dates should be announced in the *Tico Times.*

For investments, check with the National Securities Commission, Victor Chacón or Oscar Mora, 233-2840, fax 233-0969; or the Costa Rican Stock Exchange, 222-8011, fax 255-0131. Because a stock is registered doesn't mean it is approved or a good investment, but it does mean that certain minimum standards are met. Other sources of information are the Costa Rican Coalition for Development Initiatives, 220-0036, fax 220-4754; and the Center for Promotion of Exports and Investments, Oscar Ureña, 221-7166, fax 223-5722.

Doing Business via the Internet

An exciting new development in communications, the Internet, has brought Costa Rica closer to the rest of the world. This explosive technology is an important tool for all levels of government, business and academia, bringing lower communication costs and access to worldwide markets. The Costa Rican government recognizes the value of the Internet by bringing it to the country at a $30 a month hookup charge. By the beginning of 1996, the number of commercial Internet users was estimated at 5,000 and hundreds more were connecting to the country's academic node. From anywhere in the world you can connect with the Costa Rican-American Chamber of Commerce, read the *Tico Times* or *La Nación*, or contact one of the more than 100 businesses—Costa Rican and American—who currently have home pages on the Web.

If you have a computer and have access to the Internet, you might be interested in contacting my World Wide Web site. I will try to keep up to date on new laws, changes in real estate trends and events in the country which may be of interest to investors. The URL on my home page is:

http://www.hway.com/gateway/costa_rica.html

For information on buying property, setting up a corporation or opening bank accounts, see:

http://www.hway.com/gateway/crinet.html

The Costa Rican-American Chamber of Commerce has its World Wide Web page at:

http://magi.com/crica/amcham.html

Chapter Eleven

Hiring Help

During World War II, the Costa Rican government passed a series of progressive labor laws which are still on the books and are strictly enforced. These laws seek to avoid conflicts between workers and employers by setting out concrete employment rules and a system of wages and benefits. In effect, these laws take the place of union contracts between worker and employer, guaranteeing individual workers benefits they probably couldn't negotiate on their own. If you look at the rules from the viewpoint of the worker, they are only fair and certainly not unreasonable from the viewpoint of a considerate employer.

Therefore, hiring a maid, a gardener, or an employee in your business involves more than a simple understanding about wages and conditions as is the custom back home. Because we North Americans aren't used to such formal relations with employees, and because we will likely be hiring workers, even if just domestic help around the house and garden, the rules need to be spelled out in some detail. Following the laws to the letter prevents serious and unexpected problems.

Briefly, here are some ground rules: The employer is responsible for making Social Security payments for an employee as well as deducting contributions from the employee's wages. All workers are entitled to paid vacations. After a 30-day trial period of employment, an employee is entitled to severance pay as well as notice before being laid off. A Christmas bonus is not a gift or a nice gesture, but is an obligation mandated by law. The employer is required to give three months of maternity leave at half pay. All of these rules are detailed below and should be studied carefully before hiring any help.

Good Labor Relations

Recently I spoke with a lady who was visiting Costa Rica with the intention of starting some kind of business. "When hiring workers," she said, "I understand that the secret is to just hire them for 89 days, and then lay them off. That way you aren't responsible for benefits such as severance pay, vacations and such. Once they work 90 days you are obligated; so you simply hire new workers every 89 days!"

This upset me, and I told her so. Although her information was incorrect, that wasn't the point. The Costa Rican people work very hard for a fraction of the wages employees receive in the United States or Canada, and the law guarantees them certain benefits. It seems repugnant to me to try and chisel them out of their rightful wages. Attitudes like this can do nothing but tarnish the reputations of other North Americans. Those who have lived here for a long time generally realize the wisdom of paying their help more than the law requires. "I try to make it so my maid can't afford to quit," said one lady. "She is wonderful, and I couldn't stand to lose her."

Word quickly gets around the neighborhood if you are a good person to work for (or a chintzy one). If you earn a bad reputation as an employer, your job applicants will be those who can't hold a job elsewhere. Then you'll wonder why your employees are lazy, don't show up half the time or have a tendency to steal!

After I gave the newcomer a piece of my mind about her attitude, she explained that she had heard that if you lay a worker off after they've worked more than 90 days, you must pay eight years' salary as severance pay. She heard wrong again. The facts are: for each year worked, an employee is entitled to severance pay of one month's salary—up to a maximum of eight months' pay. That is eight months' salary, not eight years!

From a worker's point of view this is only fair. Let's suppose that after eight years of faithful service, it becomes necessary to let your housekeeper go. For eight years, the severance pay amounts to less than $1,500. Does that sound outrageous for eight years of loyalty and hard work? If it does, then maybe you deserve workers who are lazy, don't show up half the time or have a tendency to steal.

Roger Connor, of Plinio's hotel and restaurant in Manuel Antonio, told of his experience hiring Costa Rican workers. "It's important to gain their trust," he said. "They don't know anything about you, or how you are going to treat them. At first I had trouble attracting the best workers. But I treated people fairly and tried to keep them busy during slack seasons, so I wouldn't have to lay them off. Before long I earned a good reputation. Now, I have a waiting list of people who want to join my staff."

Conditions of Employment.

1. Length of employment. The first 30 days of employment is a trial period, and either employer or worker can terminate without notice. However, vacation pay and *aguinaldo* (Christmas bonus, described later) must be paid in addition to wages if the employee has worked over 20 days in that month's time period. Thereafter, for each month worked, one day's vacation pay is due, amounting to two weeks of vacation for a full year's work. Many employees, either by custom or through union contracts, receive three weeks' vacation. My understanding is that an employee may work through his vacation, providing he receives an additional day's pay for each day worked. (I'm not a labor lawyer, however, so you will want to confirm this point if it arises for you.)

2. Wages. Minimum wages depend on the job and skills required. As of January, 1996, the lowest minimum wage was $6.87 a day or about $35 a week. This would be for a farm worker or unskilled laborer. Construction workers earned $7.89 a day, or $39.45 a week—although in practice most are paid more than this. Bartenders, cooks and others employed in the restaurant industry have a minimum daily wage of $7.63. While these wages may seem low, bear in mind that they are more than twice those in other Central American countries!

An interesting facet of the wage structure is that a maid, gardener or chauffeur who lives in your home is considered to be receiving an additional 50 percent of their salary as "payment-in-kind." In other words, if you pay a live-in maid the present minimum wage of $121 a month, the actual salary is considered to be $181.50, or 50 percent more when figuring benefits. This is important, because the gross salary (salary plus payment-in-kind) is used to figure the *aguinaldo*, Social Security payments and severance pay. A catch here is that an hourly employee who regularly receives a lunch at your home, is also considered to be receiving a 50 percent payment in kind, so your Christmas bonus, severance pay and vacation pay has to be based on this. If you feel like you are already paying the hourly employee enough, you can save money by *not* providing lunches at home!

3. Working Hours. The maximum for domestics is 12 hours a day, although almost nobody expects more than eight. The standard is usually an eight-hour day, and a five-day week. For regular employees, other than domestics, work on Saturday and Sunday is at double-time rates. For those working in businesses or industries that traditionally operate seven days a week, the rules are a bit different.

4. Social Security. An important obligation for employers, one which is taken quite seriously by the government, is Social Security. This very important institution pays for health care, sick leave and disability pensions. You, as an employer must pay 14 percent (this deduction is scheduled to go up in January, 1997, so be sure to get a current set of guidelines from the local Seguro Social office) of the gross salary, and you must deduct nine percent of the worker's wages and pay both portions of the tax to the Caja Costarricanse del Seguro Social. Make sure your employee understands that you are withholding the money from his check, or his share could come out of your pocket. Some people pay both sides of the Social Security payments as a bonus for a good employee.

Within eight days of hiring an employee you must register his name with this bureau. This is extremely important, because should an employee become ill or injured, you could be liable for the medical bills and 50 percent of his or her pay for the duration of sickness (for life, should the disability be permanent). Once registered, you are only liable for 50 percent pay for the first three days; Social Security takes over for the rest of the time. To prevent abuse of this law, you, as the employer, are entitled to demand a health certificate from the worker (*carnet de salud*) when the employee is hired, and every six months thereafter. This is provided at no cost to the employee by the Seguro Social Hospitals.

Pregnancy is another problem, not only for the maid and her boyfriend, but for you as well. Employees are entitled to a month's rest before the baby is born and three additional months afterward—half of the salary to be paid by the employer and the other half by the government. By the way, firing a maid for being pregnant is frowned upon, and you will need to validate your reasons for firing other than pregnancy.

5. Christmas Bonus (*Aguinaldo*). Sometime between the first and 20th of December, employees are due an *aguinaldo*. For those who have worked a full year prior to December 1st, the bonus is a month's pay. For those who work more than the 30-day trial period but less than a full year, the payment is prorated over the time they worked. Thus, a person who works three months gets 3/12 of one month's pay. Remember that employees who live in, or who regularly receive at least one meal a day, also get a Christmas bonus on the payment-in-kind, or an additional 50 percent.

6. Notice and Severance Pay. Employees employed more than 90 days and less than a year are entitled to a two-week notice before being laid off. After a year, a one-month notice is required. If you don't or can't give notice, you must pay the employee full wages for the notification period.

Unless an employee quits, you are obligated to pay severance pay dependent upon length of employment: up to three months, none; from four to six months, two weeks' pay; between seven months and one year, one month's pay. Then, you must pay an additional month's pay for each year worked or fraction over six months. In no case can this payment be more than the equivalent of eight months' salary.

Again, remember this is based on gross pay (including 50 percent payment-in-kind, if applicable). It doesn't matter if the worker immediately finds a new job, you still have to pay.

A worker can be fired at any time during the first 30 days for any reason, with no obligation other than the *aguinaldo* and wages due. Furthermore, a worker who fails to give notice (*preaviso*) before quitting forfeits the *aguinaldo*.

Employee Obligations

Workers can be held responsible for damages they have caused, whether intentionally or due to imprudence, or "inexcusable neglect." A domestic worker can be discharged without receiving severance if "notorious lack of respect or civil treatment is shown," which should be backed up by witnesses. You had better have good proof though, because the Ministry of Labor tends to side with the worker in doubtful cases.

When an employee is laid off, it is usually a good practice to make things crystal clear by having him or her sign a statement (in Spanish) to the effect that all benefits have been paid. Include the severance pay, vacation pay, Christmas bonus and any salary due up to the time of separation. Have the employee sign the document in front of a witness. Should the employee be quitting voluntarily, be sure to note that in the document.

Minimum Wages

Because Costa Rica's economy is booming, there is little unemployment and much competition for good employees. Consequently, real wages are often higher than the minimum wages listed by the government. For a realistic figure, you'll need to consult your neighbors to see what they pay domestic help, or talk to other businessmen to find out what they consider appropriate salaries for employees. At the present time, construction workers are in short supply, and they earn much more than minimum. Many workers earn commissions and bonuses on top of minimum wages, so in reality, these figures are simply basic starting points for wage rates. Those North Americans who successfully operate their own businesses unanimously agree that paying good salaries means happy employees who are loyal and hard working. For an up-to-date list of minimum wages, either visit the local Surcusal Seguro Social (Social Security office) or ask your employee to get one for you. The following wages* were in effect in 1994 and have not changed substantially since then. Basically, salaries as measured in colones have risen considerably, but in dollars very little.

	Daily	**Monthly**
Bus drivers	8.26	178.97
Chauffeur, domestic	7.61	164.88
Commercial pilots	—	486.43
Computer programmer	—	327.91
Dental assistant	—	231.23
Doctor, Lawyer, Dentist, Accountant	—	434.26
Domestic Servant	—	110.40
Farm Workers	8.04	174.20
Fishermen and heavy farm workers	6.83	136.60
Graphic arts, optical lens technicians	11.12	222.00
Journalist	—	534.80
Office workers	6.72	145.60
Skilled workers	7.32	158.60
Truck or bus drivers	6.23	124.64
University professor	—	311.04
Unskilled workers	6.40	138.67

* In dollars, from Ministro de Trabajo y Seguridad Social.

Chapter Twelve

Becoming a Resident

When I first visited Costa Rica, immigration rules were rather strict. A Canadian citizen was permitted a 90-day visa, an American citizen only 30 days. Before you could get a visa or tourist card, you needed to show a return ticket and enough money to last the stay. A 30-day extension could be applied for, but it was easier to take a bus to Nicaragua or Panama, stay overnight and apply for another 30-day visa. I heard stories of visitors who overstayed their limit being placed on the next plane or bus out of the country with "no return" stamped on the passport.

Then it got to be easy. Anybody with a passport got a full 90 days, just for the asking, just for stepping off the airplane! A two-month extension was also easily obtained, allowing you a legal five-month stay. It used to be that if you waited until after the 90 days expired and applied for the two-month extension around the end of the fourth month, you'd get extra time—resulting in a hassle-free, six-month stay in Costa Rica. That covered winter, plus part of fall and spring!

There's been talk of cracking down on those who've repeatedly taken advantage of the laws allowing them to leave the country every 90 days, stay out for 72 hours and then return—those so-called "perpetual tourists." However, as of spring 1996, this law hasn't been enforced rigorously except against undesirables. You could still do the 72-hour-turnaround, but too many of

184

them in a row might draw attention. So, check out the current government policy before counting on unlimited 72-hour exits. If you are going to stay the year round in Costa Rica, you might as well consider applying for residency. Once your application is in, you don't have to worry about leaving while your residency is being processed.

Even though the rules have tightened somewhat, they are still exceedingly liberal compared with most countries. In the United States for example, if you stay one day over your visa, you will never be permitted to return! It's embarrassing to contrast the openness of Costa Rica's immigration with the closed-door policy the United States shows Costa Ricans when they want to visit Disneyland or Las Vegas. In order to receive a temporary visa, a Costa Rican must visit the embassy, hat in hand, and prove beyond a shadow of doubt that he or she has every intention of returning to Costa Rica and has no possible motive for staying in the United States. It must be a humiliating experience to be denied a visa because your job doesn't pay a salary high enough to convince an embassy employee that you're trustworthy enough to visit Hollywood and return.

For example: I have a Tica friend who won two air tickets for Miami in a raffle and went to the U.S. Embassy for a visa for her and her daughter. Now, when you apply for a tourist visa, among other things you must show a bank account book as proof of your affluence and intention of returning. Her husband is a successful contractor and always keeps large sums of money in his account to cover his payroll, materials, supplies and everyday expenses. So my friend was confident this healthy bankbook would impress the Embassy clerk who was handing out visas. But when he noticed the account held over $10,000, he tossed the bank book back at her, saying, "Drug money!" He motioned for her to step aside so he could process the next person in line.

Actually, for North Americans, Costa Rican immigration rules are even more liberal than I've just outlined. At present, if you stay longer than permitted, the penalty is a weak fine of 320 colones a month (about $1.60 at today's rates) for the overstay plus a $35 exit permit. You don't even have to go to the ICT to apply for the permits; a travel agent can take care of the tax and fine. It used to be that you had an extra 30 days after paying your fines to leave the country. But today you only have five days—certainly not unreasonable. I've met folks in Costa Rica who came several years ago on a tourist card and are still here without renewing their cards. One couple bought land, built a motel and restaurant and are operating a business, never so much as asking government permission. Again, if you plan on living here more or less permanently, you should check into becoming legal at some point.

From time to time the government declares an amnesty; those who've been in the country illegally for a certain amount of time, say two years or more, can apply for permanent residence. And those who are operating successful businesses are also sometimes permitted to apply for the residence papers. Those who qualify under amnesty rules are particularly lucky, because they don't have to certify that they won't work and therefore aren't restricted from holding jobs.

Understand, I'm not recommending that anyone overstay their visa or try to ignore Costa Rican laws. I'm simply reporting how the laws are being enforced at this point in time and how they are being applied toward foreigners with the wherewithal to support themselves, who may invest much-needed capital in the country, and who won't be taking jobs from citizens. Those who are indigent, or who get into trouble, may not find the laws applied quite so gently. Stricter enforcement could happen in the future, just as is the case for Nicaraguans and Panamanians who have slipped across the border as economic refugees.

Residency in Costa Rica

When the 30-day rules were in effect, just about the only way Americans could enjoy more than a short visit was to apply for a permanent visa. To encourage foreigners to apply for residency the government used to offer some enticing benefits to retirees. Retirees received huge exemptions from import duties on household goods, appliances and automobiles. With import taxes on automobiles running over 100 percent for a while, you could bring in a new car, drive it for five years and sell it for more than you paid for it!

For years, these valuable duty-free imports were major reasons for wanting legal residency. As you might imagine, these tax-free imports became a point of contention between Costa Ricans and foreign residents, with the local people complaining that it is unfair to pay more taxes than foreigners. Because of complaints from citizens and pressure from the World Bank and International Monetary Fund, the Costa Rican government canceled these benefits for newcomers in 1992. Those who entered the country before the laws were changed were granted "grandfather" status.

Today, with longer stays possible, the necessity of obtaining legal status is not as pressing as it once was. For someone like myself, who can be satisfied with living less than half the year in Costa Rica and the other half in his home country, there's no clear advantage to becoming a legal resident. One can own property or a business and can travel about the country with nothing more than a tourist visa. On the other hand, there are restrictions and obligations on *pensionados* and *rentistas*—not ponderous ones, but they involve a certain amount of red tape. For example, you must prove a certain amount of monthly income has been deposited in a Costa Rican bank. You must provide police certification of good conduct on a periodic basis, and you must live in Costa Rica for at least four (non-consecutive) months of the year in order to hold on to your *residente* status.

For those who will be staying pretty much full time in Costa Rica or who plan on entering business and working as a manager in the business, the resident option is probably the best way to go. Once you have the papers and as long as you fulfill the obligations of residency, you are completely legal and can enjoy all of the rights of a Costa Rican, except voting. Becoming a legal resident of Costa Rica doesn't affect your U.S. or Canadian citizenship in any way, shape or form.

Categories of Residents

Immigration and applications for residency are handled by the Costa Rican Tourist Board (ICT). Basically, they recognize three classes of legal immigre residents:

1. *Residente Pensionado*. These are retired people with pensions of $600 per month or more. This money must be deposited in a Costa Rican bank and proof of this shown to the government every year. No law says you can't take the money out of the bank right away or that you have to spend all of it; you only have to prove you've brought that amount of dollars into the country. Some people deposit the full amount at the beginning of the year to get the requirement out of the way. For a married couple, the person without the retirement income is considered a dependent and no extra income is required. This is the option most retired people go for.

2. *Pensionado Rentista.* This category is for those who are not old enough to retire, but who want to live in Costa Rica full time. Applicants must prove $1,000 a month income, deposited in a Costa Rican bank under the same rules as regular *pensionados*. The income must be guaranteed for at least five years, preferably coming from interest or dividends. Younger people and those who want to go into business choose this option.

3. *Rentista Inversionista.* Some people who are serious about going into business prefer this category. It requires a $50,000 investment in a business endorsed by the government as being in the national interest—usually in projects related to tourism. If the money is invested in an existing company, you need to submit the latest balance sheet of the company and a statement indicating its profit and loss situation. With a $150,000 investment, you can go into any business or investment you care to. Of course many foreigners invest far less and don't bother to become residents, but they are restricted to management duties and not permitted to work at ordinary tasks in the business. (This is not always enforced.)

The attractive thing about the *Rentista Inversionista* option, for those who can afford it, is its simplicity. For example: an investment of $50,000 in an authorized reforestation project provides almost instant residency. These deals are often advertised by companies promoting teak plantations. (As previously discussed, you should be cautious of over-optimistic claims; teak promoters have poor track records.)

Residents of all three statuses have the following benefits and requirements.

1. They have all the rights of citizenship except voting.

2. They can own and manage businesses, but aren't permitted to earn a salary from a Costa Rican employer or company.

3. They must reside in Costa Rica the equivalent of at least four months a year, not necessarily contiguous months.

4. They must renew proof of stable and permanent income annually.

The Red Tape

The entire question of whether to become a legal resident or to visit using a tourist card is something that varies with the individual. Some feel that four or five months is all they want to stay, so why bother with the red tape of papers? Others plan on making Costa Rica their primary home and therefore see benefits in becoming residents. It all depends upon your circumstances.

To make an application, you can either do it yourself or hire someone to go through the red tape for you. The process requires a deposit of about $100 and about $30 for fees, stamps and forms. It could take from a few months to a year before approval comes through, depending on how thorough your preparation and who is assisting you. Meanwhile, your residency status is legal and won't be challenged.

Most people find it convenient to let an attorney or someone familiar with the process handle things for them. Yes, some individuals have done it on their own, but you'll hear sad tales of woe from those who have tried it without knowing what they were doing. Few people enjoy standing in line, facing the indifferent attitudes of some clerks or the hard-to-understand questions and information in Spanish. It's even worse if you have no idea which lines to stand in!

Ask around the North American community for recommendations on a good lawyer or an experienced *tramitador* (a person who knows which lines to stand in and who to see to get your papers processed promptly). Some people I've talked to have had good experiences with *tramitadores* they located through classified ads in the *Tico Times*. But be careful; hiring someone who doesn't know what they are doing not only takes a lot more time, but could be a waste of money if they do not or cannot follow through.

I used to recommend the Costa Rican Resident's Association for their help in obtaining residency. At one time they did an excellent job of helping foreigners keep their annual papers up-to-date. But then the association began having problems. Apparently, some employees embezzled money and others fell behind in their work. Association management couldn't cope with the disorder. Folks who'd paid money to have their papers processed complained of long delays and inaction. While trying to get an update for this edition of *Choose Costa Rica*, I received no information from two faxes and one visit to the association office. So, check around the local community to see if they're reliable once again before using them.

In any event, the process of getting your resident papers is best started by you, right in your home country. It's much easier to get these at home than by mail from Costa Rica. The four main items you need are listed below, and in all cases processing must be done through your local Costa Rican Consulate. They charge about $40 per document.

1. Income Certification. This is the first and most important step; it's often complicated and difficult. Rules and proof of income differ between *residente pensionados* and *pensionado rentistas*. Social Security or other government pension money is the easiest to prove. Ask for a statement from the pension source confirming that you have at least $600 a month pension and have that notarized at a Costa Rican Consul in your country. If the pension is non-government, you'll need notarized letters that the pension is for life and two letters from bank officials testifying to the soundness of the company's pension plan.

The guarantee of income for *rentistas* is $1000 in interest and dividends from banks or investment houses. The decisions on whether your income qualifies is made on a case by case basis. You'll need statements establishing that this income is guaranteed for at least five years, and you need to renew these guarantees every succeeding five years. The Costa Rican Consul can help you with this. Again, it's important to have the notary certification and authentication of the documents done by a Consul in your home country.

2. Birth Certificate. This is needed for you and each of your dependents.

3. Marriage Certificate. Proof of previous divorce is not necessary.

4. Police Certificate of Good Conduct. Obtain this at your last place of residence, and make this the last document you receive. Have them certify a set of fingerprints, as well; ask the Costa Rican Consulate for the necessary forms. Make the good conduct verification your last step, because it's only good for six months from time of certification. If you get this document first and then spend a lot of time with the other papers, it could expire before your application gets underway. I know of people who've had to return to the United States to get another conduct certification because theirs was over six months old! You'll also need certificates of good conduct for dependents over 18.

Note also, that if you are traveling with children, some special rules apply. Apparently, these rules apply more for Costa Rican citizens than for tourists, and even though they don't seem to be strictly enforced, it's important that you be aware of them. When a child traveling without both parents stays over 30 days, the child falls under the jurisdiction of the Patronato Nacional de la Infancia, a children's welfare organization. In order for a child to leave the country without both parents, it could be necessary have a permit notarized by the Patronato offices on 19th Street and 6th Avenue in San Jose. I've never heard of any tourist being hassled for this, but, if just one parent is traveling with a child for long periods, it might be a good idea to have a notarized statement of permission from the other parent.

And remember, just having your documents notarized is not enough. The documents must be taken to the Costa Rican Consul in your country to verify the validity of the notary and his certification. Remember too, the notary isn't merely verifying your signature, she is verifying that indeed the documents are valid and that they belong to you. Not following each step correctly is responsible for the many delays and obstacles you often hear people complain about.

Other details can be taken care of in Costa Rica at the time you make a formal request for residency. You'll need 20 photographs for adults, (seven profile shots and 13 front) and 16 photos for minors (seven profile and only nine front shots). Several certified copies of your passport are required, and you'll fill out a questionnaire of personal information. You may be required to take a physical exam. As a retiree, you'll have to sign a statement that you won't work for pay while in Costa Rica (without authorization) and that you'll spend at least four months a year in Costa Rica. (As stated earlier, the months needn't be consecutive.)

From here on, it's filling out forms, standing in line, waiting for stamps and signatures, standing in more lines to put a deposit in the bank, going hither and yon, to stand in still more lines—most of which can be done by your surrogate, the *tramitador*.

Chapter Thirteen

Costa Rican Schools

Because of Costa Rica's high literacy rate and excellent educational system, a greater percentage of people speak English here than in any other Latin American country. As you try practicing your Spanish with folks you meet, you'll notice some will insist on speaking English; they love the opportunity to practice with a native English-speaker. This is good news for most North Americans; they can get by while they're trying to learn Spanish. Fluency is greatly enhanced when you can throw in an English word when the Spanish word eludes you.

Unfortunately, many North Americans live in Costa Rica for years, never learning any more words than needed to deal with the gardener or the gas station attendant. But those who take the trouble to learn Spanish will find they are appreciated by Ticos. Knowing the language opens many doors that would otherwise be closed to you. Being able to communicate with anybody, instead of only those who speak English, permits interaction with a whole new set of potential friends and acquaintances.

An excellent way to study Spanish and to learn about Costa Rica at the same time is to enroll in one of San José's many Spanish language schools. Language acquisition is big business here, with at least 20 schools in and around San José offering intensive Spanish classes. Throughout the country you'll find individuals who are happy to give private, one-on-one Spanish lessons. Some schools keep the class size to three or four students, thus ensuring each person maximum attention from the teacher.

Most schools offer programs which include living with a Costa Rican family. By interacting with a local household, you learn how to cook Costa Rican food, where and how to shop and how to deal with servants—those ordinary, everyday routines of life that can be so different from back home.

Combining school with home-stays with Costa Rican families speeds the learning process; you are in a round-the-clock Spanish environment. Weekend excursions with teachers and fellow students to various tourist locations combine learning and vacation into a very pleasant package.

In previous editions of *Choose Costa Rica*, we listed individual language schools, their facilities and tuition. But there are so many good schools today, so many opening from time to time, and all so heavily advertised that we felt it impossible to list them all. The *Tico Times*, tourist publications and newspapers are full of advertisements for language schools. Tuition is reasonable because of the competition. Ask around for recommendations and interview the schools personally to make your selection. Any school will gladly place you in a Spanish-speaking home with two meals a day and laundry. Home-stay meals are often not served on Saturday and Sunday; arrangements may have to be made individually on this. Many schools include free airport transfers. Some will pick you up at your door every morning, take you to school and return you in the afternoon.

Kindergartens, Elementary & High Schools

Recently, a friend came to me, obviously distraught. "Tell me about schools in Costa Rica," he demanded, "I'm seriously looking for an alternative to the school system here in the United States. I need to find some place where my kids have a chance to grow up safe and sane." It turned out that a young boy in his children's school had been robbing other children at knife-point and hadn't been discovered until after he had attacked a dozen or so victims. Another boy had been caught passing out samples of drugs to his classmates. "I'm ready to go anywhere to give my kids a chance," my friend insisted.

While I wouldn't want to send anybody off to a foreign country just for the sake of the children, it's my understanding that Costa Rica does have a lot to offer in the way of private education. It's also my observation that drug use and juvenile delinquency is infinitely less of a problem than in the United States. Juvenile gangs and graffiti are rare to non-existent in Costa Rica. Graffiti is mostly limited to announcements like: "Alfredo loves Alejandra." One particular piece of graffiti near downtown San José has me puzzled—it says: *"Santa Claus y Batman son socios"* ("Santa Claus and Batman are partners"). Explain that, if you please.

In the San José area, you can choose from 19 English or bilingual private schools. Some schools present classes half in Spanish, half in English, others are basically English-language schools. Some offer classes from pre-kindergarten through high school, others just the first three to seven grades. The all-English schools are very popular with upper-class Costa Rican families because they are seen as prep schools for U.S. universities. Just to give an idea of costs, herewith are a few examples of schools in the San José area. The stated tuitions are subject to change and are accurate only at the time of writing.

The **Country Day School** is a prestigious institution in Escazú, with classes from pre-kindergarten through the 12th grade. It is Costa Rican accredited and has 650 students, with classes all in English. The enrollment fee is $300 a year plus $3,510 tuition for grades one through 12. Kindergarten and preparatory school is $1,810 for a half day.

The **Costa Rica Academy** is another popular school which charges similar tuition. It is accredited by Costa Rica and in the United States by the Southern Association of Colleges and Schools. It's located in Ciudad Carari, west of San José, on the way to the airport.

The largest academy is **Lincoln School**, in Moravia, on the northeast side of San José, with 1,600 students. Tuition for high school is $128 a month; for grades seven through nine, $93 a month; and lower grades slightly less.

Escuela Britanica teaches half in English and half in Spanish, kindergarten through 11th grade. It's located in Santa Catalina on San José's west side and has 800 students. Grades nine through 11 require $147 a month tuition, lower grades less. Most schools charge an enrollment fee or a one-time family membership fee in addition to the tuition.

A new entry in the bilingual education scene is **Conbi College**, which offers pre-school, primary school and high school classes.

Universities and Foreign Students

Students from abroad are welcome at Costa Rica's many universities. There are four public universities and nine listings for private institutions. The largest of the schools is the **University of Costa Rica** (UCR), with about 35,000 students. Most of the Costa Ricans have scholarships and pay little or nothing. Located in San Pedro, on San José's northeastern edge, tuition for resident students is about $70 a semester; foreign students are charged more, with rates available on request. **The Universidad Nacional** has about 13,000 students and has several campuses scattered about the country as does UCR.

Private universities offer programs ranging from MBAs to degrees in theology, tropical agriculture and conservation. Most welcome foreign students, charging tuitions of about $100 per class and $5,600 for an MBA degree.

Chapter Fourteen

Importing vs. Buying a Car

Public transportation in Costa Rica is more than adequate, and many folks here do perfectly well without an automobile, yet having your own wheels is a luxury some refuse to forego. Since car rentals cost between $800 to $1,200 a month, after a while the savings involved in owning your own car become quite evident. The equivalent of a year's rent would purchase a nifty used, four-wheel-drive vehicle.

An additional benefit of driving your own automobile is not having to worry about collision insurance deductibles. You see, rental cars come with $750 deductible insurance, or $1,500 if the car is stolen or totaled. Every scratch they can find or invent goes on your bill. I firmly believe that some rental companies must make more money charging customers for tiny scratches than they do on car rentals. If you own your own vehicle, you can take the scratches as learning experiences, and fender benders are covered by your personal insurance on the car.

There are places in Costa Rica where it just isn't practical to visit without a vehicle. True, buses make it just about anywhere you can imagine—some places I'd hesitate to take a four-wheel-drive—but after you get there, then what do you do? If you have to walk five kilometers to the nearest store or restaurant, you are stuck. Without a car, your choice of hotel accommodations is governed by where the bus stops. With your own transportation, you can shop around for the best place to stay and then use your wheels to select the best restaurants or hunt out the nicest beaches (which are usually a long way from a bus stop).

Buy or Import?

Chapter Sixteen gives details on driving your vehicle down from the United States. That's an option for the hardy, one not to be undertaken lightly, but it can be fun, too. If you don't choose to drive, you are left with the alternatives of buying a vehicle in Costa Rica, or shipping one down from the north. There are advantages to both options. Which option is better depends on several conditions in effect at the time you need a vehicle.

One condition is import duties, which change from time to time according to the government's resolve to limit the number of additional cars coming in to clog the already over-crowded highways and byways. Another obvious factor is the current market for used cars in Costa Rica. After a wave of imports in 1994, the asking price of autos took a nose dive. People who used to make a good living importing cars from Florida suddenly began looking for other businesses to sustain them.

There are two schools of thought about buying vehicles in Costa Rica. One side claims that cars here are maintained in excellent shape because they are so expensive; folks protect their investments with loving care. The other side claims that Costa Rican roads are so full of bumps and Costa Rican drivers so wild, that cars age quickly beyond their years.

No matter which school of thought you favor, take my advice: never buy a refurbished taxicab! Taxis in Costa Rica go through absolute hell, driving all day and all night, cruising over rough streets—stop and go, stop and go—the worst kind of wear. How can you tell if a car is a rebuilt taxi? Don't ask me; you need to find an expert mechanic you trust and have him inspect the vehicle. I have a friend in San Jose who restores taxi cabs for a living. He has a great body-and-paint man and a skilled upholsterer on his staff. I've seen vehicles limp in looking hopeless, and strut out looking brand new. I've studied these cars in minute detail, but I swear, each looks showroom fresh!

Hidden Costs

At the end of this chapter you'll find thumbnail sketches of used vehicles offered for sale in the Spring of 1996 in the *Tico Times* classified section. This should give you a notion of relative values of cars compared to what they are worth in your home town. Adjust these prices to reflect the extra taxes you'd have to pay on an imported car.

Custom duties on imported cars are sky-high. Theoretically, taxes start at 100 percent of the new car price, plus sales tax, and drop down each year for about five years. Thus a six-year-old car should be taxed at about 30 percent of its list price new. This isn't as simple as it sounds, however, because lately they've decided to add in other factors. The U.S. "blue-book value" of the vehicle is considered as well as the actual condition of the automobile. Also, the amount of duties keep changing as the Congress and Ministry of Customs vacillate on how to apply customs duties. Decisions have changed several times just in the past year. Pickup trucks used to receive favorable treatment from tax collectors, but no more. My best advice is to contact a customs agency either through advertisements in the *Tico Times* or San José phone directory and request help in determining the eventual taxes.

Shipping Your Vehicle

Cars can be shipped from either Atlantic or Pacific ports to Costa Rica. But the cheapest and fastest way is from Florida or New Orleans. Most people say they paid $400 to $800, depending on the shipping line and availability of space. From California costs are higher: I paid $1,300 from San Francisco. From Florida, the destination port is Limón; from California it's Puerto Caldera (near Puntarenas). The shipping line will prepare the documents Stateside and take care of details once you deliver the car. Don't fail to ask for full coverage insurance; it's not terribly expensive. If you don't mind paying more, you can ship your car by airplane from Miami. My understanding is that it costs about $1,300. The car will be waiting for you when you arrive!

In any event, you will need a Costa Rican customs agent to handle the paperwork once the car arrives—ask around for recommendations. If you want to pick up the vehicle at the port rather than wait for it to arrive in San José, you'll need someone to accompany you to the dockside customs warehouse to attend to the paperwork there. This needn't be an expert, just a Tico who speaks good Spanish and who can ask which lines you must stand in. Some folks have used a bilingual cab driver.

My Personal Experience

I chose the option of shipping my automobile to Costa Rica rather than buying one there. I realized that it was going to cost a small fortune, but I figured it was worth the trouble; the car was in exceptional shape and had exceptionally low mileage—a 1967 Volkswagen Bug that had spent 16 years of its life in a garage.

We began the process by calling shipping companies in nearby San Francisco, shopping for the lowest cost. Estimates ranged from a high of over $2,000 to the bid we accepted of $1,300. The difference was that for $2,000 you get a container for your vehicle alone, and for $1,300 other merchandise is included in the container.

The shipping line (Maruka) handled most of the paperwork for us and gave us a date to deliver the car to the docks. We said goodbye to our little car, apprehensive of its voyage, despite the full insurance that was covered in the fee. We were told that the car would arrive 20 days later at Puerto Caldera, near Puntarenas. So we flew to Costa Rica to be ready to greet our Bug when it arrived.

After anxiously calling Puerto Caldera every day, the ship finally arrived ten days late. We found out that ten days one way or another is average for cargo ships on the West Coast. A Tico friend and I hurried to the port and began our first inquiry of a long day's asking questions, standing in line to fill out papers, getting signatures, and standing in line for more papers and signatures. We also had to drive into Puntarenas to purchase three months worth of liability auto insurance. This only cost $10, one of the lesser amounts for the day.

The most expensive cost was $85 to open the container. Another Gringo was trying to get his car at the same time, and when he complained about the $85, he was told, "You don't have to pay it. If you'd rather, you can wait until the container arrives in San José and wait until the customs officials get around to opening it. That could take a month or more." He paid the $85.

I highly recommend taking a pleasant-mannered Tico with you if you go through this process. My friend handled things very smoothly. He joked with the clerks, patted them on the back, and we bought soft drinks for a couple of helpful workers. Not once did anyone suggest a bribe, nor did we offer one. The result was, by the end of the day, we had a bevy of friends in all corners of the huge customs office. (In fact, when the ordeal was over, one of the clerks came out and towed my car to get it started when I discovered the battery was dead.)

Finally, with 15 minutes to go before the customs office was ready to close for the day, I was told, "All you need now are four copies of each of these documents, and you can pick up your car."

I eagerly rushed over to the copy machine and stood in line. Ten minutes to go, and my turn was next! But to my extreme dismay, the clerk shrugged and said, "Sorry, the machine is out of toner. You'll have to come back tomorrow!"

This is where our friendships paid off. One of the clerks we had been joking with rushed over and took the documents from my hands. "Wait here," he commanded, "I'll copy these in my boss' office." He came running back with the copies with four minutes to spare.

When I finally got my VW started, I drove to the exit gate and handed the guard a stack of documents that weighed almost as much as the car. He looked through them carefully, handed me the originals, tossed the rest into what looked like a waste basket and motioned me on.

Now the car was in the country legally, but only for 90 days. In order to make the car a naturalized "Tico" it had to go through the main customs warehouse in San José. Supposedly, this is a simple matter requiring two days in the warehouse while papers are filled out, the car inspected and license plates issued. Unfortunately, the government was in the middle of a campaign to cut the number of warehouse workers, so employees were protesting by working "by the book," as slowly as possible. In Costa Rica, this can be *very* slowly.

"When can I get my car?" I asked hopefully.

"Ordinarily, it would be two days, señor, but with this slow-down, it will take two weeks. God willing."

I called my customs agent to complain. He calmed me down by saying, "I'll talk to the chief. We can get your car in a week. God willing." I returned to the customs warehouse in two days to see if I couldn't hurry things along, and arrived just in time to hear the chief explain to another Gringo that his car would be out of hock within a month. "God willing."

I was about to inquire as to why God gets involved with Costa Rica customs, when the chief saw me and smiled broadly. "A miracle! The papers came through on your car just an hour ago." To be fair about all of this, I must point out that the strike was an untimely event, and apparently, God only works part-time for customs. Most people tell me they've had to wait no more than the expected two days for their car.

I drove away in ecstasy, thinking that my problems were over, that my car was a genuine Tico now, entitled to all the freedoms of the road of any other Tico automobile. Not so. Next, I had to go through a safety inspection in order to get papers which could then be presented to another office for clearance to get a piece of paper which is pasted on the windshield until my license plates were ready.

Eighteen months passed and still no license plates. (They're manufactured in a prison in Colombia, and clearly things are a little behind schedule there.) At this point I gave up and turned the papers over to a *tramitidora* who went to work. She knew exactly where to go, what line to stand in, and whose bread to butter. Three days later, my VW Bug was a naturalized citizen of Costa Rica! After waiting a year and a half for my license plates, I found someone who makes a good living by making plates in his garage, so for an additional 25 bucks, I now have license plates.

"Pura vida!"

Used Car Prices

The following is a typical offering of used cars listed in late 1995 from the *Tico Times* classified pages. As is the case anywhere, you can tell little about the condition or value of individual cars, but you can derive some idea of general prices and then can compare them to those in your community. Remember that having a Tico license plate is very important. If the vehicle isn't a naturalized Tico, you'll have to add lots of money on top of the purchase price, maybe 100 percent. You can generally tell from the asking price if Costa Rican plates are on the car, because if not, the price will be unusually low.

'52 WILLYS JEEP, Tico Plates. $4,000.

'63 LANDROVER excel. cond. good tires. $3,250.

'64 TOYOTA LANDCRUISER 327 Chevy engine. New paint, tires, stereo. $5,500.

'73 VOLVO 4 door sch. Very good cond. Tico Plates. $3,000.

'77 TOYOTA JEEP 4X4. Tico plates. $5,900.

'83 SENTRA WAGON Tico Plates, $4,500.

'83 VW WESTFALIA CAMPER. 97000 mi, white auto,Tico plates, $7,500.

'84 BMW, 524 turbo Diesel, 4 dr, 5 spd, sun-roof. 73,000 miles, taxes paid. $7,500.

'85 CHEVY S-10 King Cab, A/C, Auto, new paint, low miles. Alarm, Tico Plates. $7,650.

'85 FORD BRONCO, XLT. Full size, 4x4, AC, Power everything. Xlnt Hi-Fi., 5.8L, XLnt condition, low miles, full extras. $13,000.

'86 NISSAN Pick-up 4X4 D21 King Cab A/C 5 passenger. $7,500.

'86 NISSAN STANZA, 4WD. WAGON , US plates, exe. cond, extra parts. $8,000.

'86 SUBARU ST. WAG. good cond. $6,000.

'87 CB750 HONDA (US plates). $2,350.

'87 DODGE RAM AC, polarized windows. $8,144.

'87 ISUZU Trooper. Rebuilt motor, new clutch. $10,500.

'87 JEEP CHEROKEE Laredo 4L, powerful, excellent condition, taxes paid. $9,900.

'87 MERCURY SABLE 87 3.0 V6 auto. A/C power equipped, recent overhaul. $8,000.

'88 CHEVROLET S10 88 4X4 extra cab, luxurious nms, Air Cond. $8,750.

'88 HONDA ACCORD. LXI, 4 dr, 5 speed. Loaded. Exc. shape. Tico Plates. $12,000.

'88 HYUNDAI EXCEL 4 doors, great condition, excellent, taxes paid, $4,900.

'88 MITSUBISHI VAN. Automatic, air, sun-roof. Many extras. Needs C.R. plates. $5,500.

'90 NISSAN SENTRA 90, 50K mi. CD stereo, perfect condition. original owner $8,250.

'90 SUBARU 1990 Legacy All options, exc. cond., 61,000 miles. $14,000.

'90 TOYOTA 4 Runner like new $18,750.

'90 VW BUG, exe. cond: $10,000.

'95 WHITE CHEVY BLAZER LT, 4X4. 7,000 miles. $28,000.

Chapter Fifteen

Getting to Costa Rica

The most practical way to get to Costa Rica is by airplane. But for the exceptionally hardy, automobiles or inter-city buses are alternatives. It's theoretically possible to travel as far as Guatemala City by train, but the logistics of doing this are best left to wild adventurers who are willing to put up with incredibly uncomfortable and unreliable facilities.

Another mode of transportation, the passenger-carrying freighter, is all but out of the question nowadays. Waiting lists are said to be six months to a year. However, freighters are commonly used by North Americans living in Costa Rica to deliver household goods, automobiles and other items too large to carry on the airplane or to pack into the car. Regular cruise liners stop off in Costa Rica, but usually overnight, and don't allow you to purchase a one-way ticket.

Central America by Air

The quickest and easiest way to get to Costa Rica is by air, but of course this restricts the amount of belongings you can take— things you may need for a long-term stay. Those of us who live here full or part time always enter with as much luggage as we can get away with, packed with personal things we need from home and items difficult to find in Costa Rica. We send "wish lists" to our friends to carry in their luggage when they visit. They bring everything from paperbacks and video tapes to bedding and automobile parts.

A number of airlines schedule regular service to Costa Rica: American Airlines, United, and Continental, among others, and inexpensive Canadian charter flights fly from Vancouver and Montreal. Mexico's Mexicana Airlines flies to Costa Rica, as do several other Central American airlines such as TACA, Aviateca, COPA and SAM, which fly from Miami, New Orleans, Houston, San Francisco and Los Angeles.

Costa Rica's own airline, LACSA, sometimes beats the price of U.S. airlines, but generally the carriers keep their prices similar. Some lower-priced fares involve stopping several places along the way. On our last trip from Los Angeles, we stopped in Acapulco, San Salvador, Managua and, finally, San José!

Getting the best fare may involve shopping around a bit. My experience with travel agents is that some of them can't always find the least expensive way to travel. You can often save money by calling the airlines yourself and shopping for their best rates and either making your own reservations or informing your travel agent so she can make them for you (costs the same either way). I saved $160 on my last Costa Rica tickets this way. Check directory assistance for airlines' toll-free telephone listings. You'll spend time on the phone, listening to boring music while waiting for a clerk, but you could save dollars. Be sure to ask about special promotions, which can save you a bundle. Sometimes the clerk won't know until a month in advance just how much, if any, of a price discount will be available.

I don't usually recommend specific travel agents, but I will pass along the 800 numbers of a couple of agencies who deal mostly with Central American airlines and who can often beat the regular prices offered by other airlines. They also arrange tours and can make hotel reservations for you. One is Tico Travel, phone 800-493-8426, fax 305-493-8466; the other, Costa Rica Travel Exchange, phone 800-256-0124, fax 504-488-6114.

Costa Rica's Airport

Costa Rica's main international air terminal is the Juán Santamaría Airport, near San José. It's clean and modern, and customs inspection is relaxed. Airport taxis to downtown San José are plentiful and prices competitive. Ask a local person about the current fare to downtown; for a year or so the price has been around $12, and drivers will accept dollars for the trip. By the way, airport taxis aren't permitted to go to more than one hotel or address per trip, so if you share a cab with someone, you'll have to go to the same destination. If you don't have much luggage, you can take a bus to downtown San José or nearby Alajuela for about half a dollar. There's a bus stop in front of the terminal, and buses run every few minutes.

Money changers hang around the taxi stand, so this might be a convenient time to change a 20-dollar bill into colones if you can't wait until you get to your hotel. Be cautious though; street money changers can be quick-change artists. Know exactly how much money you give them and count your change carefully. Having a calculator in your hand makes them think you know what you are doing. I wouldn't change anything larger than a $20 bill, if at all. Money changers don't want travelers checks, by the way.

A brand new international airport near the Pacific coast city of Liberia is finally open for business. The catch is that it's been completed and ready to open for some time now, with the first official inauguration held 20 years ago and several other grand openings since, each time with service predicted to begin shortly. At each inauguration ceremony, officials from the tourism ministry, travel agencies and businessmen all celebrate the impending opening of this new facility. The last inauguration was in November 1995, with President Figures flying into the airport from Washington D.C. This time they are finally open for business. LACSA and Aero Tico are scheduling twice-weekly flights to kick things off. The delays can be attributed to various causes, ranging from problems with insurance and lack of infrastructure (motels, car rentals, etc) to resistance from San José hotel owners. You can imagine how unenthusiastic they would be about an international airport so far from their hotels.

With the Liberia airport in service, Guanacaste's Pacific coast towns and resorts will boom. The economy here is already healthy, but this will boost it even higher. A friend flew in from Miami the other day, with about two and a half hours flight time, and two and a quarter hours of drive time from Liberia to a Pacific beach resort—a *total* travel time of less than the drive from San José to his destination!

Central America by Bus

For those with lots of time and patience, it's entirely possible to travel from the Mexican border to Costa Rica by bus. As a matter of fact, my wife and I did exactly that during our first visit to Costa Rica 23 years ago. We didn't do it to save money (although it's an extremely cheap way to travel), we just enjoy bus travel in foreign countries, and we happened to have unlimited time for our vacation. With somebody else driving, you get to see the country-side and enjoy visiting the cities in a much different way than flying over at 33,000 feet. Like driving to Costa Rica, however, a bus trip is something I only want to do once. We flew back. It takes a stalwart traveler with a highly developed sense of adventure and lots of free time to enjoy this trip.

In Mexico, buses run at frequent intervals and are inexpensive. But the long trip to the Guatemalan border requires numerous changes and long hours on the bus. Best to break the trip up, with stopovers for sightseeing. Mexican first-class buses are okay, often having a bathroom, stereo music and sometimes even an attendant serving coffee and soft drinks.

Guatemalan buses are another story. Most are old, rickety machines, long ago discarded by U.S. school districts. The only modification is the addition of slightly wider seats, permitting the squeezing of three passengers into each seat—which were de-signed for two children. Passengers on the aisle end up with half of their bottoms hanging over empty space. If at all possible, take one of the newer buses with regular seats, or else try to be first on the bus so you can get a window seat. And, be very careful of your wallets and purses, just as you would do in any crowded place.

From Guatemala City, the bus trip becomes a different type of adventure. The bus line traveling between Guatemala and Costa Rica is the Ticabus company. Service was suspended through El Salvador for a time, but now that things are peaceful, Ticabus once again operates fairly comfortable, air-conditioned equipment. The trip to Costa Rica takes three days of driving six to eight hours a day, with overnight stops in the cities of San Salvador and Managua. With such short drives each day, you arrive more or less refreshed. The fare is a bargain, about $31 each way, last I checked. An alternate route stops over in Tegucigalpa, Honduras, instead of San Salvador.

This is not a trip for the fussy or overly fastidious, because hotel accommodations are exceptionally rustic, and you'll feel constrained to stay near your hotel and/or the bus station. I don't advise exploring the cities of San Salvador or Managua during the overnight stops, except in the company of other bus passengers— preferably Central Americans who know what they are doing.

Each terminal supports a hotel that doesn't quite reach second-class status, which passengers jokingly call the Ticabus Hilton. To describe its facilities as spartan would be charitable. Furnishings consist of twin beds with rock-hard mattresses, two worn sheets and a couple of disreputable-looking pillows. Oh yes, and a few hooks or nails to hang clothes on. You must hurry to get in line to rent one of these rooms or else you'll have to go to a nearby hotel. You may want to do that anyway, but the advantage of staying in the terminal is that you don't have to tote luggage back and forth, and you can be in front of the line for choice seat assignments the next morning.

The fun part of this bus trip is making friends with other travelers. Those passengers who live here are anxious for you to enjoy their country, and they'll point out landmarks and highlights as you cruise along. While having lunch at the rest stops, passengers make plans for having dinner together at the next overnight stop. By the time my wife and I reached San José, we had made many friends and received several invitations to visit Costa Rican families.

Chapter Sixteen

Driving to Costa Rica

One of the first questions folks ask when thinking about spending a long time in Costa Rica is: "Can I drive my car there?" The answer is, "Yes, but it ain't easy."

A few years back—before the turmoil in Central America—my wife and I drove a VW Bug to Costa Rica along the Pan-American Highway, from San Jose, California, to San José, Costa Rica. We thoroughly enjoyed ourselves. It was an interesting experience, which we wouldn't have missed for anything, but one which we would repeat only at gunpoint. (That's not quite true. I'm considering driving a four-wheel-drive vehicle to Costa Rica this year. My wife is agreeable, as long as I call home occasionally.) The roads were low-speed, mostly pavement—sometimes pockmarked, occasionally smooth with dual lanes—and occasionally stretches of gravel. In short, the roads were acceptable, as long as we didn't travel at night. Every day was a new adventure, a new challenge, full of photo opportunities and stimulating encounters with other travelers and local people.

The most annoying part of the journey was the delay and inconvenience while crossing borders. (This hasn't changed.) Sour-faced officials examine your papers with suspicious eyes, then hand out a sheaf of forms to be filled in triplicate and then rubber-stamp everything in sight. (Oh, how they love rubber stamps!) You go from one official to another for what seems an eternity. Finally, you are allowed to leave the country, only to drive

50 feet into the next country and start the process all over again at the next customs office.

I recall that during the Somoza regime, the Nicaraguan border was absolutely the worst. The Somoza officials were arrogant, corrupt and almost sadistic as they bullied travelers. One particularly nasty customs inspector searched through my book bag, looking for subversive literature. Since he read very little English, he demanded to know what each book was about. His face turned livid when he found a sociology textbook among my belongings, with the word "Sociology" prominently displayed on the cover.

"Socialism!" he shouted in a grim voice. "This book is about Socialism!" I tried to calm him down by explaining that sociology is something like psychology. But when he opened the book to the first chapter, which was titled "Revolutions in Social Theory," things hit that proverbial fan. The book stayed behind at the border, but I was permitted to enter the country, although with some reluctance. Another man had a war-surplus field jacket expropriated because it was "military equipment."

For a while, civil war in Guatemala, El Salvador and Nicaragua brought tourist automobile travel through these countries to a virtual standstill. But even then some intrepid tourists insisted on driving, merely changing the route somewhat. They traveled the Pacific coastal route through Guatemala, avoided El Salvador by detouring through Honduras and then carefully skirted trouble spots in Nicaragua.

Ironically, when the Sandinistas first took over in Nicaragua, travelers reported that the only easy border crossings were in and out of that country. Apparently, Sandinista customs inspectors were somewhat laid back, casually waving Costa Rica-bound tourists through, saying, "Have a good trip!" (Maybe General Somoza took the rubber stamps with him when he left. He took everything else.) But the Nicaraguan border guards soon learned the ways of bureaucracy, and traffic today flows with the same cold molasses consistency as the other crossings.

Today, Central America is enjoying an era of calm. Again, tourists routinely drive the Pan-American Highway as far as Costa Rica, and even into Panama. (Someday, Panama may complete the road into Colombia, and travelers will be able to drive all the way to Tierra del Fuego at the tip of South America.) With a peace accord in El Salvador, the cessation of hostilities in Nicaragua and with Guatemalan officials negotiating with its rebels, most of the region is peaceful.

Driving the Pan-American Highway isn't easy, mind you, but then it never was a journey to be taken lightly. We're talking mile after mile of marginal highways, poor hotel accommodations, frustration and red tape at every border crossing. Yet I've interviewed a dozen travelers who made the trip between 1993 and 1996; all shrugged off these inconveniences. They felt the important thing was they got their vehicles and belongings through intact, and they had fun doing it. Most described their trip as an adventure they wouldn't have missed for anything. Most also said they wouldn't care to repeat it!

One lady and her daughter made the trip in a red BMW—against my warnings and concern about two unescorted women traveling alone through countries where they couldn't speak the language. They made it, no problem, had a great time. But I noticed for the return trip the red BMW traveled by freighter from Limón to Tampa. "We were in a hurry to get back," she explained.

A couple from Arizona related their experience driving a small Ford station wagon from Phoenix to San José. "It looks like it'd be out of the way to enter Mexico at Brownsville, travel down the east coast and then cut back over to the Pacific side to cross into Guatemala at Tapachula," the husband said, "but you save almost 1,500 miles of Mexican highway driving." They reported that other than the usual potholes and construction detours, the highways were in tolerable condition. They spent between two and three hours at the major border crossings. Which border was the worst? Honduras, they both agreed.

Fees, stamps and bribes for the trip consumed about $140. The entire journey cost a little over $1,000. "We could have flown round trip for that," he noted. "But we would have missed the experience and wouldn't have had the use of our car in Costa Rica."

"We spent eight actual driving days on the road," said his wife, "and we never felt threatened. Tired and bored, sometimes, but never in danger." Would they do it again? "Maybe. We like adventure. Next time, we'll know a little more Spanish, and it'll be easier!"

The secret to stress-free traveling in Central America is to "hang loose" at the customs stops, don't get upset; try to laugh at the process. A few $5 bills handed out from time to time helps smooth over the problems.

This is perhaps the most difficult part for Americans to deal with: paying money for people to do the jobs they're already paid to do. To us, this is wrong, it's blackmail, it's theft, and it's humiliating. If you insist on looking at it this way, the border crossings are going to be bad experiences. You need to look at the process from the viewpoint of the border crossing employees. To them, accepting money to help you is a perfectly natural and legal process. The government pays customs and immigration workers minimal wages with the full knowledge that they'll make it up in tips from the travelers. So, the tougher they make it, the more travelers will be willing to pay. Like it or not, that's the way it works, and nothing you do will change the system. They see absolutely nothing wrong with the process and can become highly frustrated when confronting a stubborn, belligerent tourist who tries to single-handedly change the system by refusing to pay for quicker service.

On the Road

From the U.S. border at Brownsville to Costa Rica, the drive is 2,300 miles. From Mexicali, the distance is 3,700 miles. Your car should be in good condition, with new steel-belted tires, a spare, an emergency tool kit, road flares and flashlights with extra batteries.

Unleaded fuel is usually available nowadays, especially in larger towns. Always get out of the car and supervise the gas station attendant while he services the car. They've been known to accidentally put diesel fuel or leaded gas into a car requiring no-lead fuel. And make sure they turn the pump back to zero before they start, so you don't end up paying for gas you don't get. (I've never had this happen in Costa Rica.) You might carry a hand calculator and make sure you are paying the correct amount and getting the right change, too. Even if you don't know how to figure this out, the attendant will think you do, and he won't cheat.

You must have a valid passport. Visas aren't required in advance. However, if possible, it's a good idea to visit the consulates before you leave and have your passport stamped; you'll save time and extra tip money at the borders. Mexican, Guatemalan, Costa Rican and Honduran consulates and tourist offices have free road maps for the asking. If you can't get to the consulate or tourist office, request maps by mail.

Don't forget car insurance. Your U.S. or Canadian policy isn't recognized south of the border, but carry it with you anyway, as proof that you have a valid policy, just in case. You also will need to buy a special insurance policy for Central America. Before you cross into Mexico, contact Chris Yelland of Sanborn's Insurance, at (210) 686-0711, fax (210) 686-0732; or write to P.O. Box 310, McAllen, TX 78505-0310. This company can write Central American policies by telephone and will take credit cards. For a 15-day policy (which should be more than ample time to drive all the way to Costa Rica) the cost of full coverage on a vehicle valued at $12,000 would be $201. For 15 days of liability-only, the cost is $49. Ask for a "Travelog" with detailed directions, maps and hotel/restaurant listings for Central America (free with insurance).

Through Mexico

The first country to cross is Mexico. You will be issued a tourist card at the border without hassle, or you can obtain one in advance at your nearest consulate by showing your passport. If your vehicle is financed, you'll need a notarized statement from the bank or finance company with permission to take the vehicle out of the country. Best have it notarized at a Mexican consulate if possible. Mexico has been closely checking cars coming into the country to combat a rash of stolen automobiles. Rules are in a state of flux at the moment; you may have to post a small bond to ensure you don't sell the car in Mexico. (You must use a credit card for this bond; no cash changes hands.) When you exit the country, they'll refund this bond.

If you are carrying household goods or items you will need in Costa Rica, make sure you let customs officials know you are "in transit," and they'll so note on your car papers. Don't let them try to place you in an escorted caravan to the Guatemalan border. You'll have to stay where the police escort says, eat where you're told, and the whole thing is rushed and expensive. That's not how you want to travel through Mexico.

Unless you want to visit places like Puerto Vallarta, Acapulco or other places on the West Coast, the best route is down Mexico's east coast, entering at Brownsville or Reynosa. Although this looks like a longer route for those living on our West Coast (and it is), the better U.S. highways shorten the driving times dramatically.

Driving Mexico is, in itself, no small chore; figure three days at a minimum to make the trip to the Guatemalan border. You ought to take at least an extra week and enjoy a mini-vacation, visiting Mexico's recreational and historical sites.

Keep your eye out for speed limit signs and slow down to the posted limit; that way you won't be bothered by cops. This is pretty much true anywhere in Central America. Important: never drive at night—in Mexico or anywhere in Central America. Mexican (and Central American) highways are generally in fair condition, but they are built as cheaply as possible. The road definitely ends at the edge of the pavement; when there are shoulders it's purely by chance. In the dark, you have no idea what lays alongside the pavement—a stretch of gravel, mud, or a ten-foot drop off. You'll find no high-speed highways on this route, and the rare four-lane roads are often in worse condition than the two-lane types. Repeat after me: don't drive at night!

Guatemala

The recommended place to cross into Guatemala is near Tapachula, Mexico—at the Guatemalan town of Tecún Umanán. Good overnight accommodations can be found in Tapachula, so you'll be ready for the Guatemala run in the morning. Start early, since the border closes for siesta from 1 p.m. to 3 p.m. Sometimes earlier if the personnel feel the need of a nap.

A typical border crossing was described by Karen Bonis, remembering when she and her husband Scott drove their motorhome into Guatemala: "From the center of town we followed a steady stream of taxis filled with customers, heavy trucks and cars down a pot-holed highway to the border a few miles south. We crossed a little river and immediately were deluged with young men wanting to change money and lead us through the maze of admittance procedures for Guatemala. We exchanged a few dollars and hired a young man who led Scott into a small building to pay the bridge tax. They were gone an interminable amount of time, during which I tried unsuccessfully to stop several young men from washing our windows with oily rags, while telling young beggars they weren't going to get any dollars from me. Finally Scott and the young man returned.

"We moved another hundred yards to a modern building where a large sign said: *fumigación*. They were in this building even longer. Occasionally they would reappear at the rig, clutching even more papers. Eventually someone sprayed the tires and underside of the motorhome, and then we were confronted by customs inspectors. They weren't happy about the two TVs, didn't like the cellular phone and were adamant about not allowing the CB radio into the country. It turns out that CBs were illegal in Guatemala because they don't want rebels in the hills to get them.

"It was now well into siesta, but fortunately, no one seemed to take a break. The inspectors grabbed lunch from various food stands lining the road and continued working. Scott disappeared into the building and was gone for well over an hour negotiating with customs. He returned smiling; we would be allowed to move in just a few minutes. But the inspector returned to look at the car we were towing. Another problem. Only one vehicle per driver allowed. After showing the inspector my license, and offering to drive the car across myself, and solving a few more problems, we finally received permission to enter Guatemala. It was a short haggle over the price with our young man who helped us, settling on $5 U.S., which Scott felt was worth the price. The total time spent crossing: four and a half hours."

Alternate Routes to Costa Rica

From Guatemala City to Costa Rica, you have two choices: through Honduras or through El Salvador (which includes a few miles through Honduras). The shortest, quickest route is through El Salvador, yet until the cessation of the civil war here, most drivers preferred the slow, safe route through Honduras. Nowadays, travelers describe driving the El Salvador leg as uneventful.

The drive from Guatemala City to the city of San Salvador takes about six hours, depending upon the delay at customs at the border. At present the roads through El Salvador are the worst of all the countries, but at last report they are repairing them rapidly. From El Salvador another early start will get you across a short stretch of Honduras and into Nicaragua. Try to have a full gas tank before entering Nicaragua; gasoline shortages here aren't unknown, and fuel is more expensive here. It's only a 190-mile trip from the Honduran border to the Costa Rican border. For an overnight stay in Nicaragua, you might consider the beautiful colonial city of Granada.

An alternate way to drive from Guatemala City to Costa Rica is through Honduras, bypassing El Salvador entirely, but it is slower. A great route is through the town of Copán, where you must pause to visit the most fantastic Mayan ruins of all. Although this involves driving several kilometers of dirt road to the Honduras border crossing, there's usually only one customs guy there, so it's a snap to cross. (The road was in good shape—for a dirt road—the last time I traveled it in 1994. It may not be passable in the wet season, however.) Make sure the border official knows you're going as far as San Pedro Sula, and not just visiting the ruins for the day; otherwise he'll give you temporary papers and no transit visa. Spend a day or two exploring the ruins, then on through San Pedro Sula, turning south to the Honduras capital city of Tegucigalpa. From there you cross into Nicaragua on Highway 3 and head for Chinandega and León.

The other route through Honduras is through Agua Caliente and on to Nueva Ocotepeque, where you'll find satisfactory accommodations if you need them. When entering Honduras, be prepared to hand out money to various officials and perhaps some who are not officials, but who simply dress in a quasi-uniform and take full advantage of your not understanding the process. There are always kids hanging around who, for a fee, will run your passport and car papers around to the places where they will be rubber stamped, have stamps affixed and signatures scrawled upon them. It's difficult to tell which are legitimate charges and which are *mordidas* or bribes. The total cost is several times what it would be if you were to stand in lines and bumble about for yourself. It's a tough decision to make, to hire help or not.

If you speak good Spanish you might be better off without a *tramitador*, but you might spend a lot of time in line. If you don't speak Spanish, don't try it alone. One recent traveler reported that the border officials wouldn't deal with him until he hired a *tramitador*. Understand that all of these border conditions change from day to day; some days you'll slip through like water through a sieve, other days it'll be more like molasses. Controlling your temper and putting on a pleasant face will help. But also remember the saying, "You can get more with a smile and a five-dollar bill than you can get with just a smile."

One piece of paper is extremely important in Honduras: the *transito*, or traffic permit, a document that gives you permission to drive your car through Honduras. The cost is $10, but if you don't have one, expect another $10 payoff each and every time a cop stops you. Police cars have *transito* written on their sides, so they are easy to spot. The problem begins at the border, where the man who hands out transitos has a tendency to take your money, pocket it and forget to give you the *transito*. Don't leave customs without it!

By the time you've reached the Nicaraguan border, you'll probably be anxious to get to Costa Rica. Driving the length of Nicaragua can be done in a few hours, so there's no real need to stop over there, although you might be tempted to linger in one of the colonial cities or stay at a beach hotel not far from the Costa Rican border. Nicaragua has been plagued with strikes and protests, which can sometimes slow traffic down, so try to make the earliest border crossing possible.

Once in Costa Rica, be sure to make copies of your papers and your passport—and keep them in a separate place, just in case you lose the originals. Be sure to copy the passport page with the entry stamp for the date you entered the country.

Remember that the car permit and your insurance is good for 90 days. Unless you choose to apply for a Tico title and license plates, you'll have to take the vehicle out of the country for 72 hours and reapply for admission for another 90 days. There has been talk of clamping down on re-entering with a car after the 90-day period. The plan is to allow a short amount of time to place the car into customs for processing or remove the vehicle from the country permanently. Be sure to check with customs when crossing the border and find out the current policy.

Remember: **don't drive at night!**

Chapter Seventeen

Touring Costa Rica

Every nook and cranny of Costa Rica has something special to offer, something to dazzle the eyes or gratify the other senses. Newcomers are never satisfied until they have seen it all; long-time residents tend to repeat their travels, to see everything again and again. Fortunately, getting around the country is easy. Within a few hours, you can visit just about any section of Costa Rica you choose, and you usually have several modes of transportation available to you.

Air Transportation

The quickest way to travel about the country is by SANSA or Travelair, the airlines serving San José, Quepos, Golfito, Palmar Sur, Barra del Colorado, Nosara, Tamarindo and Sámara. Ticket prices are considerably more expensive than going by bus, but of course the trip is faster. Travelair tickets cost more than SANSA tickets, but the bottom line is that Travelair will take you to your destination even if you are the only passenger, whereas SANSA has been known to cancel flights if there aren't enough passengers. The air equipment in Costa Rica used to be old reliable, bulky DC-3s, but most planes today are those small foreign jobs that force you to hunch over as you make your way to your seat. Flights to anywhere in the country take far less than an hour, including stopovers.

Because flights are popular, and the planes tiny, they are frequently booked solid. Make reservations in advance, and be sure to reconfirm your reservations even though you have tickets. Someone else could have your boarding pass if you show up at the airport without reconfirming 24 hours in advance and arriving early.

Another air option is an "air taxi" which will take you just about anywhere a bush pilot can set down a small plane. The cost is about $300 an hour for a twin-engine plane and five passengers. For a single-engine job, the price drops to $220 an hour for the same five passengers. A $440-an-hour, seven-passenger plane can also be rented. When you consider that the country is small and flying times short, an air taxi isn't as expensive as it might appear. You'll find several companies in the phone book classified pages under the listing "Taxis Aereos."

What if you are a pilot and would like to rent a plane and fly yourself? Not so easy. Even if you are a certified pilot with a license from another country, you can't rent a Costa Rican plane until you've earned a Costa Rican license. You need to show proof of your total air hours logged in your country as well as log a certain amount of time in Costa Rica. If you own a plane, it can be kept in the country for up to six months without having to pay taxes, after which time it must be removed. However, there seems to be a question as to how many six-month permits an individual can obtain. You'll need to check this out with customs.

Trains and Buses

Guidebooks often rave about the scenic wonders of the country's train system. Especially tempting are descriptions of a spectacular railroad trip from San José to the Caribbean city of Limón. However, when you read about train trips in Costa Rica, you know the book is a bit out of date. Since the earthquake of 1991, passenger trains no longer journey to Limón, or anywhere else, for that matter. Sad, but true. Some roadbeds and a few ancient bridges slipped downhill—common occurrences in Costa Rica earthquakes—but this time the government decided not to rebuild. The lines were losing money anyway.

It's possible that, sometime in the future, service to the Pacific port of Puntarenas could be resumed, and a short commuter run to Cartago started in late 1993. There's also a short excursion to Turrialba. However, there could be a bright side to this story: the government is considering turning over the rail system to the ex-employees of the railroad. Experts are giving them training in management and business practices, in the hopes that an employee cooperative just might revitalize the train system.

Buses are another story. In addition to excellent city bus service, eight inter-city bus companies provide frequent service to just about any place you'd care to go. Unlike the United States, where monopolistic inter-city bus fares border on extortion, tickets between Costa Rican cities are downright cheap. A four-hour ride from San José to Limón, for example, is little more than $4.

San José has no central bus station; each bus line departs from its own terminal, sometimes just a curbside parking place in front of a small ticket office. For example, to go to Quepos and Manuel Antonio, you take the buses that leave from the "Coca Cola" terminal. (The Coca Cola terminal gains its name in a typical Tico fashion: there *used* to be a Coca-Cola bottling plant in the neighborhood.) Buses for Limón leave from the eastern side of the National Park on Avenida 11, but buses for Cahuita, just a few miles farther south of Limón, leave from a location a dozen blocks away. Often, reservations need to be made a day or two in advance. The better tourist guidebooks list the bus terminals, destinations and travel times.

A number of smaller bus companies (often with only one bus in the fleet) carry passengers to all imaginable sectors of the country. Few towns or villages in the republic lack bus transportation of some sort. Often, while negotiating impossible back country roads, bouncing through deep potholes, skirting boulders in the trail—wondering whether my rental car could ever make it back in one piece—a passenger-laden bus would appear from out of nowhere, sound its horn impatiently to move me aside, and then rumble past as it hurried on its way.

These country buses tend to be of an older rattle-trap variety, usually secondhand school buses bought at surplus in the United States. Sometimes the owner-drivers don't bother to change the paint, and the bus finishes its transportation career bouncing along dusty trails in Costa Rica, with the legend "Maplewood Unified School District" still painted on its side. Sometimes you'll be pleasantly surprised by a small air-conditioned vehicle of late manufacture, which makes the back country surprisingly luxurious. (Of course, there's nothing to guarantee the driver will actually turn on the air conditioning, which draws power from the engine.)

Since the distance between San José and any destination in the country is not very far, bus trips don't take too long. From San José to Quepos, a popular tourist destination, bus travel time is less than four hours. By air it is only 20 minutes or so, but by the time you get out to the airport an hour early, wait for the plane to leave (always a half-hour to an hour late) and then wait for a bus to take you from the air strip to town, you haven't saved all that much time. Plus, you've missed a lot of interesting scenery. However, be aware that different bus lines have varying schedules. For example, travel from San José to Puntarenas takes two hours by one bus line but four hours on another line.

I knew Costa Rica had a lot of competing bus companies, but for a while I was astounded at how many city bus lines there appeared to be in San José. And, it seemed that the bus lines' names were very creative. Then I discovered that the name painted on a bus's side or on the back wasn't the name of a bus company, but rather an imaginative name given to the bus by its driver as an expression of his individuality.

The *Tico Times* ran a feature article on these names, at which point I realized that the Papa Lolo bus that passed by my house every morning as I waited for my ride was not owned by the "Papa Lolo Bus Lines" but was driven by a driver with the nickname "Papa Lolo." Some buses are named after family members, other names are exercises in imagination. Other names noted were: Desert Storm, Krakatoa, El Principe Azul (the blue prince), Mil Amores (thousand loves), the Dancing Queen and El Guerrero del Camino (the road warrior).

Taxicabs Galore

Costa Rica enjoys an excellent system of taxis, with about 7,000 drivers zipping along the streets of San José and suburbs—double what there were in 1990. Almost all cabs are late-model Japanese imports, usually Toyota or Nissan. Occasionally you'll see a Volkswagen or a Volvo. By law, taxicabs are painted bright red. You can't miss them.

Not only is taxi equipment usually in good shape, but fares are inexpensive. Presently, it costs 115 colones (a little more than half a dollar U.S.) to go the first kilometer, and 50 colones for every kilometer after that—an absolute bargain! In San José, you can go practically any place in the city from downtown for about $3. Between 10 p.m. and 5 a.m. drivers are permitted to charge an additional 20 percent. Drivers don't expect tips, but I always round the bill up to the next 50 colones, and they drive away happy.

All San José taxis are supposed to have meters, and most do. Ticos refer to a taxi meter as a "maría." Why "maría"? Some years ago, Costa Rica's president decided that taxis should have meters, rather than have drivers and clients haggle over the price of each ride. So he ordered a batch of taxi meters from a company in Argentina for a trial run. The company's name contained the word María something or other. But with typical Costa Rican bureaucracy, customs officials in Limón refused to allow the contraptions into the country until all the proper papers and forms were filled in. By the time all the tax stamps had been fastened, quadruplicate copies made and signatures affixed, the meters—which were mechanical as opposed to the electronic ones they use today—had rusted in Limón's damp climate and had to be trashed. Hence the word "maría" for taximeter.

Avoid cabs parked in front of hotels or discos. The drivers will tell you that they don't have to use meters because they pay more insurance, or some other baloney. The truth is they charge from two to four times the normal rate. When in doubt, ask, *"Hay una maría?"* If the driver claims the meter isn't working, don't enter the cab until you've established a price (providing, of course, that you know about what the price should be). If the driver quotes a ridiculous price or if you haven't any idea of the correct fare, take another cab with a meter. At certain times of the day, drivers are reluctant to turn on the meters, because they know they can get all the customers they want and don't want the cab's owner to know exactly how much was taken in.

Occasionally you'll find cabs without meters, known as *piratas* or "pirates," private autos illegally operating as taxis. Usually, the fares quoted by these non-metered cabs are about what you'd pay in a legally-operated vehicle. The problem with *piratas* is that some of them aren't in safe operating condition. And unless you know what the fare should be, and you know enough Spanish to negotiate, I'd recommend waiting for a cab with a meter. All in all, I think Costa Rican taxi drivers are fairly honest. Rarely have I been overcharged, and that was during times of heavy rains or rush hours—when the extra cost was worth it to me.

Although the law says taxicabs must use meters, bear in mind that any trip over 12 kilometers is exempt. A trip from the airport to San José, for example, should cost between $10 and $15, depending on what part of the city you are going to. If you gather fellow passengers to share the cost of the trip, that's okay, but by law the driver cannot take you to different hotels or locations; he is only supposed to have one destination at a time.

Why are most cabs new? Because one side benefit of owning a taxi is that it can be purchased free of import duties, as long as it is used for three years before selling it as a used car. This means that after three years of generating income, the vehicle may be sold for as much or more than it cost in the first place.

Up to this point, we've been discussing taxi cabs around the Meseta Central. Taxis aren't only for city folk; you'll find them all over the country, sometimes in places so isolated that they would seem implausible. Not all villages will have a taxi, but most have access to one from a neighboring village. Away from the city's paved roads, four-wheel-drive taxis are the norm, in the rainy season, a must. Four-wheel-drive trucks commonly serve as a taxis, with the truck bed used to transport furniture, appliances or more passengers. In rural areas, where buses and taxis are rare or nonexistent, private autos and trucks often provide free rides to local people walking from one village to another. I do the same and find that locals appreciate rides—the hospitality enhances their opinion of foreigners.

Taxi-Chauffeurs

Driving a car around San José or through the narrow roads in the immediate countryside isn't exactly a relaxing pastime. I sometimes find myself so involved with traffic and confusion that I see very little. My passengers see even less since they spend a great deal of their time praying, cursing or shouting at me: "Watch where you're going, you dummy!" For that reason, I rarely drive in downtown San José, even though I own my own car. It takes me ten minutes of sweating and cursing to get from our condo to the center of town, whereas it only takes five minutes of sweating and cursing in the average taxi.

There is a better way to explore the Meseta Central: rent a cab! Taxi drivers much prefer the idea of one fare for the entire day, instead of wandering all over town waiting for someone to flag them down. One fare isn't nearly as hard on the cab, since passengers always want to stop, get out and spend time looking around, giving the taxi and driver a deserved rest.

It's not only convenient to let someone else drive (someone who knows what he's doing), but it costs about the same as renting a car for the day. A competent, English-speaking cab driver will chauffeur you around the Meseta Central for five or six hours for about $50. A rental car for one day—with insurance and gasoline—would cost almost $60 and a million dollars worth of tension. In other words, after you buy the driver's lunch and give a small tip, you're about even. Most any cab driver will rent hourly for about $10 per hour, but you're better off making prior arrangements with an English-speaking driver.

Taxicab rental will also save you hours of time and frustration when checking out neighborhoods for real estate. The driver can whisk you to a half-dozen suburbs in less time than you can stumble onto one. This is also a great idea for sightseeing trips around the Meseta Central. Instead of four people paying $25 to $45 per person for a five-hour commercial tour, a cab driver can show you the same sights, with individual attention, for much less. Some drivers will even take you on longer trips, anyplace in the country you care to go—Monte Verde or Manuel Antonio, for example—as long as you also take care of their hotel and meal expenses.

Not all drivers are willing to rent by the hour, and not all can speak English well enough to explain what you are seeing. To find one who does, check with your hotel clerk or a travel agency. Many English-speaking drivers are available and eager to show you around the Meseta Central.

Rental Cars in Costa Rica

This is by far the most convenient way of touring the country. When you get serious about looking for a place to live for a few months or for the rest of your life, renting a car for a week or two allows you to travel about freely in search of your dream location. You don't have to bother with bus schedules; you can check out side streets or country lanes, and you can stop whenever you find a particularly interesting view. With a car, you needn't worry about hotel reservations; chances are if one hotel is full, another will have room. You can drive around, checking out for sale or for rent signs. You can investigate for yourself instead of being under the control of a salesman, a rental agent or someone with a vested interest in showing you only their own properties.

At the present time, automobile insurance is a government monopoly, and it's mandatory that your rental car insurance be purchased through the government agency. This could change soon, bringing much-needed competition to the field. The way it is now, there's a hefty $750 deductible in case of an accident. Should the car be totaled or stolen, the deductible is $1,500. Since auto theft is at epidemic levels at the time of writing, this calls for keeping your rental car in a safe place at night.

Check with the rental company as to their policy—don't accept a car with more than $750 deductible—one company tries to impose a $1,000 floor on their liability! If you have a "Gold Card" (such as VISA or American Express) it should cover the deductible in case of an accident. Check with your credit card provider to be certain. Be sure to report a mishap to the credit card company within 20 days, even if the rental agent assures you that the other driver's insurance covers the repairs.

Accessories such as antennas, radios, tires and mirrors aren't covered by rental insurance; if they are stolen, you are liable. The answer to the insurance problem is to keep your car in a guarded parking lot overnight when in the vicinity of San José. Auto accessory theft is not common in smaller towns, but in San José and other large cities, be aware.

Important: before you accept a rental car, check the car for dents, scratches and blemishes, in minute detail! Make sure the rental car employee notes each of them on your contract—no matter how tiny the scar. Unscrupulous employees in some agencies work a scam by charging for the same trivial scratch over and over. If the damage is there, but not duly noted, you have no recourse but to pay. I've had better luck in this respect with the larger rental companies. Discuss this before you sign a contract.

Finally, insist on good tires. A sharp rock can penetrate a tire if the tread is thin and the sidewalls weak. If the tire is destroyed, you're liable for that too. So, insist on another car if the tires are not in good shape. If they give you trouble about this, consider finding another car rental agency.

On the Road

Your regular driver's license is perfectly legal in Costa Rica for 90 days from the time you enter the country. After that you need a Costa Rican license. For residents, or for those awaiting *residente* status, a license is relatively easy to get; simply apply at the local office of the Ministerio de Obras Publicas y Transportacion ("MOPT," for us Gringos; ask a friend to help you find one locally) and present several passport-sized photos. The license is issued while you wait.

However, as a tourist, you are not permitted to drive after 90 days on your home country's license. You'll have to leave the country long enough to get a fresh stamp on your passport. Take this warning seriously. The rules for foreigners applying for driver's licenses by presenting their passports changes from time to time. For a while, it was difficult, if not impossible, because of a ruling that only legal residents could get Costa Rican driver's licenses. How strict this ruling was observed is another question. Some MOPT offices issued driver's licenses to non-residents, some

PERSONAL belongings / THEFT from CARS

would not. However the advantages of having a driver's license are nebulous unless you are a resident or have made application for residency, since it's illegal to drive if your 90-day visa or extension has expired.

Always carry your passport when driving; there's a fine for not having it. A photocopy of the passport is sometimes accepted, provided you have a copy of the page showing the date you entered. The original passport is much preferred. Photocopies of your driver's license are not acceptable.

The first rule of driving in Costa Rica is one that should be followed in any country: do not leave anything stealable in the car, even out of sight. A favorite trick of thieves is to monitor the car rental desks at the airport, watch who rents a car and fills the trunk with interesting luggage. They then follow the car to the hotel and while the passengers are inside at the registration desk, the thieves open the trunk and help themselves to the luggage, extra money, cameras, etc. If at all possible, leave someone in the car during that crucial first stop. This method of stealing isn't unique to Costa Rica; it has been imported from Europe, probably originating in Italy or Spain. Once outside of San Jose, the chance of something like this happening is much less, but why take chances?

Driving through the Costa Rican countryside isn't difficult, it's just slower. With all that gorgeous scenery, who wants to travel fast? Be especially careful when passing. Make sure you have time to get around safely and be cautious near hills and curves. Always drive as though you expect trouble. That's just common sense in any country, but particularly in Costa Rica; too many drivers have a daring, gambling attitude that urges them to pass on hills and curves. For this reason, accident rates in Costa Rica are unusually high. Drive defensively and keep an eye on the speedometer. Americans, used to high-speed, paved highways, sometimes have difficulty keeping their speed under 65 mph. It doesn't seem normal to drive slower. But you must realize that 65 mph is about 110 kilometers an hour, an illegal speed anywhere in the country. Most highways have a 75-kph limit, unless posted with an 80, 90, or an occasional 100-kph limit.

N.B.

Watch for oncoming drivers who flash their headlights off and on. That means trouble ahead, usually a radar speed trap or perhaps an accident. Another sign of danger is a tree branch or piece of shrubbery laying across one lane of the pavement. That signifies an accident, a washout or some other nasty surprise that could await you ahead.

Driving in city traffic anywhere around San José can be frustrating. As you get the knack of it and learn the system, it gets easier. Theoretically, finding your way around San José should be easy because downtown city streets are logically organized on a north-south, east-west grid. *Calles*, or streets, run north to south and *avenidas*, avenues, east to west.

However, nothing in Costa Rica is as simple as it sounds. For one thing, street signs are often missing. Sometimes they'll be posted on the corner of a building, or perhaps on a signpost, but just when you need to know exactly where you are, you won't be able to find a clue. Furthermore, most downtown streets are one-way traffic, often without arrows to indicate which way! Perhaps you know that Avenida Nueve is a one-way street going west, but how do you know the street you are looking at is Avenida Nueve when there are neither street signs nor one-way signs? All you can do is wait to see which way traffic is flowing. If no cars are coming either way, you don't dare take a chance.

In the surrounding towns of the Meseta Central, traffic is lighter than in San José, but the problem of missing street signs becomes even worse. Some streets are one-way and others two-way, but too often there aren't any signs to clue you in as to which is which. An arrow painted on the pavement should indicate which direction is permissible, but sometimes the arrow isn't there. It's especially disconcerting to be driving along what you believe to be a two-way street and suddenly notice that all cars parked on both sides of the street are pointing in your direction. Since parking on either side of the street is okay in Costa Rica, you have no way of knowing if they just happen to be facing your direction or if you are traveling the wrong way again. When in doubt, park and wait for a car to drive past, then follow suit.

Away from the cities and major highways you find bumpy roads that demand slow driving. Going too fast over rocks can cut tires, marooning you several kilometers from a repair shop. You may have to change it yourself! When this last happened to me, I stood around looking perplexed until two young men stopped to change the spare for me. They refused to accept money. Next, I drove to a sort of auto repair place where two kids fixed my tire in a jiffy using strips of an old inner tube, some kind of glue and what appeared to be a steel crochet needle. They didn't even have to take the tire off the rim, as I expected. They charged the equivalent of $1.50; that included putting the repaired wheel on the car and stashing the spare in the trunk.

Automobile Ferry Schedules

Several Costa Rican communities are accessible by car only after a ferry crossing. The longest ferry voyage is across the Gulf of Nicoya from Puntarenas to the southern part of the Nicoya Peninsula. This trip offers a choice of three ferries. Each passage takes about an hour, and you have to allow an hour for waiting in line. If you aren't there at least an hour early, you could find yourself waiting for the next ferry. It always surprises me how many vehicles can fit on one of those small boats. Cargo and cattle trucks, buses and passenger cars string out in a long line from the ferry terminal in a seemingly impossible mission, yet most seem to fit aboard. Buses have priority, so the last to arrive in line could be a bus, but it will load first. A tip: truckers can gauge the line pretty accurately and can tell you whether you'll make it aboard, should you arrive late. Just ask, "*Habrá espacio para mí carro?*"

Once aboard, you can mingle with the other passengers and practice Spanish with the Ticos or compare travel agendas with the other tourists. I've met some very interesting people this way; something about a slow crossing brings out gregariousness in folks.

You have your choice of three boats to reach the southern portion of the Nicoya Peninsula, to places like Tambor, Tango Mar, Montezuma or Malpaís. All three leave from Puntarenas; follow the signs.

Puntarenas-Playa Naranjo: leaves Puntarenas at 4 a.m., 7 a.m., 10:30 a.m., 1:30 p.m. and 4:30 p.m. It leaves Playa Naranjo at 5:15 a.m., 8:30 a.m., noon, 3 p.m. and 6 p.m. The ferry has room for about 30 vehicles, depending on size. Beer, soft drinks and snacks are sold.

Puntarenas-Paquera: lands farther down the peninsula from Playa Naranjo—near the large village of Paquera—and thus cuts driving time off the trip to Tambor or to the tip of the peninsula. The disadvantage is that it doesn't sell cold beer or soft drinks. It's operated by the Hotel Playa Tambor but is open to the public. It leaves Puntarenas daily at 4:15 a.m., 8:45 a.m., 12:30 p.m. and 5:30 p.m., landing at Paquera, from which it departs at 6 a.m., 10:30 a.m., 2:30 p.m. and 7:15 p.m.

Puntarenas-Paquera: A passengers-only ferry departs daily from behind the Puntarenas market at 6 a.m. and 3 p.m. to Paquera and returns to Puntarenas at 8 a.m. and 5 p.m.

Río Tempisque Ferry: This ferry crosses to the upper (mid-peninsula) region of the Nicoya Peninsula, to the city of Nicoya and the beaches of Nosara and Sámara. It runs from 6 a.m. to 6 or 7 p.m. If you're headed for Playa Flamingo or points to the north, don't bother with the ferry; the quickest way is to continue north on the Pan-American Highway. The Tempisque Ferry takes about 25 minutes to cross and 15 minutes to load. It holds an astonishing number of vehicles, but during busy times, you may have to wait for a trip or two. Weekend and holiday traffic is the worst. Again, ask a truck driver what your waiting time will be. If it's horrendous, you might save time by returning to the highway and looping around through Liberia. On each side of the river several outdoor restaurants make the wait somewhat pleasant. A bridge across the river farther upstream has been designed and the access roads built. The only thing holding it up is money. When this bridge finally crosses the river, the peninsula will be much more accessible and property more valuable.

Río Coto Ferry: This is my favorite ferry of anywhere I've driven. You use it when you're headed for Zancudo or Pavones via the shorter route (not always the quickest). The turnoff to the ferry is about halfway between Río Claro and Golfito. The Río Coto crossing isn't very wide at this point, and a steel cable strings across the water to keep the ferry on track. When you arrive at the crossing, if nobody's tending to the ferry, you honk your horn. Soon a teenager or two will come running and start up the old Datsun engine that propels the boat across the water. The capacity is about three cars. The last time we crossed the Rio Coto, the engine was broken. How to get across? The solution was simple. Another teenager jumped into a canoe that sat alongside the ferry. He started up an outboard motor, hooked his arm through a projection of angle iron and revved up the motor. It took some time for the boat to start moving, but the trip went surprisingly fast, once underway.

Golfito-Zancudo: If you don't need to take a car with you, a quicker way to get to Playa Zancudo is via one of the many small "water taxis" that take tourists a wide variety of places around the Dulce Golfo area. Call the Asociacion de Boteros at 775-0712. There's also a passenger ferry that sails between Golfito and Puerto Jimenez, on the Oso Peninsula.

Traffic Cops and Speed Traps

I often hear reports of tourists being harassed by Costa Rican traffic cops. No doubt these things happen; as anywhere in the world, a few bad guys can get on the force. Yet, after many thousands of miles and numerous traffic tickets (all deserved), my experience is that the overwhelming majority of Costa Rican traffic police are courteous and rarely stop someone without due cause. With all the crazy drivers in this country, cops have little reason to stop somebody "for nothing at all." After all, issuing a ticket for speeding, illegal passing, no safety belt, etc., is not "police harassment." In the U.S. it's known as "law enforcement." Tourists aren't exempt from traffic laws, even if they don't thoroughly understand them. Why should they be?

Yet you'll continually hear Gringos complain that "the cops only stop rental cars. Why not Tico cars?" This is partly true, because Ticos know a little secret. When they see a speed limit sign of 60 kilometers per hour (38mph), they slow down because they know there'll probably be a radar gun ahead. Tourists, used to 65-mile-per-hour highways, blissfully pass the slowpoke Ticos in front of them. And guess what? Most Costa Rica highways have maximum limits of 75 kph (about 48mph). This may seem ridiculously slow, but Ticos know those occasional long, straight stretches of good pavement also are favorite places for radar guns. Maybe it seems sneaky—but when 75 kph is the maximum, you're asking for trouble by going any faster. I've come to love those speed traps; if it weren't for them, all Ticos would be traveling 90 miles an hour!

The latest weapon in the war against speeding is an automatic radar machine. Called the "Marom"—imported from Israel and installed in March of 1996—this device is placed along the highway a full kilometer away from the actual speed trap. It times your velocity, and if over the limit, the apparatus alerts the waiting officers and transmits a picture of your vehicle, so there can be no mistake as to the speeder's identification. The fine for speeding past this treacherous device will be $50 for ordinary speeding, or $100 for velocidad temerario (120 kilometers per hour and above). Initially, they started with three of these costly machines ($11,000 each), but if they manage to slow down traffic and save lives, you can be sure there'll be more.

Allow me to offer some advice for when you're stopped by traffic police. (I've had lots of experience in this department.)

1. Be calm, cool and courteous. After all, a ticket is no big deal. Until you're officially a resident, a traffic ticket doesn't affect your driving record or insurance. I've escaped several well-earned tickets simply by joking with the officers.

2. Do NOT get belligerent or raise your voice. Shouting won't help; it only makes things worse. When a cop feels he's being harassed for doing his job, don't be surprised if he retaliates in kind. I suspect this is where many cases of true police harassment originate: a tourist isn't aware that he's done anything wrong and becomes angry and abusive.

3. Don't offer a bribe. Even the best cops will accept money if you force it on them. This encourages a bad practice. The department has been undergoing a rigorous campaign of professionalism. Wages have been doubled, crooked cops are being dismissed and intensive training programs are underway.

4. If the cop suggests it would be easier to pay him than having to go to some distant place to pay, just politely decline and calmly wait for the ticket. Don't even discuss it with him. Again, tickets are no big deal, and you can pay at any national bank or simply save them up and turn them in to the rental company with your car. They'll pay them for you and add the fine to your credit card. Ticos routinely save their tickets and pay them once a year, just before it's time to renew their auto license plates. If a cop tries to insist on a bribe, make a good mental image of him and report the incident to the Ministry of Public Works (MOPT) at 227-2188 or at the MOPT office on Calle 9 between Avenidas 22 and 23.

I might add that since I've grown accustomed to watching the speedometer, I haven't received a ticket in almost two years, even though I make frequent 400-mile round trips to the Nicoya peninsula—past a dozen speed traps—sometimes with California plates, sometimes in a rental car. No traffic stops in two years is a Central America record for me.

Traffic tickets used to be so ridiculously cheap that drivers routinely ignored traffic laws, preferring to pay the occasional ticket rather than drive safely. This contributed to an appalling accident rate. Speeding tickets were less than $6, so why worry? Today, it's $50. Higher fines on everything from illegal parking to drunk driving should encourage safer behavior.

Finding Hotels and Lodging

The tourist boom over the last five years made the hotel situation somewhat tight at times. To compensate, new hotels were constructed and private families converted homes into bed-and-breakfasts as quickly as they could. Many North Americans joined this bed-and-breakfast boom, partly financing their retirement by renting out spare bedrooms. In smaller communities, hotels and ecotourism facilities raced to accommodate demand. Today you can often find a room in isolated places where camping was the only choice before. This trend seems to have caught up with demand, at least temporarily, because now there's an over-supply of rooms.

The tightest hotel room market in Costa Rica is during the Christmas-New Year's weeks. Not impossible, just tight. During the rush season, making reservations before you leave for Costa Rica, even if only for the first couple of nights, is a good insurance policy. After you arrive, you can check around and locate something suitable to your taste and/or the size of your pocketbook.

Around San José, hotels come in all sizes and flavors, with expensive rooms costing $100 a night and up and cheap rooms under $15. For medium-priced hotel rooms, expect to pay from $45 to $65 a night during the tourist season. I looked at one room for under $10 on my last trip, but shivers ran down my spine when I peered into the gloomy-looking room with dirty linen on the bed, in a ramshackle wooden building. For my personal tastes, a $20 room would be my bottom choice, yet many of the younger set and the backpacker brigades believe that anything over $8 is far too expensive. My wife's preferences fall into the $40 range or above.

Away from the Meseta Central, fewer hotels are available and rooms can be somewhat expensive for what you get. This is changing as competition grows. Nevertheless, I've found satisfactory accommodations for as little as $30 even in such out-of-the-way places as Golfito or Cahuita. Understand, what may be satisfactory for me could be unthinkable for someone else!

If you're on a budget—as we long-term travelers usually are—don't expect too much in the way of luxury. You may find an affordable rate for a room with a private bath, only to discover that the shower is plumbed for cold water only. When a hotel advertises hot water, you'll often find one of those rinky-dink electric heaters attached to the shower head. This contraption has a lever that can be set to one of three positions. The position that says "off" is the only one that works all the time. This encourages short but exhilarating showers, ideal for anyone considering celibacy. The secret is to let the water flow at its lowest possible volume in hopes of coaxing warmth from the heating element.

Inexpensive hotels habitually use low-wattage light bulbs, so weak you have trouble reading in bed. The solution is to carry a 75-watt bulb in your luggage and substitute it whenever you feel like reading. (Make sure you aren't into a 12-volt system!) Other items you might keep in your bag are a drinking cup, a roll of toilet paper, and some nylon string and clothes pins so you can wash out undies. Very important: a set of earplugs; I've suffered several nights made impossible by inconsiderate people partying all night or standing outside my door making plans for the next day's trip—at two in the morning! One additional item is insect repellent. A buzzing mosquito can make sleep difficult. A dozen of them can make sleep impossible.

Should you be stranded out in the country, unable to find a place to stay, your ace-in-the-hole is the local *pulpería*. This is the Costa Rican equivalent of a country "general store"; it also serves as the social center of the community. Drinks and snacks are sold, as neighbors congregate to exchange news and tidbits of gossip as well as purchase necessary items ranging from matches to machetes. The proprietor of the *pulpería* can often find you a room with a local family. This is a unique opportunity to see how country folk live in Costa Rica, but don't expect luxury. A *pulpería* is also an excellent place to inquire about real estate. If anything is for sale or rent in the neighborhood, the proprietor will know, and she probably knows the bottom-line price as well as the asking price.

Chapter Eighteen

Legal Matters

In Chapter Nine we discussed the pros and cons of buying real estate in Costa Rica. The nice part is that property ownership is open to anyone, no matter what citizenship, it's fairly easy to gain a clear title, and you can feel absolutely confident about your ownership. The nasty part is that a lot of charlatans and swindlers are out there ready to take advantage of your trusting nature. Don't worry, they haven't a chance if you do things correctly and don't skip any steps in the process.

(The following information comes to us courtesy of my friend, Carlos Umaña, of Tascan & Umaña law offices in San José. For those of you with connections to the World Wide Web, another source of Costa Rica legal information can be found at **http://www.hway.com/gateway/crinet/html**)

Your first step is to cultivate a lawyer who knows what the score is. In Costa Rica it's much easier to become an attorney than in the United States or Canada, so just because someone can legally assume the title *licenciado* doesn't guarantee he knows his backside from his big toe, or even that he's ever practiced law. You'll find many people who are entitled to call themselves attorneys, but actually practice law as an occasional sideline. A poor attorney isn't necessarily crooked; he could be inefficient or incompetent, which is just as bad.

A second important point: make certain the lawyer is working for you, exclusively for you. If you use the other person's attorney

238 / Choose Costa Rica

to represent both interests, you're facing the probability that the lawyer is primarily working for his first client and isn't on your side at all. Unlike in the U.S., this is how it can work in Costa Rica. So insist on having your attorney handle your part of the sale.

Purchasing Costa Rican Property

To make it easy to check on land ownership, all property, with a few exceptions, must be registered at the Property Department of the Public Record Office. This office is located in Zapote and is open to the public. However, it's best to have your attorney do the checking, because he knows what to look for and where.

The first step, before you hand over any money, is to run a thorough title search of the public records to see whether the property really belongs to the seller, the seller is who he claims to be, and to determine whether any mortgages, liens, encumbrances or easements come attached to the property. Mortgages and liens must be properly registered to have any effect on third parties. So, if the title is clear, you needn't worry about outstanding debts. If a lender didn't register a second deed of trust, he's out of luck. A title search should cost about $50, and it is well worth it, because if the seller was untruthful, you won't waste any more time.

You'll remember we said all property is registered, with exceptions. These exceptions are important. Let's review the three basic categories of Costa Rican properties.

1. Recorded Land: This includes all properties you'll find registered at the Public Record Office. The vast majority of properties for sale today fall into this category.

2. Non-Recorded Land: This is property that could be registered at the Public Record Office, but which has not yet been recorded. This applies to farmland, *fincas* (ranches), or homesteads, places that haven't legally changed hands for many decades, or perhaps changed through a private contract. Non-recorded land requires an attorney familiar with the procedure. It takes a judicial procedure to register land for the first time into public records. This kind of sale lacks the security granted by the Record Office.

3. Non-Registerable Land: This is property which cannot be legally recorded at the Public Registry. This is the case with most beachfront property. In some cases, beach properties can be possessed legally by individuals or corporations through a concession granted by the government. This lease is always through the government, but you must acquire possession from the previous possessor, if there is one.

Transferring Recorded Land

Any individual or company, national or foreign, may legally own land sheltered by the Record Office system. But for legal and economic reasons, you should consider placing your property in the name of a Costa Rican corporation, or *sociadad anónima* (more about this later on in this chapter).

Recorded land transfers must be granted through a public deed. That is, buyer and seller must appear before a Costa Rican Notary Public (to be chosen by the purchaser) who will insert the title transfer in his Protocol. (A notary public is a licensed attorney who is endowed with "public trust" and the right to validate and legalize all contracts and deeds. Again, to protect your investment, you should appoint your own attorney to perform as the notary public in the transaction.)

The purchase deed, as well as any liens or mortgages agreed to by the buyer, is then presented to the Public Record Office to be registered. It's also the notary's duty to complete all recording procedures necessary to provide the title transfer with full efficacy. (This is another reason to have an good attorney working for you, someone who knows what the word "efficacy" means.)

Expenses and legal fees involved may range from 6 to 7 percent of the total amount of the transaction and on the assessed price of the property. These costs are customarily shared by buyer and seller on a fifty-fifty basis—unless agreed otherwise.

Beachfront Property

Because of special regulations, some areas are not subject to private ownership. This is the case with most beachfront property, which is leased through concessions granted by the government. This is where things become complicated. Public Law No. 6043 of March 1977, established a restricted coastal zone called the "Zona

Marítimo/Terrestre." This law covers a strip of land, 200 meters deep, along both the Pacific and Atlantic coasts. The Marítimo/Terrestre restricted zone is divided into two sections:

1. The Public Zone (Zona Publica) is that first 50-meter strip of land starting at the mean high tide line. This is public property; the public has full access to the Public Zone.

2. The next 150-meter strip of land is called the Restricted Zone or Zona Restringida.

The law states that no private individual or corporation is allowed to build on or use for private purposes "any portion whatsoever" of the Public Zone. However, it's possible to obtain a lease/concession on Restricted Zone properties for private or business use. Understand, when this happens, it isn't a deed, it's a "lease concession." At first the lease is with local municipality, and later on, after a procedure, the lease is with the Instituto Costarricense de Turismo (ICT). Beneficiaries of lease concessions are granted the use, occupation, and possession of the land, including the right to build.

Now comes a sticky point. The law says, "no lease concessions are granted to non-Costa Ricans who have resided in the country less than five years, nor to foreign companies, nor to national companies of which 50 percent or more of its stock is owned by non-Costa Ricans."

While that may be the law, the fact is many if not most of the desirable Zona Restringida properties are held by Costa Rica corporations which are owned entirely by foreigners. This is, of course, difficult to verify because ownership of a Costa Rican corporation is impossible to substantiate. (Tips on how to start a corporation are found later on in this chapter.)

These lease concessions can be transferred to one person or company to another, subject to the approval of the municipality and the ICT. Leases are generally granted for periods of time that range from 5 to 20 years. The municipality is entitled to charge a small leasing fee. At the end of the leasing period, the lessee can apply for an extension of the lease concession, and extensions are normally granted with the previous approval of the ICT.

Beachfront land not regulated by this law can be found, but it's extremely unusual to find titled property in areas within the restricted 200-meter zone. True, some beachfront land isn't regulated because it was in use before the beach laws were passed. These exempt parcels are so-called "grandfathered" properties. However, be cautious; many people think that their property is "grandfathered" when it really is not. Some claim it's grandfathered when they know it is not.

Offshore Corporations

For a variety of reasons, banking secrecy laws such as those in Switzerland attract a great deal of interest among certain folks who have motives for hiding assets. As far as I know, there is no law against this as long as these accounts aren't used to defraud creditors or to evade paying taxes. Like Switzerland, Costa Rica has strict rules on non-disclosure of bank accounts.

An interesting angle of financial secrecy is the use of Costa Rican "offshore" corporations. Like bank accounts, these corporations can be started by anyone—citizen, resident or tourist—and are supposed to be totally secret. Since there's no way of knowing just whose names are on the corporation books, it's almost impossible to discover who actually controls any of these corporations. In fact, the legal term is "sociedad anónima" or "anonymous society." That's why corporation names are appended with "S.A." instead of "Inc." or Ltd. One common example of a legitimate use of a corporation is when buying or selling real estate. If the property belongs to a corporation, transfer of ownership is simple. You simply transfer the corporation's stock; the property belongs to whoever holds this stock.

Before we go any further, we need to understand a few crucial points. First of all, I am not an attorney, and even if I were, you would be foolish to accept legal advice from a book—particularly when it comes to activities as complicated as offshore corporations or foreign banking practices. Secondly, while most corporations and bank accounts in Costa Rica are legal, used for perfectly legitimate purposes, the ones used for illegal schemes are frequently toppled, sending overly creative schemers to jail. I suspect that what happens is the corporation originally starts off with legal goals in mind, and then branches out into a small tax fraud which grows until it gets out of hand. Some schemes are so obvious that the IRS has little trouble spotting the smoke and flames. My final point is a reiteration of the first: I am not a lawyer nor am I in any way urging readers to get involved in offshore corporations or secret bank accounts. I am merely reporting what Costa Rican residents and attorneys have passed along to me.

Starting a Costa Rican Corporation

Costa Rica's corporate structure allows any person (Costa Rican or not) to control a company without his name appearing in the public records. A Costa Rican lawyer (who must be a specialist in this) sets up a corporation without the real owner's name ever appearing in the record. It is called a "sociedad anónima con acciones al portador" (anonymous society with all stock owned by the bearer). This means that although there is a legal president, secretary and treasurer (often simply employees of the attorney), the actual ownership of the corporation is invested in whoever physically has the stock certificates in his or her pocket or safe-deposit box. Even the attorney has no way of knowing whether the original client still owns the stock. This arrangement is prohibited in the United States but is perfectly legal in Costa Rica.

This corporation is free to engage in many types of business activities, both in Costa Rica and in other countries. Theoretically, because it is considered a "foreign corporation" as far as the IRS is concerned, it pays no taxes in the United States. (There's talk about changing this.) Because it's a Costa Rican corporation, it pays little or nothing on what it earns outside of Costa Rica. This doesn't relieve the individual of the responsibility of reporting income and paying income taxes in his home country. New laws require that a yearly report of a corporation must be filed; should there be no income to report, there's no tax consequences—but not filing the report makes the corporation liable for a large fine. So if you already have a corporation in Costa Rica and haven't been filing reports, see your lawyer.

Advantages of a Corporation

It's always advisable for both foreigners and Costa Ricans to own land through a corporation. Among the advantages is a reduction of personal liabilities and taxes. The ownership of assets, such as real estate, boats and automobiles, is the main purpose of most registered corporations in Costa Rica. Foreigners aren't supposed to have checking accounts with a national bank, but their corporations can have an account, and checks can be written by the treasurer (you). A foreigner can't engage in commerce, but the corporation can.

A corporation may be owned by a group of shareholders or fully owned by one shareholder. This way a single individual, or a small group of people, can operate the company in a relatively simple and inexpensive manner. The asset (your house or your car) can be sold or transferred simply by handing over the shares of the corporation, because it is owned by the corporation, not the individual, even though he or she may own all of the shares. Your attorney will show you the best ways to ensure control of the company and the overall handling of corporate power.

An important point about corporations: make sure you are getting a full-fledged corporation; there are shortened versions that have some serious drawbacks. Don't go for a cut-rate, partial incorporation, because you'll not get all the required services, and it could expire at the end of a brief period of time. Later on, you'll find you have to go back and spend more money to put the company on par with other corporations. Most attorneys will charge about $650 to form a complete corporation.

As mentioned above, another advantage of incorporating is that since government banks won't open a colón account unless you are a legal resident, non-residents work around this by opening a checking account in the name of their Costa Rican corporation. Such accounts are simply for convenience of bill-paying; they pay no interest. Three national banks offer these corporate checking accounts: Banco Nacional de Costa Rica, Banco de Costa Rica, and Banco Credito Agrícola de Cartago. To open an account in a national bank, you'll be asking your attorney for help. Among other things you'll need the original letters of incorporation of your company, certification of the company's legal representatives and two recommendation letters from individuals with checking accounts in that bank. At one bank, they wanted letters from Costa Rica citizens who regularly lend me money. When I pointed out that if Ticos were gullible enough to lend me money I wouldn't need a checking account, the bank official agreed to accept a letter from my lawyer instead. The legal charges for something like this should be minimal.

Legal Details

There are four main stages in the process of forming a Costa Rican corporation.

1. Notarization of the Articles of Incorporation or Constitutive Charter of the company: This document will be prepared by your attorney. The Constitutive Charter determines the organization, administration and bylaws of the company. This is signed by all the shareholders, the appointed members of the Board of Directors, the Controller and the "Agente Residente."

2. Before registration in the Record Office, your attorney will announce the company's constitution in Costa Rica's official newspaper, *La Gaceta*. This takes about two weeks. Also, you must make a deposit of the amount of the capital stock indicated in the Constitutive Charter—usually 1,000 colones—in a national bank. The amount of shares in the corporation and their denomination is determined by the founders. All shares must have equal value and must be worth at least one colón, but there's no top limit to a share's value. The money deposited can be withdrawn once the company has been duly recorded.

3. The company must be registered in the Record Office. This registration is essential to legally constitute a corporation in Costa Rica. The registration process is performed by the Notary Public (your lawyer). The whole process takes from one to three months, depending on the time it takes for the Registry Office to approve the company's bylaws, including the books.

4. Legalization of Books: You'll receive a set of three accounting books ("Diario," "Mayor" and "Inventario y Balances") and three "legal" books (Shareholders' Record, Shareholders' Assemblies and Board of Directors Meetings). Your attorney will present the books to the Ministerio de Hacienda for their initial authorization. Once duly legalized, these books should register all internal affairs of the company (as well as stock transfers) and are kept privately by the shareholders. You can leave them with your attorney or place them in a secure place, such as a safe deposit box. Remember, whoever has the books in hand also has control of the assets.

To form a Costa Rican corporation, you need a minimum of two initial shareholders. Once the company is formed and properly inscribed in the Record Office, the shares can be transferred to a single person, who becomes the sole shareholder of the company.

The name of the company must be in Spanish, Latin or any native dialect. Of course, a name can't be identical or equivalent to existing corporations. And names with a meaning in a foreign language (i.e. English or German) are not allowed without special exceptions. Your attorney in charge of preparing the Articles of Incorporation will ask you for a list of names (in Spanish), and he'll research them and determine whether they will be accepted by the Record Office.

There must be a Board of Directors with at least the following offices: President, Secretary and Treasurer. The President must be the principal representative of the company. Other members of the Board can also be made representatives of the corporation, depending on how the founders of the company decide to do the Articles of Incorporation. The members of the Board may or may not be shareholders. The Directors must be present when the company is legally formed to personally accept their designation and sign the Corporation Charter along with the shareholders or power of attorney.

The Controller cannot be a shareholder nor a member of the Board of Directors. The person appointed as Controller has to sign the Articles of Incorporation. Usually this will be someone on your lawyer's office staff.

Every Costa Rican company must designate an "Agente Residente." The Agente Residente will probably be your Costa Rican attorney, who will be a formal representative for official matters. He has no powers to act in the company's behalf. The fee for this service is usually $100 a year.

Taxes on Corporations

Education and Culture Tax: Payable once a year, based on the value of the assets owned by the corporation. It isn't expensive, usually somewhere around $100.

Income Tax: As with individuals, the corporation must pay income tax depending on the earnings the corporation had during the past fiscal year (from Oct. 1 to Sept. 30). Companies just holding assets do not have to pay anything if there hasn't been any activity. As mentioned earlier, under a new tax law (1995) all companies must submit a tax declaration on taxes to be paid, if any. So, make sure that the declaration is presented every year before the 1st of November. The fine for not doing so can be heavy. Again, this is why you are paying your lawyer the $100-a-year fee.

Property Taxes: If the corporation owns land, it must pay the following taxes. Territorial Tax: a national tax based on the government records of land value, to be paid every four months. Municipal Taxes: local taxes for public lighting, garbage collection, etc., paid locally in the Municipalidad every four months. Land Tax: This annual tax is imposed every January and is administered on a progressive scale from 0.30 percent annually for land of 250,000 colones ($1,250) in value, up to 1.05 percent annually for values over 3,000,000 colones ($15,000). This doesn't tell you a whole lot, unless you know the assessed value of your property, which is usually far below market value.

Banking Secrecy

Traditional tax havens like the Cayman Islands, Switzerland, Luxembourg, the Channel Islands, and the Netherlands Antilles, have always tempted those looking for ways to hide assets. Secret bank accounts are often used for this purpose. I've been told that medical doctors routinely hide as much of their holdings as possible in these places to avoid disaster should a multi-million-dollar malpractice suit top their insurance limits. Like the afore-mentioned countries, Costa Rica maintains a strict policy of banking and commercial secrecy. The amount of money you have in a bank account is supposedly sacrosanct and unavailable to curious outsiders.

One banker said, "If I disclosed information about someone's account—even to a policeman or a government official—I could go to prison." The *Tico Times* illustrated this point with a story about a suspect accused of stealing and forging checks. The crime could easily be solved if authorities could access bank records and see if the stolen checks had been deposited to the suspect's account. But bank officials refused to help the police solve the crime, because in the process they would become criminals themselves!

Do not think that this secrecy deters the IRS from snooping about, and I suspect not without some success. (Realize that failing to reporting a foreign bank account on your income tax return is a law violation.) Sometimes fraud is so transparent that all the secret bank accounts or anonymous corporations in the world wouldn't help. I suspect that the IRS has its own methods of tracking down fraud without going through the Costa Rica banking system. But there is nothing illegal about U.S. or Canadian citizens owning a bank account or majority stock in an offshore corporation as long as profits are reported and taxes are properly paid.

Appendix

Business Contacts

American Chamber of Commerce of Costa Rica: P.O. Box 4946, San José; 332-1033. U.S. mailing address: SJO 1576, P.O. Box 025216, Miami, FL 33102.

Associación Nacional de Fomento Economico: Apdo. 3577, San José.

Camara de Industrias de Costa Rica: Calle 13 y 15, Avenida 6, San José; 223-2411.

Costa Rica Export Investment Promotion Center: International Trade Mart, New Orleans, LA 70130; 504-529-2282.

Dirección General de Aduanas (General Customs Bureau): Ministerio de Hacienda, Avendia 1-3, Calle 14, San José.

Economic Development Offices: c/o Embassy of Costa Rica, 2112 "S" St. N.W., Washington, DC 20008; 202-328-6628.

Ministerio de Industrias: Calle 10 Avenida 2, San José; 257-8511.

Costa Rican Consulates

Atlanta: 1870 The Exchange N.W. #100, Atlanta, GA 30339; 404-951-7025.

Chicago: 8 S. Michigan Av. #1312, Chicago, IL 60603; 312-263-2472.

Houston: 2901 Wilcrest Dr., Houston, TX 77042; 713-266-0484.

Los Angeles: 3540 Wilshire Bl. #404, Los Angeles, CA 90010; 213-380-7915.

Miami: 1600 N.W. LeJeune Rd., 3rd Flr., Miami, FL 33126; 305-871-7485.

Montreal: 7541 Louis Hernon, Montreal, Quebec, H2S 3J7 Canada; 514-393-7210.

New Orleans area: 4532 W. Napoleon Av. #112, Metairie, LA 70001; 504-467-1462.

Ottawa: 135 York St. #208, Ottawa, Ont., K1N 5T4 Canada; 613-562-2855.

New York: 80 Wall St. #1117, New York, NY 10005; 212-425-2620.

San Antonio: 2447 Lockhill-Selma, San Antonio, TX 78230; 210-308-8623.

San Diego: 8755 Aero Dr. #301, San Diego, CA 92123; (phone & fax) 619-571-6875.

San Francisco: 870 Market St. #548, San Francisco, CA 94102; 415-392-8488.

Tampa area: 2907 S.R. 590 #12, Clearwater, FL 34619; 813-726-1929.

Washington, DC: 2112 "S" St. N.W., Washington, DC 20008; 202-234-2945.

Vancouver: 600 Mesville St. #111, Vancouver, B.C., V6G 3V6 Canada; 609-669-0797.

Books and Periodicals

Costa Rica: A Natural Destination, 3rd Ed. (1994), by Ree Strange Sheck. John Muir Publications, Santa Fe, NM. A guidebook for those interested in ecology.

Costa Rica Guide, 6th Ed. (1996), by Paul Glassman. Open Road Publishing, New York, NY. Information on travel in Costa Rica, with regional maps.

Costa Rica Reader (1988), by Mark Edelman and Joanne Kenen. Grove/Atlantic, New York, NY. An excellent background source.

The Costa Ricans (1988), by Richard Mavis and Karen Biesanz. Waveland Press, Prospect Heights, IL. Useful book about Ticos and their country.

The Costa Rica Traveller, 2nd Ed. (1995), by Ellen Searby. Windham Bay Press, Occidental, CA. Covers travel in Costa Rica and descriptions of the country's attractions.

Exploring Costa Rica (1994). This Tico Times publication is available in Costa Rican bookstores and has extensive coverage of tourist activities.

Frommer's Costa Rica, Guatemala & Belize on $35 a Day, 3rd Ed. (1995). Prentice Hall Press. A comprehensive guide to budget travel in Costa Rica.

Investor's Guide to Costa Rica (1992). Costa Rican-American Chamber of Commerce. General information on investment, banking, finance and business opportunities.

Living in Costa Rica (1989). United States Mission Association. Written and produced by employees of the U.S. Embassy, this book gives excellent information on rules regulations, customs and shopping in Costa Rica.

The New Key to Costa Rica, 12th Ed. (1994), by Beatrice Blake and Anne Becher. Ulysses Press, Berkeley, CA. A popular travel guide for residents and tourists and a must for anyone considering visiting Costa Rica for more than a short vacation.

Tico Times. This weekly English-language newspaper is published in San José, Costa Rica; a three-month trial subscription is $16.50. In the U.S. or Canada, write: Dept. 717, P.O. Box 025216, Miami, FL 33102. In Costa Rica: Apdo. 4632, San José, or call: 222-8952.

Index

About the Author

During the past decade, John Howells has written nine books on places, at home and abroad, that make for comfortable, stimulating retirement. He has become increasingly well known as an authority on this subject and is much in demand as lecturer and seminar leader on retirement strategies and retirement places. He is a member of the Board of Directors of the American Association of Retirement Communities and was a featured speaker at that organization's Phoenix, Arizona, conference.

Howells was born in New Orleans and raised in suburban St. Louis. He now divides his time between homes in California and Costa Rica. At any time, however, he is just as likely to be on the road in the United States, Europe or Latin America, gathering material for a new book or an update of an older one.

He has worked on newspapers from coast to coast—more than 40 in all—and at various times has been a Linotype operator, an English teacher, a silver miner and a travel and feature writer, not to mention author of books on subjects ranging from tramp printers to prospecting for gold in addition to those on retirement.

Our books are available in most bookstores. However, if you have difficulty finding them, we will be happy to ship them to you directly. Just send your check or money order.

Retirement

Retiring, Wintering or Investing
CHOOSE COSTA RICA 3RD ED. $13.95 _____

Enjoying the Devaluation Bargains
CHOOSE MEXICO 4TH ED. $11.95 _____

Retirement Discoveries for Every Budget
CHOOSE THE SOUTHWEST   **NEW** $12.95 _____
CHOOSE THE NORTHWEST   **NOV. '96** $12.95 _____

America's Best and Most Affordable Places
WHERE TO RETIRE $14.95 _____

Strategies for Comfortable Retirement
RETIREMENT ON A SHOESTRING $8.95 _____

Travel

An Impromptu Travel Guide
FRANCE WITHOUT RESERVATIONS $12.95 _____

A Traveler's Guide to Living Affordably Abroad
EUROPE THE EUROPEAN WAY   **OCT. '96** $13.95 _____

Hiking Guides for Active Adults
WALKING EASY IN THE AUSTRIAN ALPS $10.95 _____
WALKING EASY IN THE FRENCH ALPS $11.95 _____
WALKING EASY IN THE ITALIAN ALPS $11.95 _____
WALKING EASY IN THE SAN FRANCISCO BAY AREA $11.95 _____
WALKING EASY IN THE SWISS ALPS $10.95 _____

Postage & Handling
First book.............................$1.90   _____
Each additional book..........1.00   _____
California residents add 8% sales tax   _____

Total $ _____

For Credit Card ORDERS ONLY - call toll-free 1-800-669-0773
For Information - call 510-530-0299

Please ship to:

Name _____

Address _____

City/State/Zip_____

Our books are shipped bookrate. Please allow 2 - 3 weeks for delivery. If you are not satisfied, the price of the book(s) will be refunded in full. (U. S. funds for all orders, please.)

Mail to: Gateway Books 2023 Clemens Road Oakland CA 94602